MICHEL FOUCAULT

=

THE CARE OF
THE SELF

The History of Sexuality
Volume 3

TRANSLATED FROM THE FRENCH
BY ROBERT HURLEY

PENGUIN BOOKS

PENGUIN BOOKS

Published by the Penguin Group
Penguin Books Ltd, 27 Wrights Lane, London W8 5TZ, England
Viking Penguin, a division of Penguin Books USA Inc.
375 Hudson Street, New York, New York 10014, USA
Penguin Books Australia Ltd, Ringwood, Victoria, Australia
Penguin Books Canada Ltd, 2801 John Street, Markham, Ontario, Canada L3R 1B4
Penguin Books (NZ) Ltd, 182–190 Wairau Road, Auckland 10, New Zealand

Penguin Books Ltd, Registered Offices: Harmondsworth, Middlesex, England

First published in France, under the title *Le Souci de soi,*
by Editions Gallimard 1984
This translation first published in the USA by Pantheon Books,
a division of Random House, Inc., New York, 1986
and simultaneously in Canada by Random House of Canada Ltd, Toronto
First published in Great Britain by Allan Lane the Penguin Press 1988
Published in Penguin Books 1990
3 5 7 9 10 8 6 4 2

Copyright © Editions Gallimard, 1984
This translation copyright © Random House, Inc., 1936
All rights reserved

Printed in England by Clays Ltd, St Ives plc

CONTENTS

v

Translator's Acknowledgments

My thanks go to Stephen William Foster and to
Dennis Hollier for their help with this volume of *The
History of Sexuality.*

R.H.
July 1986

PART ONE

DREAMING OF ONE'S PLEASURES

I will begin by analyzing a rather singular text. It is a "practical" work dealing with everyday life, not a work of moral reflection or prescription. Of all the texts that have survived from this period, it is the only one that presents anything like a systematic exposition of the different forms of sexual acts. By and large it does not make direct and explicit moral judgments concerning those acts, but it does reveal schemas of valuation that were generally accepted. And one notes that the latter are quite close to the general principles that, already in the classical epoch, organized the ethical experience of the *aphrodisia*. The book by Artemidorus thus constitutes a point of reference. It testifies to a perenniality and exemplifies a common way of thinking. For this very reason, it will allow us to measure what may have been uncommon and in part new in the work of philosophical and medical reflection on pleasure and sexual conduct that was undertaken in the same period.

CHAPTER ONE

===

THE METHOD OF ARTEMIDORUS

The Interpretation of Dreams by Artemidorus is the only text that remains, in full, of a literature that was abundant in antiquity: the literature of oneirocriticism. Artemidorus, writing in the second century A.D., himself cites several works that were in use in his day: those of Nicostratus of Ephesus, Panyasis of Halicarnassus, Apollodorus of Telmessus, Phoebus of Antioch, Dionysius of Heliopolis, and the naturalist Alexander of Myndus.[1] He makes favorable mention of Aristander of Telmessus, and he refers to the three books of the treatise by Geminus of Tyre, to the five books of Demetrius of Phalerum, and to the twenty-two books of Artemon of Miletus.[2]

Addressing the man to whom his work is dedicated, a certain Cassius Maximus (possibly Maximus of Tyre, or his father,[3] who he says urged him "not to surrender my wisdom to silence"), Artemidorus declares that he "has not done anything else" but employ himself "always, day and night," in the interpretation of dreams.[4] An emphatic statement of the sort that was rather customary in this kind of presentation? Perhaps. In any case Artemidorus did something quite different from compiling the most famous examples of prophetic dreams that were confirmed by reality. He undertook to write a work of method, and this in two senses: it was meant to be a manual for use in daily practice; it was also meant to be a theoretical treatise on the validity of interpretive procedures.

4

One should bear in mind that the analysis of dreams was one of the techniques of existence. Since images encountered in dreams, or some of them at least, were thought to be signs of reality or messages of the future, a high value was set on their decipherment; a reasonable life could scarcely dispense with the task. This was a very old popular tradition; it was also an accepted custom in cultured milieus. If it was necessary to consult the countless professionals of nocturnal images, it was also good to be able to interpret their signs oneself. There are innumerable testimonies showing the importance accorded the analysis of dreams as a life practice, one that was indispensable not only in dramatic circumstances but also in the everyday course of events. This was because in dreams the gods gave advice, guidance, and sometimes explicit commands. Moreover, even when the dream only announced an event without prescribing anything, even when one believed that the concatenation of future occurrences was inevitable, it was still good to have foreknowledge of things that were bound to happen, so that one might prepare for them. "Providence," says Achilles Tatius in *The Adventures of Leucippe and Clitophon,* "sometimes foreshows the future to men in dreams, not so that they may be able to avoid the sufferings fated for them, for they can never get the better of destiny, but in order that they may bear them with the more patience when those sufferings come; for when disasters come all together and unexpectedly, they strike the spirit with so severe and sudden a blow that they overwhelm it; while if they are anticipated, the mind, by dwelling on them beforehand, is able little by little to turn the edge of sorrow."[5] Later, Synesius will express a completely traditional point of view when he remarks that our dreams constitute an oracle who "dwells with us," who accompanies us "if we go abroad; she is with us on the field of battle, she is at our side in the life of the city; she labors with us in the fields and barters with us in the marketplace"; dreams are to be regarded as "a prophet who is always ready, a tireless and silent adviser." Hence we should all make an effort to interpret our dreams, whoever we may be, "men and women, old and young, rich and poor, private citizens and public officials, inhabitants of the city and of the country, artisans and orators," without regard "either to sex or age, to fortune or profession."[6] It was in this spirit that Artemidorus wrote *The Interpretation of Dreams.*

Artemidorus is mainly concerned to show the reader precisely how to go about it: How does one contrive to break down a dream into constituent parts and establish its diagnostic meaning? How does one manage also to take this whole into account in the decipherment of each of its parts? The comparison that Artemidorus makes with the divinatory techniques of sacrificers is significant: they, too, "know how each individual sign fits into the whole," and yet they "base their judgments as much on the total sum of the signs as on each individual sign."[7] His book is thus a treatise on *how to interpret.* Almost entirely centered not on the prophetic marvels of dreams but on the *technē* that enables one to make them speak correctly, the work is addressed to several types of readers. Artemidorus wishes to supply an instrument for the use of professionals and technicians of analysis. This is the vision with which he hopes to inspire his son, the addressee of the fourth and fifth books: "what has been written here, as long as it remains with you alone, will make you a more excellent interpreter of dreams than anyone."[8] He also intends to help those who, discouraged by the erroneous methods they have tried, may be tempted to give up this valuable practice. His book will serve as a salutary treatment—*therapeia sōtēriōdēs* —of those errors.[9] But he thinks, too, of the general reader who needs basic instruction.[10] In any case, he offers the book as a manual for living, a tool that can be used over the course of one's existence and adapted to life's changing circumstances: "just as there is an order and sequence in actual events" so he has made an effort to "set down everything in an orderly fashion."

This "handbook-for-daily-living" aspect is quite noticeable

when one compares Artemidorus' text with the *Tales* of Aristides, an anxious valetudinarian who spent years harkening to the god that sent him dreams through all the extraordinary ups and downs of his illness and the countless treatments he undertook. One notes that in Artemidorus there is almost no place for religious enchantments; unlike many other texts of this kind, his work does not depend on cult therapeutics, even if, using a traditional formula, he evokes Apollo of Daldis, "my own native god," who encouraged him and, appearing at his bedside, "all but commanded me to compose this work."[11] Moreover, he is careful to remark on the difference between his work and that of such oneirocritics as Geminus of Tyre, Demetrius of Phalerum, and Artemon of Miletus, who conveyed prescriptions and cures given by Serapis.[12] The typical dreamer whom Artemidorus addresses is not a worried devotee who attends to injunctions given from above. He is an "ordinary" individual: generally a man (the dreams of women are noted as an aside, as possible variants in cases where the sex of the subject happens to change the meaning of the dream); a man who has a family, possessions, quite often a trade (he runs a business; he has a shop). He is apt to have servants and slaves (but the case is considered in which he has none). And, besides his health, his chief anxieties concern the life and death of his entourage, his enrichment, his impoverishment, the marriage of his children, the functions he may be called upon to exercise in the city. In short, an average clientele. Artemidorus' text is revelatory of a type of preoccupations characteristic of ordinary people.

But the work also has a theoretical interest at stake, which Artemidorus speaks of in the dedication to Cassius: he aims to refute the adversaries of oneiromancy. He wishes to convince the skeptics who do not believe in all those forms of divination by which one attempts to decipher the signs that foretell the future. Artemidorus will seek to establish these certitudes not so much by a plain exposition of his findings as by a carefully considered procedure of inquiry and a discussion of method.

He does not mean to dispense with earlier texts; he has taken pains to read them, but not in order to recopy them, as many writers do; what interests him in the "already said" is not established authority but rather the breadth and variety of experience to be found there. And he has not searched for this experience in a few great authors, but has insisted on going to those places where it is formed. As he says in the dedication to Cassius Maximus, and later repeats, Artemidorus takes pride in the breadth of his inquiry. Not only has he compared innumerable works, he has patiently frequented the market stalls kept by dream readers and soothsayers at the crossroads of the Mediterranean world. "I, on the other hand, have not only taken special pains to procure every book on the interpretation of dreams, but have consorted for many years with the much-despised diviners of the marketplace. People who assume a holier-than-thou countenance and who arch their eyebrows in a superior way dismiss them as beggars, charlatans, and buffoons, but I have ignored their disparagement. Rather, in the different cities of Greece and at the great religious gatherings in that country, in Asia, in Italy and in the largest and most populous of the islands, I have patiently listened to old dreams and their consequences. For there was no other possible way in which to get practice in these matters."[13] With regard to all that he has brought back, Artemidorus does not intend to impart it in the form of raw data; rather, he will submit it to "experience" (peira), which is for him the "guiding principle" and "witness" of everything he says.[14] What he means by this is that he will verify the information to which he refers by matching it against other sources, by comparing it with his own practice, and by subjecting it to argument and demonstration. In this way, nothing will be said "in the air," nor by resorting to "mere conjecture." One recognizes the methods of inquiry, the notions—e.g., the notions of *historia* and *peira*—and the forms of testing and "verification" that characterized the gathering of knowledge carried out in natural history and medicine during this period, under the more or less direct influence of skeptical thought.* Artemidorus' text offers the considerable advantage of presenting a careful reflection on a vast body of traditional material.

There is no question of looking in such a document for the formulations of an austere morality or the emergence of new standards of sexual conduct. What it does offer are indications concerning current modes of valuation and generally accepted attitudes. Philosophical reflection is certainly not absent from the text, and one finds in it rather clear references to contemporary problems and debates; but these references concern the procedures of decipherment and the method of analysis, not value judgments and moral contents. The material on which the interpretations bear, the oneiric scenes they treat, as auguries, and the situations and events they announce, belong to a common and traditional landscape. One can thus expect this text by Artemidorus to provide evidence of a rather widespread moral tradition, which was doubtless rather deeply rooted in the past. But once again it must be kept in mind that while the text abounds in detail, while it presents in connection with dreams a catalog of different possible acts and relations, and is more systematic in this regard than any other work from the same period, it is not in any sense a treatise on morality, which would be primarily concerned with formulating judgments about those acts and relations. It is only indirectly, through the decipherment of the dreams, that one can discern the valuations brought to bear on the scenes and acts represented in the text. The ethical principles are not affirmed for their own sake; one can recognize them only through the

*R. J. White, in his introduction to the English edition of Artemidorus, points to several traces of the empiricist and skeptical influence on Artemidorus. A. H. M. Kessels, however, asserts that Artemidorus was only a practitioner, who just interpreted the dream that he had before him on a particular day.[15]

actual progression of the analysis, by interpreting the interpretations. This suggests that we should dwell for a moment
on the procedures of decipherment that Artemidorus brings
into play. We will then be able to decipher the ethics under-
lying his analysis of sexual dreams.

1.   Artemidorus draws a distinction between two forms of
nocturnal visions. First, there are the *enypnia,* dreams that
express the present affects of the individual and "run their
course in proximity to the mind." One is in love, one desires
the presence of the beloved, one dreams that the latter is
there; or one goes without food, one feels hungry, one
dreams of eating; or again, "a man who has stuffed himself
with food dreams that he is vomiting or choking";[16] a man
who fears his enemies dreams that he is surrounded by them.
This kind of dream has a simple diagnostic value. It is
grounded in the current state of affairs (from present to present); it shows the sleeping subject his own state; it conveys
that which is deficiency or excess in relation to the body, and
that which is fear or desire in relation to the mind.

The dream experiences called *oneiroi* are different. Their
nature and function are readily discovered by Artemidorus in
the three "etymologies" he submits. The *oneiros* is that which
to on eirei, "tells what is real." It tells what is, what is already
inscribed in time's unfolding and will come true as an event
in the not-too-distant future. It is also that which acts on the
soul and excites it—*oneirai.* The dream alters the soul, it
fashions and shapes it; it leads it into dispositions and induces
movements in it corresponding to what is shown. Further, one
recognizes in this word *oneiros* the name of the beggar of
Ithaca, Irus, who carried the messages that were entrusted to
him.[17] Term by term, then, *enypnion* and *oneiros* are opposed
to each other: the first speaks of the individual, the second of
events in the world; one originates in the states of the body and
the mind, the other anticipates the unwinding of the temporal
chain; one manifests the action of the too-little and the too-

much in the domain of appetites and aversions, the other alerts the soul and at the same time shapes it. On the one hand, the dreams of desire tell the soul's reality in its present state. On the other hand, the dreams of being tell the future of the event in the order of the world.

A second cleavage brings another form of distinction to each of the two categories of "nocturnal visions." There is that which reveals itself clearly and transparently, requiring no decipherment or interpretation, and that which displays itself only figuratively, in images telling something different from their first appearance. In state dreams, desire can be manifested by the easily recognizable presence of its object (one sees in a dream the woman one desires); but it can also be manifested by another image exhibiting a more or less distant relationship with the object in question. An analogous difference obtains in event dreams. Some of them directly designate, by showing its actual appearance, that which already exists in the future mode: one sees in a dream the sinking of a ship on which one will later suffer shipwreck; one sees oneself struck by the weapon by which one will be wounded the next day. These are the so-called theorematic dreams. But, in other cases, the relation between image and event is indirect: the image of the ship that breaks apart on the rocks may signify not a shipwreck, or even a misfortune, but, for a slave who has this dream, his emancipation in the near future. These are the "allegorical" dreams.

Now, the margin that exists between these two distinctions poses a practical problem for the interpreter. Given a particular vision in sleep, how is one to know whether one is dealing with a state dream or an event dream? How does one determine whether the image announces directly what it shows, or whether one must suppose that it stands for something else? Referring to this difficulty in the first pages of Book IV, Artemidorus emphasizes the importance of considering the individual who has the dream. It is quite certain, he explains, that state dreams will not appear to "virtuous" persons, for they have been able to subdue their irrational movements, hence their passions, their desires or fears; they also know how to keep their bodies balanced between deficiency and excess; for them, consequently, there are no disturbances, hence none of those "dreams" *(enypnia)* that are always to be understood as manifestations of affects. Moreover, it was a very frequent theme of moralists that virtue is marked by the disappearance of dreams that translate the appetites and involuntary movements of the mind and the body. "The sleeper's visions," said Seneca, "are as turbulent as his day."[18] Plutarch cited Zeno in affirming that it is a sign of progress when a person no longer dreams that he derives pleasure from indecent actions. And he alluded to those individuals who have enough strength in their waking hours to combat and resist their passions, but who at night, "throwing off opinions and laws," cease to feel any shame: then there awakens what is immoral and licentious within them.[19]

For Artemidorus, in any case, when state dreams occur they can take two forms. In most people, desire and aversion are manifested directly and without concealment; but in a man who knows how to interpret his own dreams, they are manifested only through signs. This is because his mind "plays tricks on him in a rather ingenious way." Thus a man with no experience in dream interpretation will see in a dream the woman he desires or the longed-for death of his master. The mistrustful or clever mind of the expert will, so to say, refuse to make manifest the state of desire in which he finds himself: it will resort to trickery, so that instead of simply seeing the woman he desires, the dreamer will see the image of something that signifies her: "a horse, a mirror, a ship, the sea, an animal that is female, a piece of feminine apparel." As an example, Artemidorus cites a painter from Corinth, an expert interpreter no doubt, who saw the roof of his house collapse in a dream and saw his own decapitation. One might have imagined that this was the sign of a future event, but in fact it was a state dream: the man wished for the death of his master—who is still living, Artemidorus notes in passing.[20]

As concerns the *oneiroi,* how does one recognize those that are transparent and "theorematic" in contrast to those that predict allegorically an event different from what they show? If one leaves aside the unusual images that obviously call for an interpretation, those that foretell an event are immediately confirmed by reality: the event follows them without delay. The theorematic dream opens directly onto the thing it announces, not giving interpretation any possible purchase, nor allowing it the necessary time interval. Allegorical dreams are easily recognized, therefore, by the fact that they are not followed by a direct realization, which means that one should seize the occasion to interpret them. It should be added that virtuous individuals—who do not have *enypnia* but only *oneiroi*—ordinarily experience only the clear visions of theorematic dreams. Artemidorus does not need to explain this privilege: it was traditional to suppose that the gods spoke directly to souls that were pure. Recall what Plato said in the *Republic:* "When he has quieted both spirit and appetites, he arouses his third part in which wisdom resides and thus takes his rest; you know that it is then that he best grasps reality."[21] And in the novel by Chariton of Aphrodisias, at the moment when Callirhoe is finally near the end of her trials, and when her long struggle to preserve her virtue is about to be rewarded, she has a "theorematic" dream that anticipates the conclusion of the story and constitutes both a presage and a promise on the part of the goddess protecting her: "When night came, she saw herself in a dream, once more a girl in Syracuse, entering the sacred precinct of Aphrodite and returning from it; now she was looking at Chaereas and observing her wedding day; the whole city was decked with garlands and she herself was being escorted by her father and mother to the home of the groom."[22]

* * *

We can construct a table of the relationships established by
Artemidorus between the types of dreams, their ways of signifying, and the subject's modes of being, as follows:

		state dreams		event dreams	
		direct	through signs	theorematic	allegorical
in virtuous individuals		never		usually	
in ordinary individuals	expert		usually		usually
	inexperienced	usually			

It is the last entry in the table—allegorical event dreams of
the sort that ordinary people have—that defines the domain
of oneirocriticism. It is here that interpretation is possible,
since such visions are not transparent but make use of one
image to convey another. And it is here that interpretation is
useful, since it enables one to prepare for an event that is not
immediate.

2.   Decipherment of the oneiric allegory is carried out by
means of analogy. Artemidorus returns to this point several
times: the art of oneirocriticism is based on the law of resemblance; it operates through the "juxtaposition of similari-
ties."[23] Artemidorus brings this analogy into play on two
levels. First, there is·the natural analogy between the dream
image and the elements of the future that it foretells. Artemidorus employs various means to detect this resemblance:
qualitative identity (to dream of a malaise may signify a future
"bad state" of health or fortune; to dream of mud signifies that
the body will be congested with harmful substances); identity
of words (a ram signifies authority because of the word association krios–kreiōn);[24] symbolic affinity (to dream of a lion is

a sign of victory for an athlete; to dream of tempests is a sign of misfortune); existence of a belief, a popular saying, a mythological theme (a bear indicates a woman because of Callisto the Arcadian);[25] also membership in the same category of existence: thus marriage and death may represent each other in a dream, since both are regarded as a *telos*, an end (goal or term) for a man's life;[26] and similarity of practices ("if a sick man dreams that he is marrying a maiden, it portends his death, for the same things that happen to a bridegroom happen to a dead man").[27]

There is also an analogy of value. And this is an essential point in that oneirocriticism has the function of determining whether the events that will take place are favorable or not. The whole domain of the dream's signified is marked, in Artemidorus' text, by the binary division between the good and the bad, the auspicious and the inauspicious, the fortunate and the unfortunate. The question then is this: How does the action that is represented in a dream make use of its own value to announce the event that will take place? The general principle is simple. A dream bears a favorable forecast if the action it represents is itself good. But how is this value to be measured? Artemidorus suggests six criteria. Is the represented action in conformity with nature? Is it in conformity with law? Is it in conformity with custom? Is it in conformity with the *technē*— that is, with the rules and practices that allow an action to achieve its ends? Is it in conformity with time (i.e., is it carried out at the right time and in the right circumstances)? Lastly, what of its name (does it have a name that is itself auspicious)? "It is a basic principle that everything that appears in accordance with nature, law, custom, craft, names, or time is good, but everything that is contrary to them is bad and inauspicious."[28] Artemidorus goes on to say, however, that this principle is not universal and that it involves exceptions. There can be a kind of reversal of values. Certain dreams that are "good in regard to their interior" may be "bad in regard to their exterior": the action imagined in the dream is favorable (thus, to dream that one has dinner with a god is in itself positive), but the event prefigured is negative (for if the god is Cronos, bound in chains by his sons, the image signifies that one will go to prison).[29] Inversely, other dreams are "bad in regard to their interior" and "good in regard to their exterior": a slave dreams that he is fighting in a war; this is a presage of his emancipation, for a soldier cannot be a slave. There is a considerable margin of variation, therefore, around the positive or negative signs and signifieds. What is involved is not an uncertainty that cannot be overcome, but a complex domain which demands that one take account of every aspect of the image in the dream and the circumstances of the dreamer.

Before proceeding to the analysis of sexual dreams as it was practiced by Artemidorus, this rather long detour was necessary in order to understand the mechanics of the interpretations and to determine how the moral valuations of sexual acts emerge in the divination of the dreams that represent them. It would be unwise in fact to use this text as a direct commentary on the value and legitimacy of sexual acts. Artemidorus does not say whether it is right or wrong, moral or immoral, to commit a particular act, but whether it is good or bad, favorable or ominous, to dream that one commits it. The principles that can be isolated do not therefore relate to the acts themselves but to their author, or rather to the sexual actor insofar as he represents, in the oneiric scene, the author of the dream and so enacts a presage of the good or evil that will befall him. The two main principles of oneirocriticism—namely, that the dream "tells what is real" and that it does so in the form of analogy—function here in the following way: the dream tells the event, the good fortune or misfortune, the prosperity or sorrow, that will characterize the subject's mode of being in reality, and it tells it through a relationship of analogy with the mode of being—good or bad, favorable or unfavorable—of the subject as an actor on the sexual stage of the dream. One must not look in this text for a code specifying what should and should not be done; what it reveals instead is an ethics of the subject, one that was still common in the time of Artemidorus.

CHAPTER TWO

==========

THE ANALYSIS

Artemidorus devotes four chapters to sexual dreams—not counting the many scattered notations.[1] He organizes his analysis around the distinction between three types of acts: those in conformity with the law *(kata nomon)*, those contrary to the law *(para nomon)*, and those contrary to nature *(para physin)*. This division is far from being clear: none of these terms is defined. One does not see how the categories interconnect, or whether the category of "contrary to nature" should be understood as a subdivision of acts "contrary to the law." Certain acts appear under two headings at once. We should not assume a rigorous classification that would assign every possible sexual act to the domain of the lawful, the unlawful, or the unnatural. Nevertheless, considered in detail, these groupings do have a certain intelligibility.

1. Let us consider first the acts that are "in conformity with the law." In retrospect, this chapter appears to mix together things that are quite different: adultery and marriage, frequenting of prostitutes, resorting to household slaves, a servant's masturbation. But in fact—leaving aside for now the meaning that should be given to this notion of conformity with the law—a passage from the chapter makes the progression of the analysis rather clear. Artemidorus states as a general rule that women in dreams are "symbols of things that will happen to the dreamer, so that the character and disposition of the woman determine what will happen to him.["]² It needs to be understood, then, that for Artemidorus what determines the predictive meaning of a dream, and hence in a certain way the moral value of the act dreamed of, is the condition of the partner, and not the form of the act itself. Condition should be taken here in the broad sense: it is the social status of the "other"; it is the fact that he is married or not, is free or a slave, that he is young or old, rich or poor; it is his profession, it is the place where one meets him; it is the position he holds in relation to the dreamer (spouse, mistress, slave, young protégé, etc.). One is thus able to see, beneath its apparent confusion, how the text unfolds: it follows the order of possible partners, according to their status, their connection to the dreamer, and the place where the dreamer encounters them.

The first three figures evoked by the text reproduce the traditional series of the three categories of women to which one can have access: the wife, the mistress, and the prostitute. To dream of sexual intercourse with one's own wife is a favorable sign, because the wife is in a relationship of natural analogy to the dreamer's craft or profession. As with the latter, one engages with her in a recognized and legitimate activity; one benefits from her as from a prosperous occupation; the pleasure that one derives from intercourse with her foretells the pleasure one will derive from the profits of one's trade. There is no difference in this regard between the wife and the mistress. The case of prostitutes is different. Here the analysis set forth by Artemidorus is rather curious: in themselves women, as objects from which one derives pleasure, have a positive value; and prostitutes—whom the traditional vocabulary sometimes calls "workers"—are there to furnish these pleasures, and they "give themselves without refusing anything." There is, however, "a little disgrace" in frequenting such women—disgrace and also expense—which no doubt detracts a little from the value of the event forecast by the dream that represents them. But more than anything else, it is the place of prostitution that introduces a negative value—for two reasons, one of which is linguistic in nature. If the brothel is designated by a word signifying shop or workshop *(ergastē-rion),* which has favorable implications, it is also called, like a cemetery, "a place for everyone," "a common place." The other reason touches on a point that is also frequently cited in the sexual ethics of the philosophers and physicians: the useless discharge of sperm, its waste, without the benefit of the offspring the woman can provide. Two reasons why going to prostitutes can, in a dream, portend death.

To the conventional triad of wife, mistress, prostitute, Artemidorus adds the unknown women one encounters. In this case the dream's value for the future depends on the social "value" of the woman it represents: Is she rich, well dressed, well provided with jewelry, and does she give herself willingly? If so, then the dream promises something beneficial. If she is old, ugly, poor, if she does not freely consent, the dream is inauspicious.

The household provides another category of sexual partners: servants and slaves. Here one is in the domain of direct possession. It is not by analogy that slaves signify wealth; they are an integral part of it. It stands to reason, then, that the pleasure one enjoys in a dream with this type of personage indicates that one will "derive pleasure from one's possessions, which will grow greater and more valuable." One exercises a right; one reaps benefits from one's property. Consequently, these are favorable dreams, which realize a status and a legitimacy. The sex of the partner makes little difference of course; girl or boy, what matters is that one is dealing with a slave. On the other hand, Artemidorus does bring out an important distinction concerning the position of the dreamer in the sexual act. Is he active or passive? To place oneself "beneath" one's servant in a dream, thus overturning the social hierarchy, is ominous; it is a sign that one will suffer harm from this inferior or incur his contempt. And, confirming that it is indeed a question here, not of an offense against nature, but of an attack on social hierarchies and a threat against the proper ratio of forces, Artemidorus notes the similarly negative value of dreams in which the dreamer is possessed by an enemy, or by his own brother, whether older or younger (the equality is broken).

Next comes the group comprising friends and acquaintances. It is auspicious to dream that one has sexual intercourse with a woman whom one knows if she is not married and if she is rich, because a woman who offers herself gives not only her body but also things "pertaining to the body," the things that she carries with her (clothes, jewelry, and generally speaking all the material goods she possesses). The dream is inauspicious, on the other hand, if she is a married woman, for she is under the authority of her husband. The law bars access to her and punishes adulterers, and the dreamer in this case must expect future punishment of the same type. And what if one dreams of having sex with a man? If the dreamer is a woman (this is one of the rare passages in the text where women's dreams are taken into account), the dream is favorable in every case, for it accords with the natural and social roles of women. If, however, it is a man who dreams of being possessed by another man, the distinguishing factor that enables one to decide whether the dream has a positive or a negative value is the relative status of the two partners: the dream is good if one is possessed by a man older and richer than oneself (it is a promise of gifts); it is bad if the active partner is younger and poorer, or just poorer: clearly a sign of future expenditures.

A last set of dreams in conformity with the law relates to masturbation. These dreams are very closely associated with the theme of slavery, because what is involved is a service that one renders oneself (hands are like servants who do the bidding of their master, the penis) and because the word that means "to bind to a post," used in connection with the whipping of slaves, also means "to have an erection." A slave who had dreamed he had masturbated his owner was in real life sentenced by him to a whipping. One sees the wide range of things that are "in conformity with the law." The category encompasses marital acts and sexual relations with a mistress as well as intercourse, active or passive, with another man, and masturbation.

2. The domain that Artemidorus regards as "contrary to the law" is, however, largely constituted by incest.[3] Moreover, incest is understood in the very strict sense of sexual relations between parents and children. As for incest with brothers and sisters, it is assimilated into the category of father-daughter intercourse if it occurs between a brother and his sister. Between brothers, however, Artemidorus can't seem to decide whether to place it in the category of *kata nomon* or in that of *para nomon*. In any case, he speaks of it under both rubrics.

When a father dreams that he has sex with his daughter or his son, the signification is almost always unfavorable. This may be for immediate physical reasons: if the child is very young, the physical injury resulting from such an act is a sign pointing to his or her death (if the child is less than five years old) or sickness (if more than five years old but less than ten). If the child is older, the dream is still bad, because it brings into play impossible or disastrous relations. To take sexual pleasure in one's own son, to "spend" one's semen inside him, is a useless act, a wasteful expenditure by which nothing can be gained, and which therefore portends a considerable loss of money. To have intercourse with him when he is fully grown, seeing that a father and a son cannot coexist without conflict in a household where both wish to exercise authority, is necessarily a bad omen. This kind of dream is good in a single case: when the father undertakes a journey with his son and so has a joint project to carry out with him. But if, in dreams like this, the father is in a passive position (whether the dreamer is the son or the father), the indications are ominous: the order of hierarchies, the poles of domination and activity, are overturned. The sexual "possession" of the father by the son augurs hostility and conflict.* To dream that one has sexual relations with one's own daughter is not much better for the father. Either this "expenditure" in the body of a girl who one day will marry, and thus convey the father's seed to another man, portends a substantial loss of money; or this intercourse, if the girl is already married, indicates that she will leave her husband, that she will return home, and that it will be necessary to provide for her. The dream is auspicious only in the case where, the father being poor, the daughter may return wealthy and therefore capable of providing for her father.⁵

In a way that may seem strange to us, incest with one's mother (always envisaged by Artemidorus as incest of mother with son and never of mother with daughter) is often a bearer of favorable omens. Should one conclude, based on the Artemidorean principle of a correlation between predictive value and moral value, that mother-son incest is not fundamentally reprehensible? Or should one see this as one of the exceptions, provided for by Artemidorus, to the general principle that he puts forward? There is no question that Artemidorus considers mother-son incest to be morally wrong. But it is noteworthy that he assigns it a predictive value that is often favorable, making the mother into a kind of model and matrix, as it were, of a large number of social relations and forms of activity. The mother is a man's trade; to have intercourse with her thus signifies success and prosperity in one's profession. The mother is one's native land; whoever dreams of sexual relations with her can look forward to returning home if he is in exile, or he can expect success in political life. The mother is also the fertile ground from which one came: if a man is involved in a lawsuit when he has an incest dream, this means

---

*Note, however, that in an interpretation given in Book IV, to penetrate one's son with a feeling of pleasure is a sign that he will live; to do so with a feeling of suffering is a sign that he will die. Artemidorus remarks that in this case it is the specific character of the pleasure that determines the meaning.⁴

that he will win possession of the disputed property; if he is a farmer, he will have a rich harvest. But a dream of this sort represents a danger for sick men: to penetrate into this Mother Earth means that one will die.

3. Acts "contrary to nature" occasion two successive developments in Artemidorus. The first concerns deviations from the position set by nature (and this development is appended to the interpretation of incest dreams). The second concerns relations in which it is the partner who by his own "nature" defines the unnatural character of the act.[6]

Artemidorus submits as a principle that nature has established a definite form of sexual act for each species, one and only one natural position from which animals do not deviate: "For example, some animals mount from behind, such as the horse, ass, goat, bull, stag, and the other four-footed animals. Others join their mouths first, such as the adder, the dove, and the weasel. . . . Others have no contact at all, but the females gather up the sperm that has been squeezed out by the males, as, for example, fish." Similarly, humans have received a very specific mode of union from nature: the face-to-face position, with the man extended full length on top of the woman. In this form, sexual intercourse is an act of complete possession. Provided that she "obeys" and is "willing," the man is master "of the whole body of his mate." All the other positions "have been discovered by yielding to wantonness and licentiousness." These unnatural relations always contain a portent of defective social relations (bad relationships, hostility) or a prediction of a worsening of one's economic situation (one is uncomfortable, financially "embarrassed").

Among these "variants" of the sexual act, Artemidorus gives special attention to oral eroticism. His disapproval—and here he expresses an attitude frequently attested in antiquity[7]—is vehement: an "awful act," a "moral wrong" whose representation in a dream can take on a positive value only if it refers to the professional activity of the dreamer (if he is a public speaker, flute player, or professor of rhetoric). Being a wasteful discharge of semen, this practice in a dream foretells a useless expenditure. As a custom not in harmony with nature, and one which makes it no longer possible to kiss or to share a meal, it portends a rift, enmity, and sometimes death.

But there are other ways to deviate from nature in sexual relations, by the very nature of one's partners. Artemidorus lists five possibilities: relations with gods, with animals, or with corpses; relations with oneself; and relations between women. The presence of these last two categories among the acts defying nature is more enigmatic than that of the others. Sexual intercourse with oneself is not to be understood as masturbation; the latter is mentioned among the acts that are "in conformity with the law." What is meant here by unnatural relations with oneself is penetration of the penis into one's own body, or kissing one's own sex organ, or taking the sex organ into one's mouth. The first type of dream foretells poverty, indigence, and suffering; the second promises the birth of children, if one does not yet have any, or their return, if they are absent; the last signifies that the children will die, that one will be deprived of women and mistresses (for one does not need women when one can gratify oneself), or that one will be reduced to extreme poverty.

As for sexual relations between women, one might wonder why they appear in the category of "unnatural" acts, whereas relations between men are distributed under other rubrics (and essentially under that of acts in conformity with the law). The reason for this is no doubt in the form of intercourse Artemidorus has in mind, which is penetration. By some artificial means or other, a woman contrives to usurp the role of the man, wrongfully takes his position, and possesses another woman. Between two men, penetration, the manly act par excellence, is not a transgression of nature (even if it can be considered as shameful or unseemly for one of the two to undergo it). By contrast, between two women a similar act, which is performed in defiance of what they both are and by resorting to subterfuge, is every bit as unnatural as human intercourse with a god or an animal. To dream of these acts signifies that the woman will engage in futile activities, that she will be separated from her husband, or that she will become a widow. Intercourse between two women can also signify the communication or knowledge of feminine "secrets."

CHAPTER THREE

DREAM AND ACT

Two traits should be noted because they mark the entire analysis of the sexual dream in Artemidorus. First, the dreamer is always present in his own dream. The sexual images that Artemidorus deciphers never constitute a pure and simple phantasmagoria of which the dreamer would be the spectator and which would unfold before his eyes independently of him. He always takes part, and he does so as the leading actor. What he sees is himself in his sexual activity: there is an exact correspondence between the subject dreaming of an act and the subject of the act as it is seen in the dream. Second, we may remark that in terms of his work as a whole, Artemidorus seldom treats sexual acts and pleasures as signified or presaged elements; it is relatively exceptional for an image given in a dream to forecast a sexual act or a deprivation of pleasure.[1] On the other hand, these acts and pleasures are grouped together, in the three chapters studied here, as components of the dream and as predictive elements. Artemidorus almost always has them figure on the side of the "signifiers," and almost never on the side of the "signified." They are images and not meanings, representation and not represented event. Artemidorus' interpretation will therefore place itself on a line traced between the actor of the sexual act and the dreamer of the dream, going in this way from subject to subject; and, starting from the sexual act and the role of the subject as he represents himself in his dream, the work of interpretation will have as its object to decipher what is going to happen to the dreamer once he has returned to waking life.

It is apparent at a glance that Artemidorus' interpretation quite regularly discovers a social signification in sexual dreams. True, it sometimes happens that these dreams forecast an abrupt change in the state of one's health—an illness or a recovery—and it happens, too, that they are signs of death. But in a much greater proportion, they refer to such events as success or failure in business, enrichment or impoverishment, a family's prosperity or reverse of fortune, an advantageous or disadvantageous undertaking, favorable marriages or ill-fated alliances, disputes, rivalries, reconciliations, good or bad luck in a public career, exile, condemnation. Sexual dreams foretell the dreamer's destiny in social life; the actor that he is on the sexual stage of the dream anticipates the role that he will play in the theater of family life, professional endeavor, and civic affairs.

There are, to begin with, two reasons for this. One is entirely general in nature; it concerns a feature of language Artemidorus puts to frequent use. There exists in Greek—and in many other languages as well, to varying degrees—a very pronounced ambiguity between the sexual meaning and the economic meaning of certain terms. Thus, the word *sōma*, which designates the body, also refers to riches and possessions; whence the possible equivalence between the "possession" of a body and the possession of wealth.[2] *Ousia* is substance and fortune; it is also semen and sperm: the loss of the latter may mean expenditure of the former.[3] The term *blabē*, "damage," may refer to economic setbacks, losses of money, but also to the fact that one is the victim of an act of violence and that one is a passive object in a sexual act.[4]* Artemidorus also plays on the polysemy of the vocabulary of

*See also Book IV, where it is said that to dream that one becomes a bridge signifies that one will be a prostitute: "If a woman or a handsome youth dream they turn into a bridge, they will become prostitutes and allow many to go over them." A rich man who had this same dream found himself in a situation in which he was "regarded contemptuously and was, in a certain sense, trampled under foot."[5]

debt: words signifying that one is bound to pay and one seeks to get free of the debt may also mean that one is pressed by a sexual need and that by satisfying it one is free of it. The word *anagkaion,* which is employed to designate the male organ, is at the intersection of these significations.[6]

Another reason has to do with the particular form and intended purpose of Artemidorus' work: a man's book that is addressed mainly to men in order to help them lead their lives as men. One must remember in fact that the interpretation of dreams is not regarded as a matter of pure and simple curiosity; it is an activity that is useful for managing one's existence and for preparing oneself for events that are going to occur. Since the nights tell the things of which the days will be made, it is good—if one is properly to live out his existence as a man, a master of a household, a father of a family—to be able to decipher the dreams that arise in one's life. This is the perspective of Artemidorus' books: they are a guide that will aid the responsible man, the master of his house, to conduct himself in daily life according to the signs that may prefigure that life. Hence it is the fabric of this familial, economic, and social life that he strives to rediscover in the images of dreams.

But that is not all: the interpretive practice at work in Artemidorus' discourse shows that the sexual dream itself is perceived, formalized, analyzed as a social scene. If it foretells "good things and bad" in the domain of occupation, patrimony, family, political career, status, friendships, and patronage, this is because the sexual acts that the dream depicts are made up of the same elements as that domain. By following the analytic procedures Artemidorus uses, one sees clearly that the interpretation of *aphrodisia* dreams in terms of success or failure, social good fortune or misfortune, presupposes a sort of consubstantiality between the two domains. This is apparent on two levels: that of the elements of the dream that are taken up as materials for the analysis and that of the principles that make it possible to attribute a meaning (a predictive "value") to those elements.

1. What elements does Artemidorus single out for his analysis?

The personages first of all. Concerning the dreamer himself, Artemidorus takes no account of his recent or distant past, for example, or of his state of mind, or generally of his passions either. What interests Artemidorus are the dreamer's social attributes: the age group to which he belongs, whether or not he engages in business, whether he has political responsibilities, whether he is trying to get his children married, whether he is threatened by ruin or by the hostility of those close to him, and so forth. It is also as "personages" that the partners represented are considered. The oneiric world of Artemidorus' dreamer is peopled by individuals who have few physical traits and who do not appear to have many affective or erotic ties to the dreamer himself. They figure as little more than social profiles: young people, old people (at any rate they are younger or older than the dreamer), rich people, or poor people; they are individuals who bring riches or ask for presents; they are relatives who flatter or humiliate; they are superiors to whom one had best yield or inferiors by whom one can rightfully profit; they are people from the household or from the outside; they are free men, women under a husband's control, slaves, or professional prostitutes.

As for what transpires between these personages and the dreamer, Artemidorus' restraint is nothing short of remarkable. No caresses, no complicated combinations, no phantasmagoria; just a few simple variations around one basic form —penetration. It is the latter that seems to constitute the very essence of sexual practice, the only form, in any case, that deserves attention and yields meaning in the analysis of dreams. Much more than the body itself, with its different parts, much more than pleasure, with its qualities and intensities, the act of penetration appears as a qualifier of sexual acts, with its few variants of position and especially its two poles of activity and passivity. What Artemidorus wants to know, the question that he asks constantly concerning the dreams he studies, is who penetrates whom. Is the dreaming subject (nearly always a man) active or passive? Is he the one who penetrates, dominates, enjoys? Is he the one who submits or is possessed? Whether it is a matter of relations with a son or with a father, with a mother or with a slave, the question comes back almost without fail (unless it is already implicitly answered): How did the penetration take place? Or more exactly: What was the position of the subject in regard to this penetration? All sexual dreams, even "lesbian" ones, are examined from this viewpoint and from this viewpoint alone.

Now, this act of penetration—the core of sexual activity, the raw material of interpretation, and the source of meaning for the dream—is directly perceived within a social scenography. Artemidorus sees the sexual act first and foremost as a game of superiority and inferiority: penetration places the two partners in a relationship of domination and submission. It is victory on one side, defeat on the other; it is a right that is exercised for one of the partners, a necessity that is imposed on the other. It is a status that one asserts, or a condition to which one is subjected. It is an advantage from which one benefits, or an acceptance of a situation from which others are allowed to benefit. Which brings us to the other aspect of the sexual act. Artemidorus also sees it as an "economic" game of expenditure and profit: profit, the pleasure that one takes, the agreeable sensations that one experiences; expenditure, the energy necessary for the act, the loss of semen—that precious vital substance—and the fatigue that ensues. Much more than all the variables that might come from the different possible actions, or the different sensations accompanying them, and much more than all the possible scenes that the dream might present, it is these elements relating to penetration as a "strategic" game of expenditure and benefit that are taken up by Artemidorus and used to develop his analysis.

These elements may well appear, from our vantage point, meager, schematic, sexually "colorless"; but it should be noted that they saturate the analysis from the start with socially marked elements. Artemidorus' analysis brings in personages that have been lifted fresh from a social scene, all of whose characteristics they still display; and it distributes them around an essential act that is located at one and the same time on the plane of physical conjunctions, on that of social relations of superiority and inferiority, and on that of economic activities of expenditure and profit

2. How—on the basis of these elements, taken up in this fashion and made pertinent for the analysis—will Artemidorus establish the "value" of the sexual dream? And what is meant by this is not only the type of event that is forecast allegorically, but above all—the crucial aspect for practical analysis—its "quality," that is, its auspicious or inauspicious character for the dreamer. Recall that one of the fundamental principles of the method is that the predictive quality of a dream (the favorable or unfavorable character of the event foretold) depends on the value of the foretelling image (the good or bad character of the act represented in a dream). Now, by following the analysis through a series of examples, we have been able to see that a sexual act with a "positive value" from Artemidorus' point of view is not always and not exactly a sexual act that is permitted by law, honored by opinion, and accepted by custom. There are major coincidences, of course: to dream that one has intercourse with one's own spouse or mistress is good. But there are divergences, and important ones: the favorable value of a dream of incest with one's mother is the most striking example of these. We need then to ask: What is this other way of qualifying sexual acts? What are these other criteria that enable one to say that the acts are "good" in a dream and for the dreamer, whereas they would be culpable in reality? It seems in fact that what constitutes the "value" of a dreamed-of sexual act is the relationship that is established between the sexual role and the social role of the dreamer. More precisely, we can say that Artemidorus finds "favorable" and propitious a dream in which the dreamer pursues his sexual activity with his partner according to a schema that conforms to what his relationship with the same

partner should be in social, not sexual, life. It is this adjustment to the "waking" social relation that qualifies the oneiric
sexual relation.

In order to be "good," the sexual act that one dreams needs
to obey a general rule of "isomorphism." And, speaking
schematically still, one may add that this rule takes two forms:
"analogy of position" and "economic adequation." According
to the first of these principles, a sexual act will be good to the
extent that the subject who dreams occupies in his sexual
activity with his partner a position that matches the one he
occupies in real life with this same partner (or a partner of the
same type). Thus, to be "active" with one's slave (whatever
the sex of the latter), or to be active with a prostitute (male
or female), or to be active with a boy who is young and poor,
is good; but it will be "good" to be passive with an individual
older than oneself, richer than oneself, and so on. It is by
virtue of this rule of isomorphism that the dream of incest with
one's mother is laden with so many positive values. In such
dreams the subject is indeed seen in a position of activity with
respect to a mother who gave birth to and nurtured him, and
whom he ought to cultivate, honor, serve, maintain, and en-
rich in return, like a piece of land, a native country, a city. But
for the sexual act in a dream to have a positive value, it must
also obey a principle of "economic adequation." The "cost"
and the "benefit" this activity entails must be properly regulated: in quantity (much expense for little pleasure is not good)
and in direction as well (not to spend uselessly on those individuals, male or female, who are not in a position to repay,
offer compensation, or be useful in return). It is this principle
that makes it good to dream of sexual intercourse with slaves:
one profits from one's possessions; that which one has purchased for the benefit of labor yields the benefit of pleasure
besides. It is also what gives multiple significations to dreams
in which a father has intercourse with his daughter. Depending on whether she is married or not, whether the father
himself is a widower or not, whether the son-in-law is richer
or poorer than the father-in-law, the dream will signify either

an expenditure for the dowry, or help coming from the daughter, or an obligation to provide for her after her divorce.

We can summarize all this by saying that the guiding thread of Artemidorus' interpretation, insofar as it is concerned with the predictive value of sexual dreams, implies the breaking down and ordering of such dreams into elements (personages or acts) that are, by nature, social elements; and that it indicates a certain way of qualifying sexual acts in terms of the manner in which the dreaming subject maintains, as the subject of the dreamed-of act, his position as a social subject. In the dream scene, the sexual actor (who is always the dreamer and is almost always an adult male) must, if his dream is to be good, maintain his role as a social actor (even if the act happens to be reprehensible in reality). Let us not forget that all the sexual dreams that Artemidorus analyzes are considered by him to belong to the category of *oneiros:* hence they tell "what will be"; and it so happens in this case that what "will be," and what is "told" in the dream, is the position of the dreamer as a subject of activity—active or passive, dominant or dominated, winner or loser, "on top" or "on the bottom," profit-taker or spender, deriving benefits or experiencing losses, finding himself in an advantageous position or suffering damages. The sexual dream uses the little drama of penetration and passivity, pleasure and expenditure, to tell the subject's mode of being, as destiny has arranged it.

By way of confirmation, one might refer to a passage from *The Interpretation of Dreams* which shows unmistakably the connection between that which constitutes the individual as an active subject in the sexual relation and that which situates him in the field of social activities. I am thinking of the text, in another section of the book, that is devoted to the meaning of the different parts of the body in dreams. The male organ —the one called *anagkaion* (the "necessary" part, whose needs compel us and by whose force others are compelled)— is expressive of a whole cluster of relations and activities that determine the individual's standing in the city and in the world. Among these are the individual's wealth, speech, status, political life, freedom, and even his name. "The penis corresponds to one's parents, on the one hand, because it is itself the cause of children. It signifies a wife or mistress, since it is made for sexual intercourse. It indicates brothers and all blood relatives, since the interrelationship of the entire house depends upon the penis. It is a symbol of strength and physical vigor, because it is itself the cause of these qualities. That is why some people call the penis 'one's manhood.' It corresponds to speech and education because the penis is very fertile . . . the penis is also a sign of wealth and possessions because it alternately expands and contracts and because it is able to produce and to eliminate. . . . It indicates poverty, servitude, and bonds, because it is also called 'constraining' and is a symbol of necessity. It also indicates the respect that is inspired by high rank: for it is called 'reverence' and respect. . . . If the penis is doubled, it signifies that everything will be doubled, with the exception of a wife or a mistress; these will be lost. For it is impossible to use two penises at the same time. I know of a slave who dreamt that he had three penises. He was set free and, in place of one name, he had three, since he received in addition the two names of the master who had freed him. But this happened only once. One must not base one's interpretation on rare instances but rather on the more normal cases."[7]

The penis thus appears at the intersection of all these games of mastery: self-mastery, since its demands are likely to enslave us if we allow ourselves to be coerced by it; superiority over sexual partners, since it is by means of the penis that the penetration is carried out; status and privileges, since it signifies the whole field of kinship and social activity.

The landscape evoked in the chapters in Artemidorus that deal with sexual dreams was a familiar one in antiquity. It is easy to rediscover there aspects of manners and customs that could be confirmed by many other—earlier or contemporaneous—testimonies. One is in a world very strongly marked by the central position of the male personage and by the impor-

tance accorded to the masculine role in sexual relationships. It is a world in which marriage is valued highly enough to be regarded as the best possible framework for sexual pleasures. In this world the married man can also have his mistress, avail himself of his servants (boys or girls), and frequent prostitutes. In this world, finally, sexual relations between men appear to be taken for granted—that is, provided that certain differences of age and status are respected.

We may also note the presence of several elements of a code. But it must be admitted that they are both few in number and rather nebulous—a few major prohibitions that are manifested in the form of intense repulsions: fellatio, sexual relations between women, and, above all, the usurping of the male role by a woman; a very restrictive definition of incest, conceived of essentially as intercourse between parents and children; and a reference to a standard, natural form of sexual act. But there is nothing in Artemidorus' text that refers to a permanent and complete grid of classifications among permitted and prohibited acts; nothing that draws a clear and definitive line of division between what is natural and what is "contrary to nature." Moreover, it seems that these code elements are not —at least not in dreams having a predictive function—what plays the most important and decisive role in determining the "quality" of a sexual act.

On the other hand, one does perceive, in the very way the interpretation proceeds, a different way of thinking about sexual acts and different principles for evaluating them: not with a view to the act and its regular or irregular form, but with a view to the actor, his way of being, his particular situation, his relation to others, and the position he occupies with respect to them. The main question appears to bear much less on the acts' conformity with a natural structure or with a positive regulation, than on what might be called the subject's "style of activity" and on the relation he establishes between sexual activity and the other aspects of his familial, social, and economic existence. The movement of analysis and the procedures of valuation do not go from the act to a domain such as sexuality or the flesh, a domain whose divine, civil, or natural laws would delineate the permitted forms; they go from the subject as a sexual actor to the other areas of life in which he pursues his activity. And it is in the relationship between these different forms of activity that the principles of evaluation of a sexual behavior are essentially, but not exclusively, situated.

Here one easily recognizes the principal characteristics of the ethical experience of the *aphrodisia* in the form in which it had appeared in the texts of the classical age. And, precisely insofar as it does not formulate an ethic, but uses for dream interpretation a way of perceiving and judging sexual pleasure that is contemporaneous with it, Artemidorus' book testifies to the endurance and solidity of that form of experience.

If we turn, however, to texts whose object is to reflect on the sexual practices themselves and to give advice on behavior and precepts for living, with reference to them, we can note a certain number of modifications in comparison with the doctrines of austerity formulated in the philosophy of the fourth century. Breaks, radical changes, emergence of a new form of experience of pleasure? No, this was clearly not the case. And yet there are noticeable inflections: a closer attention, an increased anxiety concerning sexual conduct, a greater importance accorded to marriage and its demands, and less value given to the love of boys: in short, a more rigorous style. But in these themes that develop, become accentuated, and gather strength, one can discern a different type of modification: it concerns the way in which ethical thought defines the relation of the subject to his sexual activity.

PART TWO

THE CULTIVATION OF THE SELF

A mistrust of the pleasures, an emphasis on the consequences of their abuse for the body and the soul, a valorization of marriage and marital obligations, a disaffection with regard to the spiritual meanings imputed to the love of boys: a whole attitude of severity was manifested in the thinking of philosophers and physicians in the course of the first two centuries. It is visible in the texts of Soranus and Rufus of Ephesus, in Musonius or Seneca, in Plutarch as well as in Epictetus or Marcus Aurelius. Moreover, it is a fact that the Christian authors borrowed extensively—with and without acknowledgment—from this body of ethical thought. And most historians today recognize the existence, strength, and intensification of these themes of sexual austerity in a society known by its contemporaries, and, more often than not, reproached, for its immorality and dissolute ways. Let us leave aside the question of knowing whether this blame was justified. Considering only those texts that talk about the "question of pleasure," and considering the place they give to it, it seems in fact that it had become more insistent. More precisely, there was greater apprehension concerning the sexual pleasures, more attention given to the relation that one might have with them. In a word, there was a more intense problematization of the *aphrodisia,* a problematization whose particular forms and motifs we must try to reconstruct.

One can appeal to various explanations in order to account

for this new accentuation. One can relate it to certain efforts on the part of political power to raise moral standards in a more or less authoritarian way. These efforts were especially forceful and explicit under the principate of Augustus; and in that instance it is true that legislative measures protecting marriage, favoring the family, regulating concubinage, and condemning adultery were accompanied by a movement of ideas—perhaps not entirely artificial—that opposed the current laxity while preaching a return to the rigor of the old customs. We cannot be satisfied with this reference, however; it would doubtless be incorrect to see in these measures and these ideas the beginning of a centuries-long evolution that would lead to a regime in which sexual freedom would be more strictly limited by institutions and laws, whether civil or religious. These political strivings were in fact too sporadic; they had objectives that were too limited; and they had too few general and lasting effects to account for the tendency toward austerity so often evinced in moral reflection over the entire course of the first two centuries. Furthermore, it is remarkable that, with rare exceptions,* this desire for rigor expressed by the moralists did not take the form of a demand for intervention on the part of public authority. One would not find in the writings of the philosophers any proposal for a general and coercive legislation of sexual behaviors. They urge individuals to be more austere if they wish to lead a life different from that of "the throngs"; they do not try to determine which measures or punishments might constrain everyone in a uniform manner. Moreover, if we are authorized to speak of an increased austerity, this is not because more rigorous prohibitions were recommended: after all, the medical regimens of the first and second centuries are, generally speaking, not much more restrictive than that of Diocles; the conjugal fidelity exalted by the Stoics is not more rigorous than that of Nicocles, who boasted of not having sexual relations with any woman other

---

*For example, Dio Chrysostom envisages certain measures that would have to be taken in order to make virtue prevail, but this is in the context of the problems posed by poverty.[1]

than his own wife; and Plutarch, in the *Dialogue on Love*, is on the whole more indulgent with regard to boys than is the strict legislator of the *Laws*. Rather, what stands out in the texts of the first centuries—more than new interdictions concerning sexual acts—is the insistence on the attention that should be brought to bear on oneself; it is the modality, scope, constancy, and exactitude of the required vigilance; it is the anxiety concerning all the disturbances of the body and the mind, which must be prevented by means of an austere regimen; it is the importance attributed to self-respect, not just insofar as one's status is concerned, but as concerns one's rational nature—a self-respect that is exercised by depriving oneself of pleasure or by confining one's indulgence to marriage or procreation. In short, and as a first approximation, this added emphasis on sexual austerity in moral reflection takes the form, not of a tightening of the code that defined prohibited acts, but of an intensification of the relation to oneself by which one constituted oneself as the subject of one's acts.[2] And the motivations of this more severe ethics cannot be examined without taking such a form into account.

One may think at this point of a phenomenon that is often alluded to: the growth, in the Hellenistic and Roman world, of an "individualism" that is said to have accorded more and more importance to the "private" aspects of existence, to the values of personal conduct, and to the interest that people focused on themselves. Thus, it was not a strengthening of public authority that accounted for the development of that rigorous ethics, but rather a weakening of the political and social framework within which the lives of individuals used to unfold. Being less firmly attached to the cities, more isolated from one another, and more reliant on themselves, they sought in philosophy rules of conduct that were more personal. Not everything is false in a schema of this sort. But we may wonder about the reality of that individualistic upsurge and the social and political process that would have detached individuals from their traditional affiliations. Civic and political activity may have, to some degree, changed its form; it nonetheless remained an important part of life for the upper classes. Broadly speaking, the ancient societies remained societies of promiscuity, where existence was led "in public." They were also societies in which everyone was situated within strong systems of local relationships, family ties, economic dependences, and relations of patronage and friendship. Further, it should be noted that the doctrines that were most attached to austerity of conduct—and the Stoics can be placed at the head of the list—were also those which insisted the most on the need to fulfill one's obligations to mankind, to one's fellow-citizens, and to one's family, and which were quickest to denounce an attitude of laxity and self-satisfaction in practices of social withdrawal.

But a more general question needs to be asked concerning this "individualism" that is so frequently invoked, in different epochs, to explain very diverse phenomena. Quite often with such categories, entirely different realities are lumped together. Three things in fact need to be distinguished here: (1) the individualistic attitude, characterized by the absolute value attributed to the individual in his singularity and by the degree of independence conceded to him vis-à-vis the group to which he belongs and the institutions to which he is answerable; (2) the positive valuation of private life, that is, the importance granted to family relationships, to the forms of domestic activity, and to the domain of patrimonial interests; (3) the intensity of the relations to self, that is, of the forms in which one is called upon to take oneself as an object of knowledge and a field of action, so as to transform, correct, and purify oneself, and find salvation. These attitudes can be interconnected, no doubt. Thus it can happen that individualism entails an intensification of the values of private life, or that the importance accorded to the relations to self is associated with an exaltation of individual singularity. But these connections are neither constant nor necessary. One could find societies or social groups—military aristocracies are a probable example of these—in which the individual is invited to assert his self-worth by means of actions that set him apart and enable him to win out over the others, without his having to attribute any great importance to his private life or to the relations of himself to himself. There are also societies in which private life is highly valued, in which it is carefully protected and organized, in which it forms the center of reference for behaviors and one of the principles of their valuation —this appears to be true of the bourgeois classes in the Western countries of the nineteenth century. But, for this very reason, individualism in such societies is weak and the relations of oneself to oneself are largely undeveloped. Finally, there are societies or groups in which the relation to self is intensified and developed without this resulting, as if by necessity, in a strengthening of the values of individualism or of private life. The Christian ascetic movement of the first centuries presented itself as an extremely strong accentuation of the relations of oneself to oneself, but in the form of a disqualification of the values of private life; and when it took the form of cenobitism, it manifested an explicit rejection of any individualism that might be inherent in the practice of reclusion.

The demands of sexual austerity expressed in imperial times do not seem to have been the manifestation of a growing individualism. Their context is characterized instead by a phenomenon that has a rather long historical range, but reached its peak at that particular moment. I am referring to the development of what might be called a "cultivation of the self," wherein the relations of oneself to oneself were intensified and valorized.

This "cultivation of the self"[3] can be briefly characterized by the fact that in this case the art of existence—the *technē tou biou* in its different forms—is dominated by the principle that says one must "take care of oneself." It is this principle of the care of the self that establishes its necessity, presides over its development, and organizes its practice. But one has to be precise here; the idea that one ought to attend to oneself, care for oneself *(heautou epimeleisthai),* was actually a very ancient theme in Greek culture. It appeared very early as a widespread imperative. At the end of his conquests, Xenophon's idealized Cyrus still does not consider his existence to be complete. It remains for him—and this he values above all else—to attend to himself: "We cannot possibly find any fault with the gods that all we wished for has not been fulfilled," he says while reflecting on his past victories. "However, if great success is to have such consequences that a man is not able to have some leisure for himself nor time to enjoy himself with his friends, I am ready to bid farewell to that sort of happiness."[4] A Lacedaemonian aphorism, reported by Plutarch,[5] stated that the reason for which cultivation of the land was entrusted to the helots was that the citizens of Sparta, for their part, wanted "to take care of themselves": no doubt it was physical and military training that was meant by the phrase. But it is used in a completely different sense in the *Alcibiades,* where it constitutes a basic theme of the dialogue. Socrates shows the ambitious young man that it is quite presumptuous of him to want to take charge of the city, manage its affairs, and enter into competition with the kings of Sparta or the rulers of Persia, if he has not first learned that which it is necessary to know in order to govern: he must first attend to himself—and right away, while he is young, for "at the age of fifty, it would be too late."[6] And in the *Apology* it is clearly as a master of the care of the self that Socrates presents himself to his judges. The god has sent him to remind men that they need to concern themselves not with their riches, not with their honor, but with themselves and with their souls.[7]

Now, it was this theme of the care of oneself, consecrated by Socrates, that later philosophy took up again and ultimately placed at the center of that "art of existence" which philosophy claimed to be. It was this theme which, breaking out of its original setting and working loose from its first philosophical meanings, gradually acquired the dimensions and forms of a veritable "cultivation of the self." What is meant by these remarks is that the principle of care of oneself became rather general in scope. The precept according to which one must give attention to oneself was in any case an imperative that circulated among a number of different doctrines. It also took the form of an attitude, a mode of behavior; it became instilled in ways of living; it evolved into procedures, practices, and formulas that people reflected on, developed, perfected, and taught. It thus came to constitute a social practice, giving rise to relationships between individuals, to exchanges and communications, and at times even to institutions. And it gave rise, finally, to a certain mode of knowledge and to the elaboration of a science.

In the slow development of the art of living under the theme of the care of oneself, the first two centuries of the imperial epoch can be seen as the summit of a curve: a kind of golden age in the cultivation of the self—it being understood, of course, that this phenomenon concerned only the social groups, very limited in number, that were bearers of culture and for whose members a *technē tou biou* could have a meaning and a reality.

1. The *epimeleia heautou,* the *cura sui,* is an injunction that one rediscovers in many philosophical doctrines. One encounters it in the Platonists: Albinus advises that one commence the study of philosophy by reading the *Alcibiades* "with a view to turning and returning to oneself," and for the purpose of learning "that which one should make into the object of his care."[8] Apuleius, at the end of the *God of Socrates,* expresses his wonder at seeing the carelessness of his contemporaries with regard to themselves: "All men should desire to live most happily, and should know that they cannot so live in any other way than by cultivating the soul, and yet leave the soul uncultivated [*animum suum non colunt*]. If, however, anyone wishes to see acutely, it is requisite that he should pay attention to his eyes, through which he sees; if you desire to run with celerity, attention must be paid to the feet, by which you run. . . . In a similar manner, in all the other members, attention to each must be paid according to one's preferences. And, as all men may easily see that this is true, I cannot sufficiently . . . wonder, in such a way as the thing deserves wonder, why they do not also cultivate their soul by reason [*cur non etiam animum suum ratione excolant*]."[9]

As for the Epicureans, the *Letter to Menoeceus* began by stating the principle that philosophy should be considered as a permanent exercise of the care of oneself: "Let no young man delay the study of philosophy, and let no young man become weary of it; for it is never too early or too late to care for the well-being of the soul."[10] It is this Epicurean theme of the need to take care of oneself that Seneca takes up in one of his letters: "Just as fair weather, purified into the purest brilliancy, does not admit of a still greater degree of clearness; so, when a man takes care of his body and of his soul [*hominis corpus animumque curantis*], weaving the texture of his good from both, his condition is perfect, and he has found the consummation of his prayers, if there is no commotion in his soul or pain in his body."[11]

Taking care of one's soul was a precept that Zeno had given his disciples from the beginning, and one Musonius was to repeat, in the first century, in a sentence quoted by Plutarch: "He who wishes to come through life safe and sound must continue throughout his life to take care of himself."[12] The fullness assumed, in Seneca, by the theme of application of oneself to oneself is well known: it is to this activity, according to him, that a man must devote himself, to the exclusion of other occupations. He will thus be able to make himself vacant for himself *(sibi vacare)*.[13] But this "vacation" takes the form of a varied activity which demands that one lose no time and spare no effort in order to "develop oneself," "transform oneself," "return to oneself." *Se formare, sibi vindicare, se facere, se ad studia revocare, sibi applicare, suum fieri, in se recedere, ad se recurrere, secum morari*[14]—Seneca commands a whole vocabulary for designating the different forms that ought to be taken by the care of the self and the haste with which one seeks to reunite with oneself *(ad se properare)*.[15] Marcus Aurelius also feels the same haste to look after himself: neither reading nor writing must keep him any longer from the direct attention he must give to his own being: "No more vague wanderings. You are not likely to read your memoranda, your histories of Greece and Rome, or the extracts from books which you put aside for your old age. Hasten then to the end, discard vain hopes, and if you care for yourself at all, rescue yourself [*sautōi boēthei ei ti soi meleî sautou*] while you still may."[16]

It is in Epictetus no doubt that one finds the highest philosophical development of this theme. Man is defined in the *Discourses* as the being who was destined to care for himself. This is where the basic difference between him and other creatures resides. The animals find "ready prepared" that which they need in order to live, for nature has so arranged things that animals are at our disposal without their having to look after themselves, and without our having to look after them.[17] Man, on the other hand, must attend to himself: not, however, as a consequence of some defect that would put him in a situation of need and make him in this respect inferior to the animals, but because the god [Zeus] deemed it right that he be able to make free use of himself; and it was for this purpose that he endowed him with reason. The latter is not to be understood as a substitute for natural faculties that might be lacking; on the contrary it is the faculty that enables one to use, at the right time and in the right way, the other faculties. In fact, it is this absolutely singular faculty that is capable of making use of itself, for it is capable of "contemplating both itself and everything else."[18] By crowning with this reasoning faculty all that is already given to us by nature, Zeus gave us the possibility and the duty to take care of ourselves. It is insofar as he is free and reasonable that man is the natural being that has been committed to the care of himself. The god did not fashion us out of marble, like Phidias his Athena, who forever extends the hand on which Victory came to rest immobile with wings outspread. Zeus "not only made you, but entrusted and committed you to yourself alone."[19] The care of the self, for Epictetus, is a privilege-duty, a gift-obligation that ensures our freedom while forcing us to take ourselves as the object of all our diligence.[20]

But the fact that the philosophers advise that one give heed to oneself does not mean that this zeal is reserved for those who choose to live a life similar to theirs, or that such an attitude is required only during the time one spends with them. It is a valuable principle for everyone, all the time and throughout life. Apuleius points out that one can, without shame or dishonor, ignore the rules that make it possible to paint and to play the zither, but to know how "to perfect one's own soul with the help of reason" is a rule "equally necessary for all men." The case of Pliny can serve as a concrete example in this regard: aloof from all strict doctrinal adherences, leading a regular career replete with honors, absorbed by his activities as a lawyer, he is not on the point of breaking his ties to society—far from it. And yet, throughout his life he does not cease to speak of the care he intends to devote to himself as perhaps the most important matter with which he could be concerned. When, as a very young man still, he is sent to Syria to do military service, his first thought is to visit with Euphrates, not just to hear his lectures, but little by little to get to know him, "win his affection," and benefit from the admonitions of a master who knows how to go after faults without attacking individuals.[21] And later, in Rome, when he has occasion to take a period of rest in his villa at Laurentum, it is in order to be able to attend to himself, "reading and writing and finding time to take the exercise which keeps my mind fit," and "sharing my thoughts with no one but my own writings."[22]

Hence there is no right age for attending to oneself. "It is never too early nor too late to care for the well-being of the soul," to quote Epicurus again. "The man who says that the season for this study has not yet come or is already past is like the man who says it is too early or too late for happiness. Therefore, both the young and the old should study philosophy, the former so that as he grows old he may still retain the happiness of youth in his pleasant memories of the past, the latter so that although he is old he may at the same time be young by virtue of his fearlessness of the future."[23] "Spend your whole life learning how to live" was an aphorism—

Seneca cites it—which asked people to transform their existence into a kind of permanent exercise. And while it is good to begin early, it is important never to let up.[24] Those to whom Seneca or Plutarch offer their counsel are in fact no longer the eager or timid adolescents whom the Socrates of Plato or Xenophon urged to attend to themselves. They are men. Serenus, to whom the moral essay *De tranquilitate* is addressed (in addition to the *De constantia* and perhaps the *De otio*) is a young relative under Seneca's protection, but nothing like a boy pursuing his studies. At the time of the writing of *De tranquilitate,* he is a provincial who has just arrived in Rome, and who is still trying to decide on a career and a way of life; but he already has behind him a certain philosophical itinerary. His perplexity relates essentially to the way in which he might bring it to a conclusion. As for Lucilius, apparently he was only a few years younger than Seneca. He is procurator in Sicily when, starting in 62, they exchange the intimate correspondence in which Seneca reveals to him the principles and practices of his wisdom, tells him of his own weaknesses and his still unfinished battles, and occasionally even asks for his help. Nor is he embarrassed to tell him that when more than sixty years old, he himself went to hear the lectures of Metronax.[25] The correspondents to whom Plutarch addresses his treatises—which are not just general considerations on virtues and faults, on the happiness of the soul and the misfortunes of life, but advice on conduct, often in reference to very specific circumstances—are men as well.

This extreme eagerness of adults to look after their souls, the zeal with which, like schoolboys grown old, they sought out philosophers so that they might be shown the way to happiness, irritated Lucian, and many others with him. He makes fun of Hermotimus, who is seen muttering lessons in the street, lessons he must not forget. Hermotimus is no longer a young man, however: it has been twenty years already since he decided no longer to mingle his life with that of unfortunate humans, and he estimates that it will take him another twenty years to reach the state of bliss. Now (he mentions this himself a little further on), he began to philosophize at the age of forty. So it is the last forty years of his life that he will have devoted to caring for himself, under the direction of a master. And his interlocutor Lycinus, for his own amusement, pretends to discover that for him, too, the time has come to study philosophy, seeing that he has just turned forty: "Act as my crutch," he says to Hermotimus, and "lead me by the hand."[26] As Ilsetraut Hadot says in reference to Seneca, all this activity of spiritual direction is in the category of adult education—of *Erwachsenerziehung*.[27]

2.   It is important to understand that this application to oneself does not require simply a general attitude, an unfocused attention. The term *epimeleia* designates not just a preoccupation but a whole set of occupations; it is *epimeleia* that is employed in speaking of the activities of the master of a household, the tasks of the ruler who looks after his subjects, the care that must be given to a sick or wounded patient, or the honors that must be paid to the gods or to the dead.[28] With regard to oneself as well, *epimeleia* implies a labor.

It takes time. And it is one of the big problems of this cultivation of the self to determine the portion of one's day or one's life that should be devoted to it. People resort to many different formulas. One can set aside a few moments, in the evening or in the morning, for introspection, for examining what needs to be done, for memorizing certain useful principles, for reflecting on the day that has gone by. The morning and evening examination of the Pythagoreans is encountered again, doubtless with a different content, in the Stoics. Seneca, Epictetus, and Marcus Aurelius refer to those moments that ought to be devoted to turning one's thoughts to oneself.[29] One may also from time to time interrupt one's ordinary activities and go into one of those retreats that Musonius, among so many others, strongly recommended.[30] They enable one to commune with oneself, to recollect one's bygone days, to place the whole of one's past life before one's eyes, to get to know oneself, through reading, through the precepts and examples that will provide inspiration, and, by contemplating a life reduced to its essentials, to rediscover the basic principles of a rational conduct. It is possible too, in the middle or at the end of one's career, to unburden oneself of these activities and, taking advantage of these declining years when desires are calmed, give oneself up entirely—like Seneca in his philosophical work or Spurrina in the tranquillity of a pleasant existence[31]—to the possession of oneself.

This time is not empty; it is filled with exercises, practical tasks, various activities. Taking care of oneself is not a rest cure. There is the care of the body to consider, health regimens, physical exercises without overexertion, the carefully measured satisfaction of needs. There are the meditations, the readings, the notes that one takes on books or on the conversations one has heard, notes that one reads again later, the recollection of truths that one knows already but that need to be more fully adapted to one's own life. Marcus Aurelius thus gives an example of "a retreat within oneself": it is a sustained effort in which general principles are reactivated and arguments are adduced that persuade one not to let oneself become angry at others, at providence, or at things.[32] There are also the talks that one has with a confidant, with friends, with a guide or director. Add to this the correspondence in which one reveals the state of one's soul, solicits advice, gives advice to anyone who needs it—which for that matter constitutes a beneficial exercise for the giver, who is called the preceptor, because he thereby reactualizes it for himself.[33] Around the care of the self, there developed an entire activity of speaking and writing in which the work of oneself on oneself and communication with others were linked together.

Here we touch on one of the most important aspects of this activity devoted to oneself: it constituted, not an exercise in solitude, but a true social practice. And it did so in several ways. It often took form within more or less institutionalized structures. The neo-Pythagorean communities are an example of this, or those Epicurean groups about whose practices we have some information by way of Philodemus: a recognized hierarchy gave the most advanced members the task of tutoring the others (either individually or in a more collective fashion). But there were also common exercises that allowed one, in the attention he gave to himself, to receive the help of others: this was the task defined as *to di' allēlōn sōzesthai.*[34] Epictetus taught in a setting that was more like that of a school. He had several categories of students: some were there for only a short stay; others would remain longer in order to prepare for the life of an ordinary citizen or even for important activities; and finally a few others, who intended to become professional philosophers themselves, were there to be trained in the rules and practices of spiritual direction.[35] One also found—particularly in Rome, in aristocratic circles—the practice of the private consultant who served in a family or a group as a life counselor, a political adviser, a potential intermediary in a negotiation: "Some wealthy Romans found it useful to keep a philosopher, and men of distinction did not find the position humiliating. They expected to be able to give moral advice and comfort to their patrons and their families, while their patrons could draw strength from their approval."[36] Thus Demetrius was the spiritual guide of Thrasea Paetus, who had him participate in the staging of his suicide, so that he might in this final moment help him give his life its finest and most accomplished form. Furthermore, these different functions of professor, guide, adviser, and personal confidant were not always distinct—far from it: in the practice of the cultivation of the self, the roles were often interchangeable, and they could be played in turn by the same person. Musonius Rufus had been the political adviser of Rubellius Plautus; in the exile that followed the latter's death, he drew visitors and loyal supporters around him and held a kind of school. Under Vespasian, he returned to Rome, where he gave public lectures and was part of Titus' entourage.

But all this attention to the self did not depend solely on the existence of schools, lectures, and professionals of spiritual direction for its social base; it found a ready support in the whole bundle of customary relations of kinship, friendship, and obligation. When, in the practice of the care of the self, one appealed to another person in whom one recognized an aptitude for guidance and counseling, one was exercising a right. And it was a duty that one was performing when one lavished one's assistance on another, or when one gratefully received the lessons the other might give. Galen's text on curing the passions is significant from this point of view: he advises anyone who wishes to take proper care of himself to seek the aid of another; he does not, however, recommend a technician known for his competence and learning, but simply a man of good reputation, whose uncompromising frankness one can have the opportunity of experiencing.[37] But it is sometimes the case, too, that the interplay of the care of the self and the help of the other blends into preexisting relations, giving them a new coloration and a greater warmth. The care of the self—or the attention one devotes to the care that others should take of themselves—appears then as an intensification of social relations. Seneca addresses a letter of consolation to his mother, during the period when he is in exile, in order to help her support his present misfortune, and perhaps greater misfortunes in the future. The Serenus to whom he addresses the long moral essay on tranquillity of mind is a young provincial relative whom he has under his protection. His correspondence with Lucilius deepens a preexisting relationship between the two men, who are not separated by a very great difference in age, and tends little by little to transform this spiritual guidance into a shared experience, from which each derives a benefit for himself. In the thirty-fourth letter, Seneca, who is able to say to Lucilius: "I claim you for myself; you are my handiwork," immediately adds: "I am cheering on one who is in the race and so in turn cheers me on." And, already in the next letter, he alludes to the reward of perfect friendship in which each one will be for the other that constant help which will be the subject of letter 109: "Skilled wrestlers are kept up to the mark by practice; a musician is stirred to action by one of equal proficiency. The wise man also needs to have his virtues kept in action; and as he prompts himself to do

things, so he is prompted by another wise man."[38] The care of
the self appears therefore as intrinsically linked to a "soul
service," which includes the possibility of a round of exchanges with the other and a system of reciprocal obligations.

3. In keeping with a tradition that goes back a very long
way in Greek culture, the care of the self is in close correlation
with medical thought and practice. This ancient correlation
became increasingly strong, so much so that Plutarch is able
to say, at the beginning of *Advice about Keeping Well,* that
philosophy and medicine are concerned with "a single field"
(mia chōra). [39] They do in fact draw on a shared set of notions,
whose central element is the concept of "pathos." It applies
to passion as well as to physical illness, to the distress of the
body and to the involuntary movement of the soul; and in both
cases alike, it refers to a state of passivity, which for the body
takes the form of a disorder that upsets the balance of its
humors or its qualities and which for the soul takes the form
of a movement capable of carrying it away in spite of itself.
On the basis of this shared concept, it was possible to construct a grid of analysis that was valid for the ailments of the
body and the soul. For example, there was the schema proposed by the Stoics, which determines the degrees of development and the chronicity of diseases. The first distinction made
in this schema is the predisposition to disease, the *proclivitas*
that exposes one to the possible illnesses. Next there is the
affection, the disorder, which in Greek is called *pathos* and in
Latin *affectus;* then the illness *(nosēma, morbus)* that is established and declared when the disorder has taken hold of the
body and the soul. More serious, more lasting, is the *aegrotatio*
or *arrhōstēma* that constitutes a state of sickness and debility.
Finally, there is the inveterate disease *(kakia, aegrotatio in-
veterata, vitium malum)* for which no cure is possible. The
Stoics also presented schemas that mark the different stages or
different possible forms of the cure. Thus Seneca distinguishes
between sick persons who are cured of all or part of their vices
and those who are rid of their ills but not yet rid of their

affections; and there are those who have recovered their health but are still frail because their predispositions have not been corrected.[40] These notions and schemas are intended to serve as a common guide for the medicine of the body and the therapeutics of the soul. They make it possible not only to apply the same type of theoretical analysis to physical troubles and moral disorders alike, but also to use the same kind of approach in attending to them, treating them, and, if possible, curing them.

A whole series of medical metaphors is regularly employed to designate the operations necessary for the care of the soul: put the scalpel to the wound; open an abscess; amputate; evacuate the superfluities; give medications; prescribe bitter, soothing, or bracing potions.[41] The improvement, the perfecting of the soul that one seeks in philosophy, the *paideia* the latter is supposed to ensure, increasingly assumes a medical coloration. Educating oneself and taking care of oneself are interconnected activities. Epictetus lays stress on this point: he does not want his school to be considered as just a place of education where one can acquire knowledge useful for a career or a reputation, before returning home to derive advantage from it. The school should be thought of as a "dispensary for the soul": "The philosopher's school is a physician's consulting-room [*iatreion*]. You must leave it in pain, not in pleasure."[42] He insists that his disciples be mindful of their condition, regarding it as a pathological state; that they not consider themselves first and above all as students who have come to gain knowledge from the man who possesses it; that they present themselves as patients, as though one had a dislocated shoulder, the other an abscess, the third a fistula, and the next one headaches. He takes them to task for coming to him not in order to be treated (*therapeuthēsomenoi*) but in order to have their judgments amended and corrected (*epanorthōsontes*). "You wish to learn syllogisms? You must first attend to your ulcers, and stay your flux, and arrive at peace in your mind."[43]

In return, a physician like Galen considers it within his

competence not only to cure the great aberrations of the mind (love madness was traditionally within the purview of medicine), but to treat the passions ("an irrational power within us which refuses to obey reason") and the errors (which "arise from a false opinion"). Moreover, "both are commonly called errors in a generic sense."[44] Thus he undertakes to cure a traveling companion who was too easily disposed to lose his temper. Or again, he grants the request of a young man he knew who had come one day to ask him for medical advice: the young man had in fact imagined himself to be immune to the agitation of the passions, however minor they might be; but he had been obliged to recognize that he was more troubled by matters of no importance than was his teacher Galen by momentous ones, so he came to him for help.[45]

The increased medical involvement in the cultivation of the self appears to have been expressed through a particular and intense form of attention to the body. This attention is very different from that manifested by the positive valuation of physical vigor during an epoch when gymnastics and athletic and military training were an integral part of the education of a free man. Moreover, it has something paradoxical about it since it is inscribed, at least in part, within an ethics that posits that death, disease, or even physical suffering do not constitute true ills and that it is better to take pains over one's soul than to devote one's care to the maintenance of the body.[46] But in fact the focus of attention in these practices of the self is the point where the ills of the body and those of the soul can communicate with one another and exchange their distresses: where the bad habits of the soul can entail physical miseries, while the excesses of the body manifest and maintain the failings of the soul. The apprehension is concentrated above all on the crossover point of the agitations and troubles, taking account of the fact that one had best correct the soul if one does not want the body to get the better of it, and rectify the body if one wants it to remain completely in control of itself. It is to this point of contact, the weak point of the individual, that the attention one gives to the physical ills, discomforts, and complaints is directed. The body the adult has to care for, when he is concerned about himself, is no longer the young body that needed shaping by gymnastics; it is a fragile, threatened body, undermined by petty miseries—a body that in turn threatens the soul, less by its too-vigorous requirements than by its own weaknesses. The letters of Seneca offer many examples of this attention focused on health, on regimen, on the malaises and all the troubles that can circulate between the body and the soul.[47] The correspondence between Fronto and Marcus Aurelius—to say nothing of the *Sacred Tales* of Aelius Aristides, which give altogether different dimensions to the narrative of illness and an entirely different value to its experience—shows very well the place occupied by concern for the body in these practices of the self, but it also shows the style of this preoccupation: fear of excess, economy of regimen, being on the alert for disturbances, detailed attention given to dysfunction, the taking into account of all the factors (season, climate, diet, mode of living) that can disturb the body and, through it, the soul.[48]

But there is something more important perhaps: on the basis of this rapprochement (practical and theoretical) between medicine and ethics, there is the inducement to acknowledge oneself as being ill or threatened by illness. The practice of the self implies that one should form the image of oneself not simply as an imperfect, ignorant individual who requires correction, training, and instruction, but as one who suffers from certain ills and who needs to have them treated, either by oneself or by someone who has the necessary competence. Everyone must discover that he is in a state of need, that he needs to receive medication and assistance. "This, then, is where the philosophic life begins," says Epictetus, "in a man's perception of the state of his ruling faculty [*aisthēsis tou idiou hēgemonikou pōs echei*]: for when once you realize that it is in a feeble state, you will not choose to employ it anymore for great matters. But, as it is, some men, finding themselves unable to swallow a mouthful, buy themselves a treatise, and set about eating it whole, and in consequence they vomit or have indigestion. Hence colics and fluxes and fevers. They ought first to have considered whether they have the faculty."[49] And the establishment of the relation to oneself as a sick individual is all the more necessary because the diseases of the soul—unlike those of the body—do not announce themselves by the suffering that one perceives; not only can they go undetected for a long time, but they blind those whom they afflict. Plutarch remarks that the disorders of the body can generally be detected by the pulse, bile, temperature, and pains; and further, that the worst physical illnesses are those in which—as in lethargy, epilepsy, or apoplexy—the individual is not aware of his state. The insidious thing about the diseases of the soul is that they pass unnoticed, or even that one can mistake them for virtues (anger for courage, amorous passion for friendship, envy for emulation, cowardice for prudence). Now, what physicians desire is "that a man should not be ill; and, if he is ill, that he should not be unaware that he is ill."[50]

4. In this practice, which is at once personal and social, self-knowledge occupies a considerable place, of course. The Delphic principle is often recalled; but it would not be sufficient to see this merely as the influence of the Socratic theme. In reality, a whole art of self-knowledge developed, with precise recipes, specific forms of examination, and codified exercises.

a. We can thus begin by isolating—very schematically and subject to a more thorough and systematic study—what might be called the "testing procedures." These have the dual role of moving one forward in the acquisition of a virtue and of marking the point one has reached. Hence their progressive character, emphasized by Plutarch and Epictetus alike. But it is important to note that the purpose of these tests is not to practice renunciation for its own sake; it is to enable one to do without unnecessary things by establishing a supremacy over oneself that does not depend on their presence or absence. The tests to which one subjects oneself are not successive stages of privation. They are a way of measuring and confirming the independence one is capable of with regard to everything that is not indispensable and essential. They bring one back, momentarily, to the basic needs, revealing in this manner the actual basis of all that is superfluous and the possibility of doing without it. In *Socrates' Daemon,* Plutarch reports on a test of this kind, the value of which is affirmed by the character in the dialogue who represents the themes of neo-Pythagoreanism. One began by whetting the appetite through the practice of some sport; next one placed oneself in front of tables laden with the most succulent dishes; then, having gazed on these, one left them to the servants and made do with the kind of food that slaves ate.[51]

Exercises in abstinence were common to the Epicureans and the Stoics, but this training did not have the same meaning for both groups. In the tradition of Epicurus, it was a matter of showing how, in this satisfaction of the most elementary needs, one could find a fuller, purer, more stable pleasure than in the delight one might take in all that is superfluous; and the test served to mark the threshold where privation could start to make one suffer. On certain days, Epicurus, whose diet was extremely abstemious already, would take only a reduced ration in order to see how much his pleasure would be diminished.[52] For the Stoics, it was primarily a matter of preparing oneself for possible privations by discovering how easy it was, finally, to dispense with everything to which habit, opinion, education, attention to reputation, and the taste for ostentation have attached us. With these reductive tests, they wished to show that we can always have at our disposal those things that are strictly necessary, and that one should guard against the least apprehension at the thought of possible privations: "In days of peace the soldier performs maneuvers, throws up earthworks with no enemy in sight, and wearies himself with gratuitous toil, in order that he may be equal to unavoidable toil. If you would not have a man flinch when the crisis comes, train him before it comes."[53] And Seneca alludes to a practice which he also speaks of in another letter: brief training periods of "fancied poverty" to be done every month and in the course of which, by voluntarily placing oneself "within the confines of destitution" for three or four days, one experiences a bed of straw, coarse clothing, and bread of the lowest quality: "not a game, but a test" *(non lusus, sed experimentum).* [54] One does not deprive oneself for a moment in order to sharpen one's taste for future refinements but to convince oneself that the worst misfortune will not deprive one of the things one absolutely needs, and that one will always be able to tolerate what one is capable of enduring at times. [55] One makes oneself familiar with the minimum. This is what Seneca wishes to do according to a letter written a short time before the Saturnalia of the year 62. Rome is "in a sweat" and "licentiousness is officially sanctioned." Seneca asks himself if one ought to take part in the festivities or not; it would be proof of one's self-control if one broke with the general attitude and refrained. But one would be acting with a still greater moral force if one did not withdraw oneself; the best thing would be "to do what the crowd does, but in a different way." And this "different way" is the way that one learns ahead of time by means of voluntary exercises, periods of abstinence, and poverty treatments. These exercises make it possible to celebrate the festival like everyone else but without ever falling into *luxuria.* Thanks to them, one can keep a detached mind in the midst of abundance: "We shall be rich with all the more comfort, if we once learn how far poverty is from being a burden." [56]*

   b. In conjunction with these practical tests, it was considered important to subject oneself to self-examination. This custom formed part of Pythagorean teaching, [58] but it had become quite widespread. It seems that the morning examination served mainly as an occasion to consider the tasks and obligations of the day, so as to be sufficiently prepared for it. The evening examination for its part was devoted much more

---

*Compare: "Study cannot be helpful unless you take pains to live simply; and living simply is voluntary poverty." [57]

specifically to reviewing the day that had gone by. The most detailed description of this exercise, which was regularly prescribed by numerous authors, is given by Seneca in *De ira.* [59] Seneca traces the practice of it to Sextius, that Roman Stoic whose teaching he knew by way of Papirius Fabianus and Sotion. He presents Sextius' practice as being centered mainly on the evaluation of one's progress at the end of the day. When he had retired for the night, Sextius would question his soul: "What bad habit have you cured today? What fault have you resisted? In what respect are you better?" Seneca, too, undertakes an examination of this kind every evening. Darkness—"when the light has been removed from sight"—and quiet—"when my wife has become silent"—are its external conditions. And he is mindful of the need to prepare for a blissful sleep: "Can anything be more excellent than this practice of thoroughly sifting the whole day? And how delightful the sleep that follows this self-examination—how tranquil [*tranquillus*], how deep [*altus*] and untroubled [*liber*], when the soul has either praised or admonished itself." At first glance, the examination to which Seneca subjects himself appears to constitute a sort of small-scale judicial drama, which is clearly evoked by such phrases as "appear before the judge," "give report of my own character," "plead my cause." These elements seem to indicate the division of the subject into a judging authority and an accused individual. But the process as a whole also calls to mind a kind of administrative review, where it is a matter of evaluating a performed activity in order to reactivate its principles and ensure their correct application in the future. As much as the role of a judge, it is the activity of an inspector that Seneca evokes, or that of a master of a household checking his accounts.

The words employed are significant. Seneca means to "scrutinize" the entire day that has just unfolded (the verb *executere,* "to shake out," "to knock so as to make the dust fall," is used to denote the scrutiny by which one locates the errors in an account); he intends to "inspect" it, to "remeasure" the acts that were committed, the words that were spoken (*re-*

metiri, as one might do after a piece of work is finished, to see if it is up to the standards set for it). The subject's relation to himself in this examination is not established so much in the form of a judicial relationship in which the accused faces the judge; it is more like an act of inspection in which the inspector aims to evaluate a piece of work, an accomplished task. The word *speculator* (one needs to be a *speculator sui*) designates this role exactly. Further, the examination practiced in this manner does not focus, as if in imitation of the judicial procedure, on "infractions"; and it does not lead to a verdict of guilty or to decisions of self-castigation. Seneca, in the example he gives here, singles out such actions as arguing too intensely with ignorant people, whom one cannot convince in any case, or vexing, through reproaches, a friend whom one would have liked to help improve. Seneca is dissatisfied with these ways of behaving insofar as, in order to achieve the goals that one must in fact set for oneself, the means employed were not the right ones: it is good to want to correct one's friends, if need be, but reproof is too extreme and gives offense instead of helping; it is good to convince those who don't know, but it is necessary first to choose such people as are capable of being taught. The purpose of the examination is not therefore to discover one's own guilt, down to its most trifling forms and its most tenuous roots. If one "conceals nothing from oneself," if one "omits nothing," it is in order to commit to memory, so as to have them present in one's mind, legitimate ends, but also rules of conduct that enable one to achieve these ends through the choice of appropriate means. The fault is not reactivated by the examination in order to determine a culpability or stimulate a feeling of remorse, but in order to strengthen, on the basis of the recapitulated and reconsidered verification of a failure, the rational equipment that ensures a wise behavior.

c. Added to the foregoing is the necessity of a labor of thought with itself as object. This work will have to be more than a test for measuring what one is capable of, and something other than the assessment of a fault in relation to rules of conduct; it should have the form of a steady screening of representations: examining them, monitoring them, sorting them out. More than an exercise done at regular intervals, it is a constant attitude that one must take toward oneself. To characterize this attitude, Epictetus employs metaphors that will have a long career in Christian spirituality, but they will take on quite different values in it. He asks that one adopt, vis-à-vis oneself, the role and posture of a "night watchman" who checks the entries at the gate of cities or houses;[60] or further, he suggests that one exercise on oneself the functions of a "tester of coinage," an "assayer," one of those money-changers who won't accept any coin without having made sure of its worth: "You all see in the matter of coinage . . . how we have even invented an art, and how many means the tester employs to test the coinage—sight, touch, smell, finally hearing: he throws the denarius down and then listens to the sound and is not satisfied with the sound it makes on a single test, but, as a result of his constant attention to the matter, he catches the tune, like a musician." Unfortunately, Epictetus continues, these precautions that we willingly take when it is a matter of money, we neglect to take when it is a question of our soul. Now the task of philosophy—its principal and primary *ergon*—will be precisely to exercise this control *(dokimazein).* [61]

In order to formulate what is both a general principle and an attitudinal schema, Epictetus refers to Socrates and to the aphorism stated in the *Apology:* "An unexamined life [*anexetastos bios*] is not worth living."[62] In reality, the examination Socrates was talking about was the one to which he intended to subject both himself and others apropos of ignorance, knowledge, and the non-knowledge of this ignorance. The examination Epictetus talks about is completely different: it is an examination that deals with representations, that aims to "test" them, to "distinguish" *(diakrinein)* one from another and thus to prevent one from accepting the "first arrival." "We ought not to accept a mental representation unsubjected to examination, but should say, 'Wait, allow me to see who you are and whence you came' (just as the night-watch say, 'Show me your tokens'). 'Do you have your token from nature, the one which every representation which is to be accepted must have?' "[63] However, it should be made clear that the control point will not be located in the origin or in the very object of the representation, but in the approval that one should or should not give to it. When a representation enters the mind, the work of discrimination, of *diakrisis,* will consist in applying to it the famous Stoic canon that marks the division between that which does not depend on us and that which does. In the former case, the representations will not be accepted since they are beyond our understanding; they will be rejected as not being appropriate objects of "desire" or "aversion," of "attraction" or "repulsion." This inspection is a test of power and a guarantee of freedom: a way of always making sure that one will not become attached to that which does not come under our control. To keep constant watch over one's representations, or to verify their marks the way one authenticates a currency, is not to inquire (as will be done later in Christianity) concerning the deep origin of the idea that presents itself; it is not to try and decipher a meaning hidden beneath the visible representation; it is to assess the relationship between oneself and that which is represented, so as to accept in the relation to the self only that which can depend on the subject's free and rational choice.

5.   The common goal of these practices of the self, allowing for the differences they present, can be characterized by the entirely general principle of conversion to self—of *epistrophē eis heauton.* * The expression has a Platonic cast, but it generally covers meanings that are considerably different. It is to be understood first of all as a change of activity: not that one must cease all other forms of occupation and devote oneself entirely and exclusively to oneself; but in the activities that one ought to engage in, one had best keep in mind that the chief objective

*The expressions *epistrophē eis heauton* and *epistrephein eis heauton* appear in Epictetus.[64]

one should set for oneself is to be sought within oneself, in the relation of oneself to oneself. This conversion implies a shift of one's attention: the latter must not be dissipated in an idle curiosity, either that of everyday agitations and of absorption in the lives of others (Plutarch devoted a whole treatise to this *polypragmosyne*), or that which seeks to discover the secrets of nature furthest removed from human existence and from the things that matter for it. (Demetrius, quoted by Seneca, held that nature, keeping only useless secrets, had placed within reach and in sight of human beings the things it was necessary for them to know.) But the *conversio ad se* is also a path by which, escaping all the dependences and enslavements, one ultimately rejoins oneself, like a harbor sheltered from the tempests or a citadel protected by its ramparts: "The soul stands on unassailable grounds, if it has abandoned external things; it is independent in its own fortress; and every weapon that is hurled falls short of the mark. Fortune has not the long reach with which we credit her; she can seize none except him that clings to her. Let us then recoil from her as far as we are able."[65]

This relation to self that constitutes the end of the conversion and the final goal of all the practices of the self still belongs to an ethics of control. Yet, in order to characterize it, moralists are not content with invoking the agonistic form of a victory over forces difficult to subdue and of a dominion over them that can be established beyond question. This relation is often conceived in terms of the juridical model of possession: one "belongs to himself," one is "his own master" (*suum fieri, suum esse* are expressions that recur often in Seneca);[66] one is answerable only to oneself, one is *sui juris;* one exercises over oneself an authority that nothing limits or threatens; one holds the *potestas sui.*[67] But apart from this rather political and judicial form, the relation to self is also defined as a concrete relationship enabling one to delight in oneself, as in a thing one both possesses and has before one's eyes. If to convert to oneself is to turn away from the preoccupations of the external world, from the concerns of ambition, from fear of the future, then one can turn back to one's own past, recall it to mind, have it unfold as one pleases before one's own eyes, and have a relationship with it that nothing can disturb: "This is the part of our time that is sacred and set apart, put beyond the reach of all human mishaps, and removed from the dominion of fortune, the part which is disquieted by no want, by no fear, by no attack of disease; this can neither be troubled nor snatched away—it is an everlasting and unanxious possession."[68] And the experience of self that forms itself in this possession is not simply that of a force overcome, or a rule exercised over a power that is on the point of rebelling; it is the experience of a pleasure that one takes in oneself. The individual who has finally succeeded in gaining access to himself is, for himself, an object of pleasure. Not only is one satisfied with what one is and accepting of one's limits, but one "pleases oneself."[69] This pleasure, for which Seneca usually employs the word *gaudium* or *laetitia,* is a state that is neither accompanied nor followed by any form of disturbance in the body or the mind. It is defined by the fact of not being caused by anything that is independent of ourselves and therefore escapes our control. It arises out of ourselves and within ourselves.[70] It is characterized as well by the fact that it knows neither degree nor change, but is given as a "woven fabric," and once given no external event can rend it.[71] This sort of pleasure can thus be contrasted point by point with what is meant by the term *voluptas.* The latter denotes a pleasure whose origin is to be placed outside us and in objects whose presence we cannot be sure of: a pleasure, therefore, which is precarious in itself, undermined by the fear of loss, and to which we are drawn by the force of a desire that may or may not find satisfaction. In place of this kind of violent, uncertain, and conditional pleasure, access to self is capable of providing a form of pleasure that comes, in serenity and without fail, of the experience of oneself. *"Disce gaudere,* learn how to feel joy," says Seneca to Lucilius: "I do not wish you ever to be deprived of gladness. I would have it born in your house; and it is born there, if only it is inside of you . . . for

it will never fail you when once you have found its source
. . . look toward the true good, and rejoice only in that which
comes from your own store [*de tuo*]. But what do I mean by
'your own store'? I mean your very self and the best part of
you."[72]

It was against the background of this cultivation of the self,
of its themes and practices, that reflection on the ethics of
pleasure developed in the first centuries of our era. It is in that
direction that one must look in order to understand the transformations that may have affected that ethics. What may be
regarded, at first sight, as a more pronounced severity, an
increased austerity, stricter requirements, should not in fact be
interpreted as a tightening of interdictions. The domain of
behaviors that might be forbidden did not expand to any
appreciable extent, and there was no attempt to organize systems of prohibition that would be more authoritarian and
efficacious. The change had much more to do with the manner
in which the individual needed to form himself as an ethical
subject. The development of the cultivation of the self produced its effect not in the strengthening of that which can
thwart desire, but in certain modifications relating to the
formative elements of ethical subjectivity. A break with the
traditional ethics of self-mastery? Clearly not, but rather a
shift, a change of orientation, a difference in emphasis.

Sexual pleasure as an ethical substance continues to be governed by relations of force—the force against which one must
struggle and over which the subject is expected to establish his
domination. But in this game of violence, excess, rebellion,
and combat, the accent is placed more and more readily on the
weakness of the individual, on his frailty, on his need to flee,
to escape, to protect and shelter himself. Sexual ethics requires, still and always, that the individual conform to a certain art of living which defines the aesthetic and ethical criteria
of existence. But this art refers more and more to universal
principles of nature or reason, which everyone must observe
in the same way, whatever their social status. As for the

definition of the work that must be carried out on oneself, it too undergoes, in the cultivation of the self, a certain modification: through the exercises of abstinence and control that constitute the required *askēsis,* the place allotted to self-knowledge becomes more important. The task of testing oneself, examining oneself, monitoring oneself in a series of clearly defined exercises, makes the question of truth—the truth concerning what one is, what one does, and what one is capable of doing—central to the formation of the ethical subject. Lastly, the end result of this elaboration is still and always defined by the rule of the individual over himself. But this rule broadens into an experience in which the relation to self takes the form not only of a domination but also of an enjoyment without desire and without disturbance.

One is still far from an experience of sexual pleasure where the latter will be associated with evil, where behavior will have to submit to the universal form of law, and where the deciphering of desire will be a necessary condition for acceding to a purified existence. Yet one can already see how the question of evil begins to work upon the ancient theme of force, how the question of law begins to modify the theme of art and *technē,* and how the question of truth and the principle of self-knowledge evolve within the ascetic practices. But we need first to try to discover in what context and for what reasons the cultivation of the self developed in this way, precisely in the form that we have just considered.

PART THREE

SELF AND OTHERS

The work of historians suggests several reasons for this development of the cultivation of the self and for the concurrent modulation in the ethics of pleasure. Two factors seem especially important: changes in marital practice and modifications in the rules of the political game. In this brief section, I shall simply review some aspects of these two themes, borrowing from previous historical research, and outline a tentative general hypothesis. Is it not the case that the new importance of marriage and the couple, together with a certain redistribution in political roles, gave rise, in what was essentially a male ethics, to a new problematization of the relation to the self? These developments may very well have occasioned, not a withdrawal into the self, but a new way of conceiving oneself in one's relation to one's wife, to others, to events, and to civic and political activities—and a different way of considering oneself as the subject of one's pleasures. Hence the cultivation of the self would not be the necessary "consequence" of these social modifications; it would not be their expression in the sphere of ideology; rather, it would constitute an original response to them, in the form of a new stylistics of existence.

CHAPTER ONE

===

THE MARITAL ROLE

It is difficult to determine, for the different regions and the different social strata, the actual extent of marital practice in Hellenistic or Roman civilization. Historians have been able, however, to identify—where the documentation makes this possible—certain transformations affecting either the institutional forms, the organization of conjugal relationships, or the meaning and moral value that could be given to the latter.

The institutional perspective first of all. As a private act, a matter for the family to decide, coming under its authority, under the rules it followed and recognized as its own, marriage did not call for intervention by public powers, either in Greece or in Rome. In Greece, it was a practice "designed to ensure the continued existence of the *oikos*." Of its two basic and vital acts, the first marked the transfer to the husband of the tutelage exercised up to that moment by the father, and the second marked the actual handing over of the bride to her marriage partner.[1] It thus constituted "a private transaction, a piece of business concluded between two heads of family, the one actual, the girl's father, the other virtual, the husband-to-be." This private affair was "unconnected with the political and social organization."[2] The same was true of Roman marriage. J. A. Crook and Paul Veyne point out that it was originally only a *de facto* condition "dependent on the intention of the

72

parties," "marked by a ceremony," and "producing legal effects," but without being "a juridical act."[3]

In the Hellenistic world, marriage gradually made a place for itself within the public sphere. It thus overstepped the bounds of the family, with the paradoxical result that the authority of the latter found itself "publicly" sanctioned but also relatively limited. In Claude Vatin's view, this evolution was aided by recourse to religious ceremonies, which served as a kind of intermediary between the private and the public institution. Summing up this transformation, whose results can be observed in the second and first centuries B.C., he writes: "It is clear that marriage has now gone beyond the limits of the familial institutions, and Alexandrian religious marriage, which is perhaps a vestige of the ancient religious marriage, is also a civic institution. It is always the entire city that sanctions marriage, whether this is through an official or a priest." And comparing the data for the city of Alexandria with the data for rural society, he adds: "One sees in the *chorā* and in the capital a rapid evolution, with variants, from a private into a public institution."[4]

In Rome, one notes an evolution that is of the same general type, although it takes different paths and although marriage continues, until quite late, to be essentially "a private ceremony, a celebration."[5] A set of legislative measures marks little by little the hold of public authority on the marriage institution. The famous law *de adulteriis* is one of the manifestations of this phenomenon. A manifestation all the more interesting because in condemning for adultery the married woman who has sexual intercourse with another man and the man who has intercourse with a married woman (and not the married man who has relations with an unmarried woman), this law offers nothing new in the way of legal definition of acts. It reproduces precisely the traditional schemas of ethical valuation, merely transferring to public power a sanction previously under familial authority.

This gradual "publicizing" of marriage accompanies many other transformations, of which it is at once the effect, the

relay, and the instrument. It appears, to the extent that the
documents allow us to form a judgment, that the practice of
marriage, or regular concubinage, became general or at least
widespread in the dominant strata of the population. In its
ancient form, marriage held no interest, had no reason for
being, except insofar as, although a private act, it had legal
effects or at least effects relative to status: handing down a
name, instituting heirs, organizing a system of alliances, joining fortunes. This meant something only to those who were
capable of developing strategies in such domains. As Paul
Veyne says: "In pagan society, everyone did not marry, far
from it. . . . Marriage, when one did marry, corresponded to
a private objective: to transmit the estate to one's descendants,
rather than to other members of the family or to the sons of
friends; and it corresponded to a politics of castes: to perpetu-
ate the caste of citizens."[6] As John Boswell puts it, this was
a kind of marriage which "for the upper classes was largely
dynastic, political, and economic."[7] As for the lower classes,
as little informed as we are concerning their marital practice,
we may suppose with S. B. Pomeroy that two contradictory
factors were able to play a part, both of which were connected
with the economic functions of marriage: the wife and children could form a useful source of labor for a free man who
was poor. On the other hand, "there is an economic level below
which a man may not hope to support a wife and family."[8]

The economico-political imperatives that governed marriage (making it necessary in some cases, and in others, useless) must have lost some of their importance when, in the
privileged classes, status and fortune came to depend on proximity to the prince, on a civil or military "career," on success
in "business," more than simply on the alliance between family groups. Less encumbered with various strategies, marriage
became "freer": free in the choice of a wife; free, too, in the
decision to marry and in the personal reasons for doing so. It
could be, too, that in the underprivileged classes, marriage
became—beyond the economic motives that could make it
attractive—a form of tie that owed its value to the fact that

it established and maintained strong personal relationships, implying the sharing of life, mutual aid, and moral support. In any case, the study of tomb inscriptions has been able to show the relative frequency and stability of marriages in milieus that were not those of the aristocracy,[9] and we have statements attesting to the marriage of slaves.[10] Whatever response is given to the question of the extent of marital practice, it seems that the latter became more accessible; the thresholds that made it "interesting" were lowered.

Hence marriage appeared more and more as a voluntary union between two partners whose inequality diminished to a certain extent but did not cease to exist. It does seem that in the Hellenistic world, and taking many local differences into account, the wife's status gained in independence compared with what it was in the classical period—and above all compared with the Athenian situation. This relative modification was due first of all to the fact that the position of the citizen-husband lost some of its political importance. It was also due to a strengthening of the role of the wife—of her economic role and her juridical independence. According to some historians, the documents show that the intervention of the wife's father became less and less decisive in marriage. "It was common for a father to give a daughter in marriage in his role of formal guardian, but some contracts were made simply between a woman and a man agreeing to share a common life. The right of the married daughter to self-determination against paternal authority began to be asserted. According to Athenian, Roman and Egyptian law, the authority of the father over a married daughter was curtailed by judicial rulings stating that the wishes of the woman were the determining factor. If she wished to remain married, she could do so."[11] Marriage was concluded more and more clearly as a voluntary agreement entered into by the partners, who pledged themselves personally. The *ekdosis* by which the young woman was ceremoniously handed over to the husband by the father or guardian "tended to disappear," and the contract that traditionally accompanied it, which was basically financial in character, ended up existing only in the case of written marriages, where it was supplemented by clauses relating to the persons. Not only did women receive their dowry, which they disposed of more and more freely within marriage, with certain contracts providing for restitution to them in case of divorce, but they also collected their share of inheritance.

As for the obligations marriage contracts imposed on husbands, Claude Vatin's study shows a significant evolution for Hellenistic Egypt. In documents dating from the end of the fourth century B.C. or from the third, the wife's pledges implied obedience to the husband; prohibition from leaving the house, day or night, without the husband's permission; exclusion of any sexual relations with another man; and the obligation not to ruin the household and not to dishonor her husband. The latter in turn must support his wife, must not establish a concubine in the house, must not mistreat his wife, and must not have children from relationships he might maintain on the outside. Later, the contracts studied specify much stricter obligations on the part of the husband. The obligation to provide for the needs of his wife is stipulated; but it is also expressly forbidden for him to have a mistress or sweetheart, and to own another house (in which he might maintain a concubine). As Vatin notes, in this type of contract "it is the sexual liberty of the husband that is in question; the woman will now be just as exclusive as the man." Developed in this way, marriage contracts bring the husband and the wife into a system of duties or obligations that are not equal, certainly, but are shared. And this sharing occurs not in the name of the respect due to the family, which each of the two marriage partners represents, as it were, in the state of marriage, but on behalf of the couple, its stability and its internal regulation.[12]

Such explicitly affirmed obligations demanded and revealed forms of conjugal life that were much more closely defined than in the past. The prescriptions could not have been formulated in the contracts if they did not already correspond to a new attitude; and at the same time they must have carried such weight for each of the marriage partners that they impressed on their life, much more clearly than in the past, the reality of the couple. The institutionalization of marriage based on mutual consent, says Vatin, "engendered the idea that there existed a conjugal community and that this reality, constituted by the couple, had a value greater than that of its component parts."[13] Paul Veyne has called attention to a somewhat analogous evolution in Roman society: "Under the Republic, both spouses had a specific role to play and beyond the satisfactory performance of this role affective relations between husband and wife were whatever they happened to be. . . . Under the Empire . . . the very functioning of the marriage was supposed to depend on mutual understanding and the law of the heart. In this way a new idea came into being: the couple composed of the master and mistress of the house."[14]

So there were many paradoxes in the evolution of this marital practice. It looked to public authority for its guarantees; and it became an increasingly important concern in private life. It threw off the economic and social purposes that had invested it with value; and at the same time it became a general practice. It became more and more restrictive for spouses, and gave rise at the same time to attitudes that were more and more favorable—as if the more it demanded, the more attractive it became. It appears that marriage became more general as a practice, more public as an institution, more private as a mode of existence—a stronger force for binding conjugal partners and hence a more effective one for isolating the couple in a field of other social relations.

Obviously it is difficult to measure accurately the scope of this phenomenon. The available documentation covers only a few privileged geographic areas, and it throws light only on certain strata of the population. It would be speculation to make it into a universal and massive movement, even though, notwithstanding their lacunary and scattered character, the indications are rather convergent. In any case, if we are to give credence to the other texts from the first centuries of our era, marriage appears to have become—for men, that is, since we have only their testimony—a focus of experiences that were more important, more intense, but also more difficult and more problematic. And by marriage what is meant is not just the institution that is useful to the family or the city, or the domestic activity that is carried out in the context and according to the rules of a good household, but also the "state" of marriage as a form of living, a shared existence, a personal bond, and a respective position of the partners in this relationship. It is not, as we have seen, that matrimonial life according to the old schema excluded closeness and feeling between spouses. But it does seem that in the ideal set forth by Xenophon these feelings were tied directly (which did not rule out serious commitment or intensity) to the exercise of the husband's status and to the authority granted to him. Rather paternal toward his young wife, Ischomachus patiently taught her what she had to do; and to the degree that she performed well in the role that went with her duties as mistress of the household, he had a respect and an affection for her that would not diminish to the end of their days. In the literature of the imperial epoch, one finds testimonies to a far more complex experience of marriage; and the search for an ethics of "conjugal honor" is clearly manifested in the reflection on the role of the husband, on the nature and form of the bond that attached him to his wife, on the interplay between a superiority at once natural and statutory and an affection that could extend to the point of need and dependence.

It might be useful, then, to look at the image that Pliny, in certain of his letters, gives of himself as a "conjugal individual," and compare it with the portrait of that other good husband, Ischomachus. Thus, in the famous letter he addresses to his wife bemoaning her absence, what is shown is not simply, as in other letters, a man who calls his admiring and docile spouse to witness his literary labors and his successes as a tribune; it is a man who feels an intense attachment to his wife and a physical desire so strong that he cannot keep from looking for her night and day even though she is no longer there: "You cannot believe how much I miss you. I love you so much, and we are not used to separations. So I stay awake most of the night thinking of you, and by day I find my feet carrying me (a true word, carrying) to your room at the times I usually visited you; then finding it empty I depart, as sick and sorrowful as a lover locked out. The only time I am free of this misery is when I am in court and wearing myself out with my friends' lawsuits. You can judge then what a life I am leading, when I find my rest in work and distraction in troubles and anxiety."[15] The formulas of this letter merit our attention. The specific character of a personal, intense, and affective conjugal relationship, which does not depend on status, marital authority, or household responsibility, is clearly evident. Love is carefully differentiated from the habitual sharing of existence, even if both rightfully contribute to making the presence of the wife precious and her absence painful. Moreover, Pliny avails himself of several of the traditionally acknowledged signs of amorous passion: the images that haunt the night, the involuntary comings and goings, the search for the lost object. Now, these behaviors that belong to the classic and negative image of passion are presented in a positive light; or rather, the husband's suffering, the passionate movement in which he is taken up, the fact that he is ruled by his desire and his sorrow are offered as positive tokens of conjugal affection. Finally, between matrimonial life and public activity, Pliny suggests, not a common principle unifying the government of the household and authority over others, but a complex process of substitution and compensation: failing to find at home the happiness that his wife provided him, he immerses himself in public affairs. But the hurt he feels must be extreme for him to find comfort for his private sorrows in the worries of this external life.

In many other texts as well, one sees the relation between husband and wife detach itself from matrimonial functions, from the status-determined authority of the husband and the reasonable government of the household, and take on the character of a singular relation having its own force, its own difficulties, obligations, benefits, and pleasures. One could cite other letters of Pliny and point to other indications of this in Lucian or Tacitus. One could also refer to the conjugal love poetry that is exemplified in Statius. There the state of marriage appears as the merging of two destinies in an undying passion wherein the husband recognizes his emotional bondage: "For it is you—you, whom Venus of her grace united to me in the springtime of my days, and in old age keeps mine; you, who while I yet roved in youth nor knew nothing of love did transfix my heart. You it is whose rein in willing submission [*libens et docilis*] I obeyed, and yet press the bit once put within my mouth, without ever thought of change. . . . This land bore me for you [*creavit me tibi*], and bound me to you in partnership forever."[16]

Of course it is not in texts like these that one should look for a representation of what matrimonial life may have really been like in the period of the Empire. The sincerity they display does not have the value of evidence. They are texts that go out of their way to proclaim an ideal of conjugality. They should be taken not as the reflection of a situation, but as the formulation of an exigency, and it is precisely on this account that they form part of reality. They show that marriage was interrogated as a mode of life whose value was not exclusively, nor perhaps even essentially, linked to the functioning of the *oikos,* but rather to a mode of relation between two partners. They also show that, in this linkage, the man had to regulate his conduct, not simply by virtue of status, privileges, and domestic functions, but also by virtue of a "relational role" with regard to his wife. Finally, they show not only that this role was a governmental function of training, education, and guidance, but that it was involved in a complex interplay of affective reciprocity and reciprocal dependence. Now, while it is true that moral reflection on proper conduct in marriage had long sought its principles in an analysis of the "household" and its intrinsic necessities, one sees how a new type of problem emerged, where it was a matter of defining the way in which the husband would be able to form himself as an ethical subject within the relation of conjugality.

CHAPTER TWO

THE POLITICAL GAME

The decline of city-states as autonomous entities starting in the third century B.C. is a well-known fact. It is often seen as evidence of a general withdrawal from political life in a place where civic activities had constituted for citizens a true vocation. It is given as the reason for the decadence of the traditionally dominant classes. And its consequences are sought in a movement of retreat into the self by which the representatives of these privileged groups would have transformed this real loss of authority into a voluntary retirement, attributing in this way more and more value to personal existence and private life. "The collapse of the city-state was inescapable. On the whole, people felt themselves in the grip of world powers which they could not control or even affect. . . . Chance ruled. . . . The philosophies of the Hellenistic Age, for all their nobility, were essentially philosophies of escape, and the principal means of escape lay in the cultivation of autarky."[1]

While the city-states—where they existed—did lose, from the third century on, a portion of their autonomy, it would clearly be questionable to reduce the structural transformations that took place in the political domain, during the Hellenistic and Roman epochs, essentially to that phenomenon. It would also be inadequate to search there for the main explanatory principle behind the changes that occurred in moral reflection and in the practice of the self. In actual fact—and on this point one must refer to the work of historians who have

81

gone a long way toward dismantling the great nostalgic figure
of the city-state that the nineteenth century took pains to
construct—the organization of the Hellenistic monarchies,
then that of the Roman Empire, cannot be analyzed simply in
the negative terms of a decline of civic life and a confiscation
of power by state authorities operating from further and further away. It needs to be emphasized, on the contrary, that
local political activity was not stifled by the establishment and
strengthening of those great overarching structures. City life,
with its institutional rules, its interests at stake, its struggles,
did not disappear as a result of the widening of the context in
which it was inscribed, nor as a consequence of the development of a monarchical type of power. Apprehension before a
universe become too vast and having lost its constituent communities could well be a feeling that has been imputed retro-
spectively to the people of the Greco-Roman world. The
Greeks of the Hellenistic period did not have to flee from "the
cityless world of the great empires" for the very good reason
that "Hellenism was a world of cities." Furthermore, criticizing the idea that philosophy constituted, after the collapse of
the system of cities, "a shelter from the storm," F. H. Sandbach observes that, in the first place, "the city-state had never
given security," and second, "it remained the standard primary form of social organization even after military power
had passed into the hands of the great monarchies."[2]

Rather than imagining a reduction or cessation of political
activities through the effects of a centralized imperialism, one
should think in terms of the organization of a complex space.
Much vaster, much more discontinuous, much less closed
than must have been the case for the small city-states, it was
also more flexible, more differentiated, less rigidly hierarch-
ized than would be the authoritarian and bureaucratic Empire
that people would attempt to organize after the great crisis of
the third century. It was a space in which the centers of power
were multiple; in which the activities, the tensions, the con-
flicts were numerous; in which they developed in several dimensions; and in which the equilibria were obtained through

a variety of transactions. It is a fact, at any rate, that the Hellenistic monarchies sought much less to suppress, curb, or even completely reorganize the local powers than to lean on them and use them as intermediaries and relays for the levy of regular tributes, for the collection of extraordinary taxes, and for supplying what was necessary to the armies.[3] It is a fact as well that by and large Roman imperialism tended to prefer solutions of this kind to the exercise of a direct administration. The policy of municipalization was a rather constant line, whose effect was to stimulate the political life of the cities within the larger framework of the Empire.[4] While the speech Dio Cassius places in the mouth of Maecenas presents anachronisms with respect to the policy that had been recommended to Augustus and actually pursued by him, it nevertheless represents certain of the major tendencies of the imperial government in the course of the first two centuries: look for "assistants and allies," persuade "those subjects under your rule that you are not treating them as slaves" but that you are making sure that they share advantages and authority, that "they live as it were in a single city."[5]

Can one still speak, then, of a decline of the traditional aristocracies, of their political dispossession, of a consequent withdrawal into the self? There were economic and political factors of transformation, to be sure: the elimination of opponents and confiscations of property played their part. There were also stabilizing factors: the importance of wealth in land and in holdings of estates,[6] or the fact that in societies of this kind, fortunes, influence, prestige, authority, and power were always interconnected. But the most important and determining phenomenon for the new emphases of moral reflection did not relate to the disappearance of the traditionally dominant classes, but to the changes that could be observed in the conditions of the exercise of power. These changes concerned recruitment first of all, since it was a matter of addressing the needs of an administration that was both complex and extensive. Maecenas is supposed to have said as much to Augustus: the number of senators and knights must be increased to the extent necessary to govern at the right time and in the right way.[7] And we know that in fact these groups grew appreciably larger in the course of the first centuries A.D., even if they never constituted more than a tiny minority of the total population.[8] Changes also affected the role they were led to play and the position they occupied in the political game: with respect to the emperor, to his entourage, to his councilors, to his direct representatives; within the hierarchy, where competition played a major part but in a different fashion from that found in agonistic societies; in the form of revocable offices which depended, often quite directly, on the pleasure of the prince; and nearly always in an intermediary position between a higher power whose orders must be conveyed or carried out, and individuals or groups whose obedience must be obtained. What the Roman administration needed was a "managerial aristocracy," as R. Syme says, a service aristocracy, which would furnish the different kinds of agents necessary to "administer the world": "officers in the army, financial procurators, and senatorial governors of provinces."[9]

And if one wishes to understand the interest that was directed in these elites to personal ethics, to the morality of everyday conduct, private life, and pleasure, it is not all that pertinent to speak of decadence, frustration, and sullen retreat. Instead, one should see in this interest the search for a new way of conceiving the relationship that one ought to have with one's status, one's functions, one's activities, and one's obligations. Whereas formerly ethics implied a close connection between power over oneself and power over others, and therefore had to refer to an aesthetics of life that accorded with one's status, the new rules of the political game made it more difficult to define the relations between what one was, what one could do, and what one was expected to accomplish. The formation of oneself as the ethical subject of one's own actions became more problematic.

R. MacMullen has underscored two essential features of Roman society: the public character of existence and the very pronounced "verticality" of differences in a world where the gulf separating the very small number of wealthy people and the very large mass of poor people did not cease to widen.[10] One understands the importance attributed, at the intersection of these two traits, to status differences, to their hierarchy, to their visible signs, to their careful and ostentatious staging.[11] We may suppose that starting from the moment when new conditions of political life modified the relations between status, functions, powers, and duties, two opposite phenomena occurred. One discovers them in fact—and in their very opposition—as early as the beginning of the imperial epoch. On the one hand, there is an accentuation of everything that allows the individual to define his identity in accordance with his status and with the elements that manifest it in the most visible way. One seeks to make oneself as adequate as possible to one's own status by means of a set of signs and marks pertaining to physical bearing, clothing and accommodations, gestures of generosity and munificence, spending behavior, and so on. With regard to these behaviors by which one affirms oneself in the superiority one manifests over others, MacMullen has shown how common they were in the Roman aristocracy and the degree of exaggeration to which they could be carried. But at the opposite extreme one finds the attitude that consists, on the contrary, in defining what one is purely in relation to oneself. It is then a matter of forming and recognizing oneself as the subject of one's own actions, not through a system of signs denoting power over others, but through a relation that depends as little as possible on status and its external forms, for this relation is fulfilled in the sovereignty that one exercises over oneself. To the new forms of the political game, and to the difficulties of conceiving oneself as an acting subject placed between birth and functions, tasks and rights, prerogatives and subordinations, one was able to respond by intensifying all the recognizable marks of status or by seeking an adequate relationship with oneself.

These two attitudes were often perceived and described in strict opposition to one another. Seneca offers an example of this: "What we have to seek for then, is that which does not each day pass more and more under the control of some power which cannot be withstood. And what is this? It is the soul—but the soul that is upright, good, and great. What else should you call such a soul than a god dwelling as a guest in a human body? A soul like this may descend into a Roman knight just as well as into a freedman's son or a slave. For what is a Roman knight or a freedman's son or a slave? They are mere titles, born of ambition or of wrong. One may leap to heaven from a slum. Rise then."[12] It is this way of being, too, which Epictetus endorses in opposing it to that of an imagined or real interlocutor: "You make it your concern how to live in a palace, how slaves and freedmen are to serve you, how you are to wear conspicuous raiment, how you are to have a multitude of huntsmen, minstrels, players. Do I lay claim to any of these? But you, for your part, have you concerned yourself with judgments? Have you concerned yourself with your own rational self?"[13]

The importance assumed by the theme of the return to oneself or of the attention that must be given to oneself, in Hellenistic and Roman thought, is often interpreted as the alternative that was offered to civic activity and political responsibilities. It is true that in certain philosophical currents one finds the recommendation to turn aside from public affairs, from the troubles and passions to which they give rise. But it is not in this choice between participation and abstention that the principal line of division lies; and it is not in opposition to the active life that the cultivation of the self places its own values and practices. It is much more concerned to define the principle of a relation to self that will make it possible to set the forms and conditions in which political action, participation in the offices of power, the exercise of a function, will be possible or not possible, acceptable or necessary. The important political transformations that took place in the Hellenistic and Roman world may have induced certain withdrawal behaviors. But, above all, they brought about, in a much more general and essential way, a problematization of political activity. It can be characterized briefly as follows.

1. A relativization. In the new political game, the exercise of power is relativized in two ways. First, even if by one's birth one is marked out for public offices, one no longer identifies sufficiently with one's status to consider it a foregone conclusion that one will accept such responsibilities; or in any case, if many reasons, and the best of reasons, incline one toward public and political life, it is good to enter it precisely for those reasons and as a consequence of a personal act of choice. The treatise Plutarch addresses to the young Menemachus is characteristic in this regard. He condemns the attitude that would make politics into an occasional activity, but he refuses to treat it as the necessary and natural consequence of a status. One must not, he says, regard political activity as a sort of pastime *(scholē)* in which one would engage because one has nothing else to do and because circumstances are favorable, only to abandon it when difficulties arise.[14] Politics is "a life" and a "practice" *(bios kai praxis).*[15] But one cannot devote oneself to it except by a free and deliberate choice. (Here Plutarch employs the technical expression of the Stoics: *proairesis.*) And this choice must be based on judgment and reason *(krisis kai logos):*[16] only in this way can one deal firmly with the problems that may be posed. The exercise of political activity is indeed a "life," implying a personal and lasting commitment. But the foundation, the link between oneself and political activity, that which establishes the individual as a political actor, is not—or not merely—his status; it is, in the general context defined by his birth and his standing, a personal act.

But one can also speak of relativization in another sense. Short of being the prince himself, one exercises power within a network in which one occupies a key position. In a certain way, one is always the ruler and the ruled. Aristotle, in the *Politics,* also evoked this game, but in the form of an alternation or rotation: one is now the ruler, now the ruled.[17] On the other hand, in the fact that a man is one and the other at the same time, through an interplay of directions sent and received, of checks, of appeals of decisions taken, Aristides sees the very principle of good government.[18] Seneca, in the preface of Book IV of the *Natural Questions,* speaks of this "intermediary" situation of the high Roman official. He reminds Lucilius that the power he has to exercise in Sicily is not a supreme authority, an *imperium,* but the delegated power of a *procuratio,* the limits of which must not be exceeded—which is, in his view, the condition for being able to take pleasure *(delectare)* in the exercise of such an office and to profit from the leisure time it might leave.[19] Plutarch presents the converse, as it were, of this situation. It is not enough that the young aristocrat to whom he addresses his advice is in the first rank among his own people: he must also relate to the "rulers" —*hēgemones*—that is, to the Romans. Plutarch criticizes those who, in order better to establish their power in their own city, show servility in their dealings with the representatives of the imperial administration. He counsels Menemachus to carry out the necessary duties with respect to them and to form such friendships with them as are useful, but never to humiliate his native land or be anxious to ask for authorization apropos of everything.[20] Anyone who exercises power has to place himself in a field of complex relations where he occupies a transition point.* His status may have placed him there; it is not this status, however, that determines the rules to follow and the limits to observe.

2. Political activity and moral agent. It was one of the most constant themes of Greek political thought that a city could be happy and well governed only if its leaders were virtuous; and inversely, that a good constitution and wise laws were decisive factors for the right conduct of magistrates and citizens. The ruler's virtue, in an entire line of political thought in the imperial epoch, is still regarded as necessary, but for somewhat different reasons. It is not as an expression or effect of the general harmony that this virtue is indispensable; but because, in the difficult art of ruling, amid so many obstacles,

---

*See also the passage in which Plutarch says that one must be able to entrust certain specific tasks to subordinates.[21]

traits he draws of him, Marcus Aurelius recalls that he received three lessons: first, not to identify with the political role that one plays ("see to it that you do not become Caesarized, or dyed with that coloring"); second, to practice the virtues in their most general forms ("treasure simplicity, goodness, purity, dignity, lack of affectation, justice, piety, kindliness, graciousness, and strength for your appropriate duties"); third, to hold to the precepts of philosophy such as that of revering the gods, protecting men, and being mindful of how short life is.[24] And when, at the beginning of the *Meditations,* Marcus Aurelius draws a more detailed portrait of Antoninus, which stands as a model for his own life, he shows how these same principles regulated his way of exercising power. By avoiding useless outbursts, satisfactions of vanity, transports of anger and violent displays, by eschewing everything in the way of vindictiveness and suspicion, by keeping flatterers away and giving access only to wise and frank counselors, Antoninus showed how he rejected the "Caesarean" mode of being. Through his practice of self-restraint (whether it was a matter of food, clothes, sleep, or boys), through the moderate use he made of the comforts of life, through the absence of agitation and the equanimity of his soul, and through the cultivation of friendships without inconstancy or passion, he trained himself in the art of sufficing to himself without losing his serenity. And it was in these conditions that the exercise of imperial responsibilities could appear as the practice of a serious occupation, and one that demanded a good deal of effort: examining matters closely, never leaving a dossier incomplete, not incurring useless expenses, carefully planning one's projects and seeing them through. A whole elaboration of the self by oneself was necessary for these tasks, which would be accomplished all the better because one did not identify in an ostentatious way with the trappings of power.

Epictetus, for his part, had set forth the principles that ought to guide an official—of relatively high rank—in the performance of his tasks. On the one hand, he must fulfill his the ruler will still have to be guided by his personal reason. It is in knowing how properly to conduct himself that he will be able to lead others properly. A man, says Dio of Prusa, who observes the law and equity, who is more courageous than common soldiers, who works more diligently than those who are under coercion, who refrains from any sort of sensual excess (obviously, it is a question of virtues that anyone might possess, but that need to be carried to a higher degree when one aims to govern)—such a man, who is not just good for himself but for others as well, has a *daimōn*. [22] The rationality of the government of others is the same as the rationality of the government of oneself. This is what Plutarch explains in *To an Uneducated Ruler:* one will not be able to rule if one is not oneself ruled. Now, who then is to govern the ruler? The law, of course; it must not, however, be understood as the written law, but rather as reason, the *logos,* which lives in the soul of the ruler and must never abandon him.[23]

In a political space where the political structure of the city and the laws with which it is endowed have unquestionably lost some of their importance, although they have not ceased to exist for all that, and where the decisive elements reside more and more in men, in their decisions, in the manner in which they bring their authority to bear, in the wisdom they manifest in the interplay of equilibria and transactions, it appears that the art of governing oneself becomes a crucial political factor. We are aware of the importance assumed by the problem of the emperors' virtue, of their private life, and of their ability to control their passions, which is seen as the guarantee that they will themselves be able to set a limit on the exercise of their political power. But this principle applies to anyone who governs: he must attend to himself, guide his own soul, establish his own *ēthos.*

It is in Marcus Aurelius that one finds the clearest formulation of an experience of political power that, on the one hand takes the form of an occupation separate from status and, o the other, requires the careful practice of personal virtue From the emperor Antoninus, in the briefest of the two po obligations without regard to his personal life or interests: "You have been given a post in an imperial city, and not in some mean place; not for a short time, either, but you are a senator for life. Do you not know that a man in such a post has to give only a little attention to the affairs of his own household, but for most of his time has to be away, in command, or under command, or serving some official, or in the field, or on the judge's bench?"[25] But even though the magistrate must leave aside his personal life and that which attaches him to it, it is his personal virtues as a reasonable man that will need to serve him as a guide and regulative principle in governing others. "Beating an ass," explains Epictetus to an inspector of cities, "is not governing men. Govern us as rational beings by pointing out to us what is profitable, and we will follow you; point out what is unprofitable, and we will turn away from it. Bring us to admire and emulate you. . . . 'Do this; do not do this; otherwise I will throw you in prison.' Say that and you cease to be a government as over rational beings. No, rather say, 'As Zeus has ordained, do this; if you do not do so, you will be punished, you will suffer injury. What kind of injury? No injury but that of not doing what you ought.' "[26] It is the modality of a rational being and not the qualification of a status that establishes and ought to determine, in their concrete form, relations between the governors and the governed.

Such a modeling of political work—whether it concerned the emperor or a man who exercised an ordinary responsibility —shows clearly how these forms of activity became detached from status and appeared as a function to fill; but—and this is not the least important consideration—that function was not defined in terms of laws belonging to an art of governing others, as if it were a question of a "profession" with its particular skills and techniques. It was to be exercised on the basis of the individual's "retreat within himself"; that is, it depended on the relationship he established with himself in the ethical work of the self on the self. Plutarch says this to the prince who is not yet educated: as soon as he takes power, the man who governs must "set his soul straight" and properly establish his own *ēthos.*[27]

3. Political activity and personal destiny. The precariousness of good fortune—too much success provokes the jealousy of the gods, or the people are fond of withdrawing favors they once granted—was clearly a traditional theme of meditation. In reflection on political activity, during the first centuries of the Empire, this precariousness inherent in the exercise of power is associated with two other themes. First, it is perceived as being linked to the dependence that one experiences in relation to others. It is not so much the particular cycle of good and bad fortune that explains this fragility, but the fact that one is placed under what Seneca calls the *potentia aliena* or the *vis potentioris.*[28] In the complex network of power, one is never alone facing one's enemies. One is exposed on all sides to influences, intrigues, conspiracies, losses of favor. To be secure, one will have to be careful not to "give offence. It is sometimes the people that we ought to fear; or sometimes a body of influential oligarchs in the Senate . . . and sometimes individuals equipped with power by the people and against the people. It is burdensome to keep the friendship of all such persons; it is enough not to make enemies of them." Between the prince, the Senate, and the populace giving and taking away their favors according to circumstances, the exercise of power depends on an unstable conjuncture: "You have held the highest offices; but have you held any as great, as unlooked for, as comprehensive as those of Sejanus? Yet on the day on which the Senate played the escort, the people tore him to pieces! Of the man who had heaped upon him all that gods and men were able to bestow, nothing was left for the executioner to drag to the river!"[29]

For these reversals and for the anxiety that they cause, one must prepare oneself by setting a prior limit on the ambitions that one entertains: "Nothing can free us from these mental waverings so effectively as always to establish some limit to advancement and not leave to Fortune the decision of when it shall end, but halt of our own accord."³⁰ And if the occasion presents itself, it is good to withdraw from these activities when they become disturbing and prevent one from attending to oneself. If misfortune suddenly strikes, if one falls from favor and is exiled, one ought to tell oneself—this is the advice Plutarch addresses no doubt to the same Menemachus whom he had encouraged, several years before, to enter politics "by free choice"*—that one is finally free from obedience to governors, from liturgies that are too costly, from services to render, from ambassadorial missions to accomplish, and from taxes to pay.³¹ And to Lucilius, who is not under any threat, however, Seneca gives the advice to disengage himself from his duties, gradually and at the right time, just as Epicurus counseled, so as to be able to place himself at his own disposal.³²

The basic attitude that one must have toward political activity was related to the general principle that whatever one is, it is not owing to the rank one holds, to the responsibility one exercises, to the position in which one finds oneself—above or beneath other people. What one is, and what one needs to devote one's attention to as to an ultimate purpose, is the expression of a principle that is singular in its manifestation within each person, but universal by the form it assumes in everyone, and collective by the community bond it establishes between individuals. Such is, at least for the Stoics, human reason as a divine principle present in all of us. Now, this god, "a guest in a mortal body," can be found in the form or a Roman knight as well as in the body of a freedman or a slave. From the viewpoint of the relation to the self, the social and political identifications do not function as authentic marks of a mode of being; they are extrinsic, artificial, and unfounded signs. How could one be a Roman knight, a freedman, a slave? These were names that one used, born of pride and injustice.³³ "Each man acquires his character for himself, but accident assigns his duties."³⁴ It was according to this law, therefore,

---

*The treatise on exile is thought to be addressed to the same personage as the *Praecepta gerendae reipublicae*.

that one would have to assume responsibilities, and that one would need to rid oneself of them.

Clearly, then, it would not be adequate to say that political activities, in moral reflection, were conceived primarily in the form of a simple alternative: to participate or to abstain. It is true that the question was framed in such terms rather often. But this alternative itself derived from a more general problematization. The latter concerned the manner in which one ought to form oneself as an ethical subject in the entire sphere of social, political, and civic activities. It concerned how one determined which of these activities were obligatory or optional, natural or conventional, permanent or provisional, unconditional or recommended only under certain conditions. It also concerned the rules that must be applied when one engaged in them, and the way in which one ought to govern oneself in order to take one's place among others, assert one's legitimate share of authority, and in general situate oneself in the complex and shifting interplay of relations of command and subordination. The question of the choice between retreat and activity was indeed posed in a recurrent fashion. But the terms in which it was posed and the solution so often given to it show very well that it was not purely and simply a matter of translating a general waning of political activity into an ethics of withdrawal. It was a matter of elaborating an ethics that enabled one to constitute oneself as an ethical subject with respect to these social, civic, and political activities, in the different forms they might take and at whatever distance one remained from them.

In view of these changes in matrimonial practice and in the political game, one can see how the conditions under which the traditional ethics of self-mastery asserted itself were transformed. Self-mastery had implied a close connection between the superiority one exercised over oneself, the authority one exercised in the context of the household, and the power one exercised in the field of an agonistic society. It was the practice of superiority over oneself that guaranteed the moderate and reasonable use that one could and ought to make of the two other superiorities.

Henceforth one was in a world where these relations could no longer operate in the same way: the relation of superiority exercised in the household and over the wife had to be associated with certain forms of reciprocity and equality. As for the agonistic game by which one sought to manifest and ensure one's superiority over others, it had to be integrated into a far more extensive and complex field of power relations. Consequently, the principle of superiority over the self as the ethical core, the general form of "heautocratism," needed to be restructured. Not that it disappeared; but it had to make room for a certain balance between inequality and reciprocity in married life. In social, civic, and political life, it had to bring a certain dissociation into play between power over the self and power over others. The importance given to the problem of "oneself," the development of the cultivation of the self in the course of the Hellenistic period, and the apogee it experienced at the beginning of the Empire manifested this effort of reelaboration of an ethics of self-mastery. The reflection on the use of pleasure that was so directly linked to the close correlation between the three types of authority (over oneself, over the household, and over others) was modified in the very course of this elaboration. A growth of public constraints and prohibitions? An individualistic withdrawal accompanying the valorization of private life? We need instead to think in terms of a crisis of the subject, or rather a crisis of subjectivation—that is, in terms of a difficulty in the manner in which the individual could form himself as the ethical subject of his actions, and efforts to find in devotion to self that which could enable him to submit to rules and give a purpose to his existence.

PART FOUR

THE BODY

It has often been remarked how intense and prevalent was the taste for things medical in the period of the Flavians and the Antonines. Medicine was widely recognized as a practice that was of interest to the public.[1] It was also recognized as a high form of culture, on the same level as rhetoric and philosophy. G. W. Bowersock observes that the medical model accompanied the development of the Second Sophistic and that a number of important rhetors had received medical training or manifested interests in that field.[2]* It had long been established that philosophy was closely related to medicine, even though the demarcation of boundaries posed doctrinal problems and gave rise to territorial rivalries. In the first lines of *Advice about Keeping Well*, Plutarch echoes these debates: the physician is wrong, he says, when he claims to be able to do without philosophy, and one would be quite mistaken to reproach philosophers with crossing their own boundaries when they concern themselves with health and its regimen. One must consider, Plutarch concludes, that medicine is in no way inferior to the liberal arts (*eleutherai technai*) in elegance, distinction, and the satisfaction it yields. To those who study it, it gives access to a knowledge of great importance since it concerns health and the preservation of life.'

Thus, medicine was not conceived simply as a technique of

*Celsus, in his treatise *De Medicina*, explains the birth of medicine by the development of the *litterarum disciplina*.'

intervention, relying, in cases of illness, on remedies and oper-ations. It was also supposed to define, in the form of a corpus of knowledge and rules, a way of living, a reflective mode of relation to oneself, to one's body, to food, to wakefulness and sleep, to the various activities, and to the environment. Medi-cine was expected to propose, in the form of regimen, a volun-tary and rational structure of conduct. One of the points of discussion related to the degree and form of dependence that this medically informed life ought to manifest with regard to the authority of physicians. The way in which the latter some-times took control of their clients' existence in order to man-age it in the least detail was an object of criticism, for the same reasons as was the spiritual direction practiced by philoso-phers. And Celsus, as convinced as he was of the high value of regimen medicine, was against subjecting oneself to a physi-cian if one was in good health.* The literature of regimen was meant to ensure this self-reliance. It was in order to avoid too-frequent consultations—because they were not always possible and they were often not desirable—that it was neces-sary to equip oneself with a medical knowledge that one could always use. Such is the advice that Athenaeus gives: acquire when young sufficient knowledge to be able, throughout one's life and in ordinary circumstances, to be one's own health counselor. "It is advisable, or rather, necessary, for everyone to learn, among the subjects that are taught, not only the other sciences but also medicine, and to hear the precepts of this art, so that we may often be our own accomplished counselors in matters useful to health; for there is almost no moment of the night or the day when we have no need of medicine. Thus, whether we are walking or sitting, whether we are oiling our body or taking a bath, whether we are eating, drinking—in a word, whatever we may do, during the whole course of life and

*Celsus, in the preface of his treatise *De Medicina*, distinguishes one kind of medicine by regimen (*victu*), another by medicaments (*medicamentis*), and a third by opera-tions (*manu*). Those who teach the first, "by far the most famous authorities, endeav-oring to go more deeply into things, claim for themselves a knowledge of nature." This did not mean that a man in good health needed to subject himself to the physicians' authority.'

in the midst of life's diverse occupations, we have need of advice for an employment of this life that is worthwhile and free of inconvenience. Now, it is tiresome and impossible always to consult a physician concerning all these details."[6] One easily recognizes in this passage one of the basic principles of the practice of the self: be equipped with, have ready to hand, a "helpful discourse," which one has learned very early, rehearses often, and reflects on regularly. The medical *logos* was one such discourse, dictating at every moment the correct regimen of life.

A reasonable discourse could not unfold without a "health practice"—*hygieinē pragmateia* or *technē*—which constituted the permanent framework of everyday life, as it were, making it possible to know at every moment what was to be done and how to do it. It implied a medical perception of the world, so to speak, or at least a medical perception of the space and circumstances in which one lived. The elements of the milieu were perceived as having positive or negative effects on health. Between the individual and his environs, one imagined a whole web of interferences such that a certain disposition, a certain event, a certain change in things would induce morbid effects in the body. Conversely, a certain weak constitution of the body would be favorably or unfavorably affected by such and such a circumstance. Hence there was a constant and detailed problematization of the environment, a differential valuation of this environment with regard to the body, and a positing of the body as a fragile entity in relation to its surroundings. One can cite as an example the analysis submitted by Antyllus of the different medical "variables" of a house, its architecture, its orientation, and its interior design. Each element is assigned a dietetic or therapeutic value; a house is a series of compartments that will be harmful or beneficial as regards possible illnesses. Rooms on the ground floor are good for acute illnesses, hemoptyses, and headaches; upper-floor rooms are favorable in cases of pituitary illnesses; rooms with a southerly exposure are good except for patients who need cooling; westerly facing rooms are bad, in the morning because they are gloomy, in the evening because they provoke headaches; whitewashed walls are too dazzling, painted walls cause nightmares in those who are delirious due to fever; stone walls are too cold, brick walls are better.[7]

The different periods of time—days, seasons, ages—are also, in the same perspective, bearers of varying medical values. A careful regimen must be able to determine precisely the relations between the calendar and the care that needs to be given to oneself. This is the advice that Athenaeus offers for confronting the winter season: in the city as well as in the house, one should wear thick clothing, "one should breathe while keeping a part of one's garment in front of the mouth." As for food, one should choose food that "can heat the parts of the body and dissolve the liquids that have been congealed by the cold. Drinks should consist of hydromel, honeyed wine, and white wine, old and sweet-smelling; in general, they should be substances capable of drawing out all the excess moisture; but one should reduce the quantity of drink. The dry foods should be easy to prepare, thoroughly worked, well-cooked, pure, and should be mixed with fennel and ammi. For pot vegetables, one should eat cabbage, asparagus, leeks, boiled tender onions and boiled horseradish; as concerns fish, rockfish are good, for they are easily assimilated by the body. In the meat category, one should eat poultry and, among the other kinds, young goat and young pork. As concerns sauces, those that are prepared with pepper, mustard, winter cress, garum, and vinegar. One should take up moderately strenuous exercise, practice holding one's breath, and undergo rather vigorous rubdowns, especially those that one applies to oneself by the fireside. It is also good to resort to hot baths, whether these be taken in the bathing pool or in a small bathtub, etc."[8] And the summer regimen is no less meticulous.

This preoccupation with the environment, with places and times, called for a constant attention to oneself, to the state one was in and to the acts that one performed. Addressing that category of people considered to be especially fragile, the city-dwellers, and above all, those who devote themselves to study *(litterarum cupidi),* Celsus prescribes a keen vigilance: if one has digested well, one should rise early; if one has digested poorly, one should continue to rest, and in case one is obliged to get up all the same, one should go back to sleep; and if no digestion has taken place, one should remain completely inactive, and "neither work nor take exercise nor attend to business." One will know if one is in good health "if his morning urine is whitish, later reddish; the former indicates that digestion is going on, the latter that digestion is complete." When one is kept busy all day by one's affairs, one should nevertheless set aside a little time for the *curatio corporis.* The exercises that should be practiced are "reading aloud, drill, handball, running, walking; but this is not by any means most useful on the level, since walking up and down hill varies the movement of the body, unless indeed the body is thoroughly weak; but it is better to walk in the open air than under cover; better, when the head allows it, in the sun than in the shade; better under the shade of a wall or of trees than under a roof; better a straight than a winding walk. . . . The proper sequel to exercise is: at times an anointing, whether in the sun or before a brazier; at times a bath, which should be in a chamber as lofty, well lighted and spacious as possible."⁹

In a general way, all these themes of dietetics had remained remarkably continuous since the classical period. It is clear that the general principles stayed the same; at most, they were developed, given more detail, and refined. They suggested a tighter structuring of life, and they solicited a more constantly vigilant attention to the body. The evocations of their everyday life that one can find in the letters of Seneca or in the correspondence between Marcus Aurelius and Fronto testify to this mode of attention to the self and to one's body. An intensification, much more than a radical change; an increase of apprehension and not a disparagement of the body; a change of scale in the elements to which one needed to direct one's attention and not a different way of perceiving oneself as a physical individual.

It was in this overall context, so strongly marked by concern for the body, health, environment, and circumstances, that medicine framed the question of sexual pleasures: the question of their nature and their mechanism, that of their positive and negative value for the organism, that of the regimen to which they ought to be subjected.[10]

CHAPTER ONE

====

GALEN

1. Galen's analyses concerning the *aphrodisia* are situated within the ancient thematic of the relations between death, immortality, and reproduction. For him, as for a whole philosophical tradition, the necessity of the division of the sexes, the intensity of their mutual attraction, and the possibility of generation are rooted in the lack of eternity. This is the general explanation given by the treatise *On the Usefulness of the Parts of the Body.* [1] Nature, doing her work, encountered an obstacle, a sort of intrinsic incompatibility in her task. Her plan, what she strove *(espoudase)* to do, was to construct an immortal work. But the substance she had to work with did not permit this; she could not make arteries, nerves, bones, and flesh using an "incorruptible" material. Galen discerns at the very core of the demiurgic work—the *dēmiourgēma*—an internal limit and a kind of "failure" due to an unavoidable inadequacy between the immortality that was planned and the corruptibility of the material used. The *logos* that builds the natural order is in a situation rather similar to that of the founder of a city: the latter may very well bring men together to form a community; however, the city will disappear, will fall into oblivion, if one does not discover how to make it endure beyond the death of its first citizens. A means is necessary to surmount this fundamental difficulty. Galen's vocabulary is both insistent and significant. It is a question of finding an aid, of contriving a means *(boētheia),* of discovering an art

105

(technē), of using an enticement *(delear),* to ensure the salvation and protection of the species. In short, something ingenious *(sophisma)* is needed.[2] To bring her work to its logical conclusion, the demiurge, in creating living beings and giving them a means to reproduce, had to perfect a ruse: a ruse of the *logos* that presides over the world, in order to overcome the unavoidable corruptibility of the material of which this very world is made.

This ruse brings three elements into play. First, the organs that are given to all animals and are used for fertilization. Next, a capacity for pleasure that is extraordinary and "very keen." Lastly, in the soul, the longing *(epithumia)* to make use of these organs—a marvelous, inexpressible *(arrhēton)* desire. The "sophism" of sex does not therefore reside simply in a subtle anatomical arrangement and in carefully planned mechanisms; it also consists in their association with a pleasure and a desire, the singular force of which is "even beyond words." To overcome the incompatibility between her plan and the limitations of her materials, Nature had to place the principle of a force, an extraordinary *dynamis,* in the body and soul of the living creature.

Hence the wisdom of the demiurgic principle, which, knowing very well the substance of her work and consequently its limits, invented this mechanism of excitement—this "sting" of desire. (Here Galen repeats the traditional image, by which one spoke metaphorically of the uncontrolled vehemence of desire.[3]) So that, experiencing this sting, even those animals that are incapable of understanding the purpose of Nature in her wisdom—because they are young, foolish *(aphrona),* or without reason *(aloga)*—do in fact accomplish it.[4] By their intensity the *aphrodisia* serve a rationality which those who engage in them do not even need to know.

2. The physiology of sexual acts in Galen is still marked by some fundamental traits found in the earlier traditions.

In the first place, there is the isomorphism of these acts in the man and the woman. For Galen, it rests on the principle of an identity of the anatomical apparatus in the two sexes: "Consider first whichever parts you please, turn outward the woman's, turn inward, so to speak, and fold double the man's, and you will find them the same in both in every respect."⁵ He assumes the emission of sperm by the woman as well as by the man, the difference being that the production of this humor is less perfect in the woman and less complete—which explains its minor role in the formation of the embryo.

One also finds in Galen the traditional model of the paroxysmal process of excretion that traverses the body, shakes it, and exhausts it. But the analysis he gives of this phenomenon deserves nonetheless to be examined. It has the double effect of linking, very closely, the mechanisms of the sexual act with the organism as a whole, while making it a process in which the individual's health, and possibly his very life, is at risk. At the same time that it inserts the act into a dense and unbroken physiological web, it invests it with a high potential for danger.

This is brought out very clearly in what we might call a "physiologization" of desire and pleasure. Chapter Nine of Book XIV of *On the Usefulness of the Parts* poses the question: "Why is a very great pleasure coupled with the exercise of the generative parts?" From the outset Galen rejects the idea that the vehemence of desire and the intensity of pleasure could simply have been associated with the sexual act by the will of the creating gods as a means of inciting men to its performance. Galen does not deny that the demiurgic power so arranged things that there would be that intensity which sweeps us along. He means that it was not added in the soul as a supplement, but that it was most certainly planned as an integral consequence of the mechanisms of the body. Desire and pleasure are direct effects of anatomical dispositions and physical processes. The final cause—which is the continuation of the generations—is pursued through a material cause and an organic arrangement: "For animals acquired this desire and pleasure not simply because the gods that formed us wished a vehement desire for love to be born in us or a vehement pleasure to be coupled with it, but because a suitable material and instruments had been prepared for this purpose."[6] Desire is not just a movement of the soul, nor is pleasure a reward added in as something extra. They are the effects of a pressure and a sudden evacuation. Galen sees several pleasure factors in this mechanism. First, there is the accumulation of a humor of such a nature that it provokes intense sensations in those parts where it collects. "It is the sort of thing that happens when serous humors are heated, as they frequently are, especially when acrid humors collect under the skin of the animal and then itch and make it scratch and enjoy the scratching."[7] One must also take into account the heat that is particularly strong in the lower part, and singularly so on the right side because of the nearness of the liver and the large number of vessels that come from it. This dissymmetry with regard to heat explains the fact that boys are formed most frequently in the right uterus and girls in the left.[8] It also explains why the parts on the right side are more apt to be the locus of intense pleasure. In any case, Nature gave the organs of this area a special sensitivity, much greater than that of the skin, despite their having the same functions. Lastly, the much thinner humor coming from the glandular bodies Galen calls *parastata* constitutes an additional material factor of pleasure. This humor, by permeating the parts involved in the sexual act, makes them more elastic and heightens the pleasure they experience. There is, then, a whole anatomical disposition and a whole physiological design that inscribe in the body and its specific mechanisms pleasure with its excessive vigor *(hyperochē tēs hēdonēs)*, which cannot be resisted: it is *amēchanos.*[9]

But even though the formation of pleasure is firmly anchored and precisely localized in this way, it is no less true that, by virtue of the elements it brings into play and the consequences it entails, the sexual act involves the entire body. Galen does not hold, as does the Hippocratic author of *De generatione,* that the sperm is formed by agitation occurring in the bloodstream; nor does he believe, as does Aristotle, that it constitutes the final state of digestion. In his view, it combines two elements: first, the product of a certain "coction" of the blood that is effected in the coils of the spermatic channels (it is this slow elaboration that gradually gives it its color and consistency); and second, the presence of the pneuma: it is the pneuma that swells the sexual organs, it is the pneuma that seeks to exit violently from the body and escapes in the sperm at the moment of ejaculation. Now, this *pneuma* is formed in the complex labyrinth of the brain. The sexual act, when it takes place and thus withdraws sperm and pneuma, acts on the general mechanism of the body, where all the elements are linked "as in a chorus." And, "when, as a result of venereal excesses, all the sperm has been evacuated, the testicles draw from the veins above them all the seminal fluid which they contain. Now, this liquid is found there only in small quantities, mixed with the blood in the form of dew." These veins, "violently deprived of this fluid by the testicles, which have a more energetic action than they, in turn draw the liquid away from the veins situated above them, these draw it from the next ones, and the latter from those that are adjacent to them. This movement of attraction does not stop before the transfer has been propagated in all parts of the body." And if this expenditure continues, the body is not simply deprived of its seminal fluid: "all the parts of the animal find themselves robbed of their vital breath."[10]

3. We can thus understand the cluster of relations that are established in Galen's thought between the sexual act and the phenomena of epilepsy and convulsions: relations of affinity, analogy, and causality.

The sexual act belongs, by reason of its mechanism, to the large family of convulsions, the theory of which is given in the treatise *On the Affected Parts*.[11] In that work Galen analyzes the process of convulsion as being of the same nature as any other involuntary movement; the difference lies in the fact that the traction exerted by the nerve on the muscle does not originate in the will but in a certain condition of dryness (which draws the nerve tight, like a leather cord left in the sun) or repletion (which by swelling the nerves shortens them and pulls excessively on the muscles). It is to this last type of mechanism that the spasm peculiar to the sexual act is assimilated.

In this large family of convulsions, Galen identifies a particular analogy between epilepsy and the sexual act. For him, epilepsy is caused by a congestion of the brain, which finds itself completely filled by a thick humor: whence the obstruction of the channels that leave the ventricles where the pneuma resides. The latter is therefore imprisoned by this accumulation and it tries to escape, just as it strains to get out when it has collected with the sperm in the testicles. It is this attempt that is the source of the agitation of the nerves and muscles that one can witness, with varying proportions, in epileptic seizures or in the performance of the *aphrodisia.*

Finally, there is, between the *aphrodisia* and convulsive attacks, a relation of causality that can be established in either direction. The epileptic convulsion can lead to a spasm in the sexual organs: "From severe attacks of epilepsy," says Galen in the treatise *On the Usefulness of the Parts,* "and from the disease called gonorrhea you may learn how great a power the spasm, so to speak, of the parts that accompanies the sexual act has to expel what they contain. For in violent attacks of epilepsy semen is expelled because the whole body and with it the generative parts are strongly convulsed."[12] Conversely, indulgence in the sexual pleasures at the wrong time can induce illnesses of the convulsive type by causing a gradual drying and an ever greater tension of the nerves.

In the great edifice of Galenic theory, the *aphrodisia* appear to be situated on three successive planes. First, they are firmly anchored in the order of demiurgic providence: they were conceived and positioned at that precise point where the creator's wisdom came to the rescue of her power, in order to transcend the limits she encountered in death. Second, they are placed within an interplay of complex and constant correlations with the body, both by the precise anatomical location of their processes and by the effects they produce in the overall economy of the pneuma, which ensures the unity of the body. Lastly, they are situated in a vast field of affinity with a group of diseases, within which they maintain relations of analogy and a relationship of cause to effect. A clearly visible thread extends, in Galen's analyses, from a cosmology of reproduction to a pathology of spasmodic excretions. And from the natural foundation of the *aphrodisia,* it leads to an analysis of the perilous mechanisms that constitute their intrinsic nature and associate them with dread diseases.

CHAPTER TWO

ARE THEY GOOD?
ARE THEY BAD?

This ambiguity in medical thought concerning the sexual pleasures is not peculiar to Galen, although it is more discernible in him than elsewhere. It characterizes the essential part of what remains of the medical texts of the first and second centuries. In reality it is an ambivalence rather than an ambiguity, for what is involved is the interweaving of two antithetical valuations.

First, on the positive side, there is the valorization of semen, of sperm—that precious substance which Nature, when she designed the human body, took so many precautions in forming. It gathers up all that is powerful in life and transmits it, thereby enabling us to cheat death. It is in the male that it reaches its greatest strength and its highest perfection. And it is this substance that gives him his superiority. It contributes "to health, strength, courage, and generation."[1] The male is preeminent because he is the spermatic animal par excellence.

There is also a valorization of the act for which, in both sexes, the organs were so carefully arranged. Sexual union is a fact of nature; it cannot be considered bad. Rufus of Ephesus expresses a general opinion when he says that sexual intercourse is a natural act, and that consequently it cannot be harmful in itself.[2]

But in a sense it is only the possibility and the principle of the act that are validated in this way. For as soon as the act takes place, it is, in its unfolding, regarded as intrinsically

112

dangerous. Dangerous because it is a wasting of that precious substance whose accumulation nevertheless incites one to commit it—it allows all the life force that the semen has concentrated to escape. Dangerous, too, because its very unfolding makes it akin to a disease. Aretaeus had a meaningful phrase for this: the sexual act, he said, "bears the *symbola*" of epilepsy.[3] Caelius Aurelianus compared, term by term, the unfolding of the sexual act and the development of an epileptic seizure, finding exactly the same phases in both: "various parts are subjected to spasms, and at the same time there occur panting, sweating, rolling of the eyes and flushing of the face, and finally a feeling of malaise along with pallor, weakness, or dejection."[4] Such is the paradox of the sexual pleasures: the high function Nature assigned them, the value of the substance they have to transmit and therefore lose—this is the very thing that relates them to sickness. The physicians of the first and second centuries were not the first nor the only ones to formulate this ambivalence. But around it, they described an entire pathology, more developed, more complex, and more systematic than that attested in the past.

1. The pathology of sexual activity itself is constructed around two elements by which the dangers of the sexual act are usually characterized: an involuntary violence of tension and an indefinite, exhausting expenditure.

On the one hand, there is the disease that is marked by a constant excitation, which restrains the act while indefinitely prolonging the mechanism of stimulation. In the male version of this kind of affliction—designated as satyriasis or priapism—all the mechanisms that prepare the sexual act and ejaculation (tensions, agitations, heatings) are brought together and maintained in a continuous fashion, whether or not there is an evacuation of sperm: a sexual erethism that is never resolved. The patient is in a state of constant convulsion, traversed by extreme attacks, which closely resemble epilepsy. Aretaeus' description can serve as a testimony of the way in which people perceived this strange disease where the sexual act is as though left to itself in a timeless and boundless movement; its convulsive, epileptic nature is revealed there in the raw state, as it were: "It is a disease in which the patient has erection of the genital organ. . . . It is an unrestrainable impulse to connection; but neither are they at all relieved by those embraces, nor is the tentigo soothed by many and repeated acts of sexual intercourse. Spasms of all the nerves, and tension of all the tendons, groins, and perineum, inflammation and pain of the genital parts." This constant state is punctuated by attacks. The patients then lose "all restraint of tongue as regards obscenity, and likewise all restraint in regard to the open performance of the act . . . ; they vomit much phlegm. Afterwards, froth settles on their lips, as is the case with goats in the season of rutting, and the smell likewise is similar." Their minds lapse into madness, and they do not come to their ordinary senses again until the paroxysm has ended.[5] Galen, in his treatise *On the Affected Parts,* gives a much more sober description of satyriasis: "Priapism is an increase in the length and circumference of the male genitalia without sexual desire and without the acquired increase in heat which some people experience in the recumbent position. Other physicians describe it in the following manner, which is a shorter definition: a persisting increase of the external genitals or a persisting swelling."[6] The cause of this disease is to be understood, according to Galen, from the mechanisms of erection, which means that it will be found in "the dilated orifices of the arteries" or in "the formation of the pneuma in the nerve." Actually, Galen allows for both causes and their convergence in the genesis of symptoms. But he is most often inclined to blame the dilation of arteries, which is, according to him, a phenomenon that occurs much more frequently than that involving the pneuma "in the cavernous nerve." This kind of disease is found in those who "have too much sperm" and who, contrary to their usual habits, "abstain from intercourse" (unless they find a means of "dissipating in numerous occupations the surplus quantity of their blood"), or in those who, while practicing self-control, imagine sexual pleasures after seeing certain spectacles or as a result of recurring memories.

Satyriasis in women is sometimes mentioned. Soranus encounters the same type of symptoms in such cases; they take the form of an "intense itching of the genitals." Women afflicted with this ailment are moved by "an irresistible desire for sexual intercourse," which "throws aside all sense of shame."[7] But it is doubtless hysteria that best represents the excessive tension of the sexual organs. In any case, that is how Galen describes an affliction in which he declines to see a movement of the uterus. The changes that have made some people think that the desiccated organ draws up toward the diaphragm in search of the moisture it lacks are due, according to him, either to retention of the menstrual flow or to retention of sperm. The obstruction of the vessels may cause them to become enlarged and hence shortened. A traction is thus brought to bear on the uterus. But it is not this process in itself which provokes the set of other symptoms; these all stem from the retention of humors that occurs, either when menstruation is suspended or when the woman interrupts her sexual relations: whence the hysteria that one can observe in widowed women, "particularly those who previously menstruated regularly, had been pregnant, and were eager for intercourse, but were now deprived of all this."[8]

The other pole of the pathology is constituted by unlimited expenditure. This is what the Greeks call *gonorrhea* and the Latins *seminis effusio.* Galen defines it thus: "an involuntary discharge of sperm," or "to be more definite, a continuous discharge of semen without erection of the penis." Whereas satyriasis attacks the penis, gonorrhea affects the spermatic vessels, paralyzing their "retentive faculty."[9] Aretaeus describes it at length in *On the Causes and Signs of Chronic Diseases* as the exhaustion of the vital principles, its three effects being a general loss of strength, premature aging, and a feminization of the body. "Young persons, when they suffer from this affection, necessarily become old in constitution, torpid, dull, spiritless, enfeebled, shriveled, inactive, pale whitish, effeminate, loathe their food, and become frigid; they have heaviness of the members, torpidity of the legs, are powerless, and incapable of all exertion. In many cases, this disease is the way to paralysis; for how could the nervous power not suffer when nature has become frigid in regard to the generation of life? For it is the semen, when possessed of vitality, which makes us men, hot, well-braced in limbs, hairy, well-voiced, spirited, strong to think and to act, as the characteristics of men prove. For when the semen is not possessed of its vitality, persons become shriveled, have a sharp tone of voice, lose their hair and their beard, and become effeminate."[10] With gonorrhea it is virility, the life principle, that is lost via the genitals. Hence the traits that are traditionally associated with it. It is a shameful disease—no doubt because it is often induced by a quantitative excess of sexual activity. But it is also shameful in itself because of the appearance of emasculation it produces. It is a disease that leads inevitably to death. Celsus says that in a short time it causes the patient to die of consumption.[11] Finally, it is a disease that is perilous not just for the individual but, according to Aretaeus, for his offspring as well.[12]

2. Beyond the particular sphere of their pathology, sexual acts are placed, by the medicine of the first two centuries, at the junction of a complex pathology. On the one hand, sexual acts are susceptible of being affected, in their unfolding and their satisfactory conclusion, by an abundance of diverse factors: there is the temperament of the individuals; there is the climate, the time of day; there is the food that one has ingested, its quality and amount. The acts are so fragile that the least deviation, the least malaise, risks perturbing them. As Galen says, to experience the sexual pleasures, one ought to be in an exactly medial state, at the zero point, as it were, of all the possible organic variations: "beware of repletion and deficiency," avoid "fatigue, indigestion, and anything, moreover, which might be suspect in consideration of a person's health."[13]

But if the *aphrodisia* constitute such a fragile and precarious activity, they in return exert a substantial and quite extensive influence on the entire organism. The list of ailments, malaises, and diseases that can be engendered by the sexual pleasures if one commits a deviation, with respect either to time or measure, is virtually open. "It is not difficult," says Galen, "to recognize that sexual relations are fatiguing for the chest, the lungs, the head and the nerves."[14] Rufus submits a table in which are juxtaposed, as effects of an abuse of sexual relations, digestive disorders, a weakening of sight and hearing, a general weakness of the sense organs, and memory loss; convulsive trembling, pains of the joints, a stabbing pain in the side; aphtha in the mouth, toothaches, inflammation of the throat, spitting of blood, and kidney and bladder diseases.[15] It is concerning hysteria that Galen meets the objection of those who cannot believe that symptoms so numerous, so extensive, and so violent can be due to the retention or alteration of such a small amount of humor, which remains in the body as a result of the suspension of sexual relations. To which Galen replies by comparing the noxious powers of corrupted sperm to those of the virulent poisons that one observes in nature: "We can see that the entire body is affected by the bite of the venemous spider, although only an insignificant amount of venom enters through a very small opening." The effect produced by the scorpion is more surprising still, for the most violent symptoms declare themselves immediately; and yet, "a truly minimal amount or absolutely nothing is injected by the attacking stinger, the point of which seems to be without perforation." The torpedo-fish is another example of this fact that "a minute quantity of some substance elicits a most painful effect simply by contact." And Galen concludes: "When, however, an affection involving our body originates inside and resembles the effect of the administration of a dangerous poison, then it is not astonishing that an abnormally composed semen or an equally abnormal menstrual discharge produces serious symptoms by stagnation or putrefaction in persons susceptible to such diseases."[16] The organs, the humors, and sexual acts constitute both a surface that is receptive and especially sensitive to anything capable of disturbing the organism, and a very active focus for inducing a long series of polymorphous symptoms throughout the body.

3.   Sexual activity is a source of therapeutic effects as well as pathological consequences. Its ambivalence makes it capable of healing in certain cases. In others, on the contrary, it is likely to lead to illnesses. But it is not always easy to determine which of the two effects it will have: a question of individual temperament; a question, too, of particular circumstances and of the transitory state of the body. In general, theorists subscribe to the Hippocratic teaching that "sexual intercourse is excellent against diseases due to the phlegm." And Rufus comments: "Many individuals who are emaciated as a result of an illness are restored by means of this practice. Some of them thereby regain an easy respiration, which had been obstructed, others recover the appetite for food which they had lost, still others achieve the cessation of contrary nocturnal emissions."[17] He also credits the evacuation of sperm with positive effects on the soul when the latter is troubled and needs, like the body, to be purged of that which encumbers it: intercourse dissipates fixed ideas and pacifies violent fits of anger. This is why there does not exist a more eminently useful remedy against melancholy and misanthropy. Galen also attributes to sexual relations a number of curative effects, on the soul as well as the body: "this act predisposes the soul to tranquillity. Indeed it restores the melancholy and furious man to a more sensible state, and in an amorous individual it dampens the too immoderate ardor, even when this man has intercourse with a different woman. Further, animals that are ferocious when they have given birth become calm after copulation." As to their effectiveness for the body, Galen sees a proof of their action in the fact that, once sexual practice has begun, boys become "hairy, large, manly," whereas before they were "smooth-skinned, small, and feminine."[18]

But Galen also remarks o... ...
relations may have according ...
subject finds himself: "intercour... ...
ness those whose strength is incons... ...
strength is intact and who are sick t... ...
phlegm will not be struck down by int... ...
ment "it makes weak people warm agai... ...
chills them considerably"; or further, wherea...
in their early youth, become instantly enfee... ...er-
course. Others, if they do not have regular sexu... ...ations,
feel heavy in the head, become nauseated and feverish, have
a poor appetite and bad digestion."[19] And Galen even mentions the case of certain temperaments for which the evacuation of sperm provokes illnesses or malaises despite the fact
that its retention is harmful: "Certain people have an abundant, warm sperm which incessantly arouses the need for
excretion; however, after its expulsion, people who are in this
state experience a languor at the stomach orifice, exhaustion,
weakness, and dryness in the whole body. They become thin,
their eyes grow hollow and if, because they have suffered these
effects after intercourse, they abstain from sexual relations,
they feel discomfort in the head and at the stomach orifice
along with nausea, and they do not derive any significant
advantage from their self-control."[20]

Around these positive or negative effects, several debates
developed concerning certain precise questions. For example,
the question of nocturnal emissions. Rufus reports the opinion
of those for whom these losses of semen during sleep are "less
distressing." But for his part, he opposes this conception,
being of the opinion that "emissions relax the body even more,
when it is already relaxed in sleep."[21] And Galen does not see
that anything is gained by those who, abstaining from intercourse because of its harmful effects, experience nocturnal
emissions as a result.[22] More important no doubt was the
debate concerning children's convulsions and their cessation
at the age of puberty. It had often been held that, because of
the affinity between ejaculation and spasm, young boys

...nvulsions could be cured by the first sexual
...his is the thesis of Rufus, who believes that epilepsy
...headaches come to an end when a boy reaches puberty.[23]
As a therapy against these spasms, some physicians recommended making the age of the first sexual relations earlier for
those children. Aretaeus criticizes this method, because it
violates the designs of Nature, who appointed the proper
times, and because it produces or prolongs the disease it aims
to cure: physicians who give such advice "are ignorant of the
spontaneous law of Nature by which all cures are accomplished. For along with every age she produces that which is
proper for it in due season. At a given time there is the maturity of semen, of the beard, of hoary hairs. For on the one hand
what physician could alter Nature's original change in regard
to the semen, and, on the other, the appointed time for each?
But they also offend against the nature of the disease; for being
previously injured by the unseasonableness of the act, they are
not possessed of seasonable powers at the proper commence-
ment of the age for coition."[24] If in fact the convulsions disappear at puberty, this is due not to the enjoyment of sexual
pleasures, but to a general modification in the balance and role
of the humors.

4.   But the most important consideration is doubtless the
tendency to attribute positive effects to sexual abstention. It is
true, as we have seen, that the physicians call attention to the
disorders that can result from the practice of self-restraint.
But they generally observe them in subjects who were accustomed to frequent sexual relations and in whom the cessation
amounts to a sudden change of regimen. This is the case
reported by Galen in the treatise *On the Affected Parts,* involving a man who, breaking with all this previous habits, had
given up sexual activity.[25] They are also observed in subjects
whose sperm is affected by qualities that make its evacuation
necessary. Galen has seen men who, through the effect of this
deprivation, became "dull and inactive," and others who, "for

no evident reason, had a sad and hopeless expression on their faces like melancholics." These observations allow him to state that "the retention of sperm does considerable harm to young and strong individuals, in whom the sperm is naturally abundant and formed of humors that are not entirely faultless, who lead a somewhat lazy life, who had quite frequently indulged in sexual intercourse before, and who suddenly practice continence."[26] That abstention from all sexual relations is harmful to the organism is therefore not regarded as a general fact that might be observed in anyone, no matter who they might be, but rather as the consequence of certain particular facts pertaining either to the state of the organism or to a habitual mode of living. In itself, and without any other factor entering in, abstinence that retains the spermatic substance cannot reasonably be considered harmful.

As concerns men, the high vital value granted to the spermatic humor had long enabled people to attribute positive effects to the kind of rigorous self-restraint practiced by athletes. The example is still regularly cited. It was precisely in order to follow this model that a patient of Galen's had decided to refrain from all sexual activity, without considering that up to then he had led a very different life and that the effects of this abstention could not therefore be comparable. Aretaeus, describing the beneficial effects of semen, that "vivifying humor"—it makes one manly, courageous, full of fire, robust; it gives a deep tone to the voice and makes one capable of vigorous action—asserts that a self-controlled man "who retains his semen" thereby becomes "bold, daring, and strong as wild beasts." He recalls the example of athletes or animals that are all the more vigorous because they keep their semen; thus, "such as are naturally superior in strength, by incontinence [*akrasia*] become inferior to their inferiors; while those by nature much their inferiors by continence [*enkrateia*] become superior to their superiors [*kreittones*]."[27]

On the other hand, the values of abstinence were much less likely to be granted for women, given the fact that they were considered to be socially and physiologically destined for marriage and procreation. Yet Soranus, in his *Gynecology,* cites the arguments of a debate, which seems to have been important in his day, on the advantages and disadvantages of virginity. Those who criticize it call attention to the diseases that are due to humors that do not flow out and desires that are not extinguished by abstinence. The advocates of virginity point out, to the contrary, that women thereby avert the dangers of childbearing, are unacquainted with desire since they do not know pleasure, and keep within themselves the force that semen possesses. Soranus, for his part, concedes that virginity can have disadvantages. But he observes them for the most part in women who live "shut inside the temples" and are deprived of "the necessary exercises." He contends that as a rule permanent virginity is healthy for both sexes.[28] Hence sexual union would not in his view have any natural justification in the health of individuals; only the obligation to maintain the human race makes its practice necessary. It is "the general principle of nature" that requires it, more than personal regimen.

Sexual abstinence was not regarded as a duty, certainly, nor was the sexual act represented as an evil. But we see how, in the development of these themes that were already explicitly formulated by the medical and philosophical thought of the fourth century, a certain inflection occurred: an insistence on the ambiguity of the effects of sexual activity, an extension of the correlations attributed to it throughout the organism, an accentuation of its peculiar fragility and its pathogenic power, and a valorization of abstinent behaviors, for both sexes. In times past the dangers of sexual activity were perceived in connection with involuntary violence and careless expenditure. They are now described more as the effect of a general fragility of the human body and its functioning.

We can understand, given these conditions, the importance that the regimen of the *aphrodisia* was apt to assume in the management of one's personal life. On this point, Rufus makes a noteworthy statement, which links together, quite explicitly, the danger of sexual practice and the fundamental principle of the care of the self: "Those who indulge in sexual relations and especially those who indulge without much caution need to take care of themselves in a much more rigorous fashion than others, so that, by putting their body in the best possible condition, they might experience less the harmful effects of these relations" *(hē ek tōn aphrodisiōn blabē).* [29]

CHAPTER THREE

=====

THE REGIMEN OF PLEASURES

Sexual acts must therefore be placed under an extremely careful regimen. But this regimen is very different from a prescriptive system that would try to define a "natural," legitimate, and acceptable form of practice. It is remarkable that almost nothing is said in these regimens about the type of sexual acts that one may engage in or about those which Nature disfavors. Rufus, for example, mentions relations with boys in passing. He also alludes to the positions the partners can take, but he translates the dangers of these positions directly into quantitative terms: they would demand a greater expenditure of strength than the others.[1]* Remarkable, too, is the fact that these regimens are more "concessive" than "normative." Rufus sets forth his regimen after having evoked the pathogenic effects of sexual activity—if it is exaggerated and practiced unduly—and after submitting that these acts "are not harmful absolutely, in every respect, provided that one considers the opportuneness of the act, the limit that is to be put on it, and the hygienic constitution of the person who performs it."[2] And Galen says, also with a view to limitations, that he would not want that "people were completely prohibited from practicing sexual intercourse."[3]† These are circumstantial regimens, which demand that one take great care to

---

*Rufus also notes that the standing position is tiring.
†Note, however, in Celsus, a moderate judgment: "Coition is neither to be desired overmuch, nor overmuch to be feared."[4]

determine the conditions that will least affect the whole combination of balances. Four variables are singled out: the auspicious occasion for procreation, the age of the subject, the time frame (the season or the hour of the day), and individual temperament.

1. The regimen of the aphrodisia *and procreation.* An entirely traditional theme said that noble offspring—*euteknia*—could not be engendered unless one took a certain number of precautions. The disorders of conception would be reflected in one's progeny. Not only because the descendants would resemble their parents, but because they would bear the characteristics of the act that brought them into existence. We recall the recommendations of Aristotle and Plato on this point.[5] That the sexual act, in its procreative finality, requires a good deal of care and a meticulous preparation is a principle that one finds again in the medical regimens of the imperial epoch. These regimens prescribe a long-term preparation first of all. This involves a general conditioning of the body and the soul designed to produce or maintain in the individual the qualities with which the semen will need to be imbued and by which the embryo will need to be marked. One must form oneself as the prior image of the child one wishes to have. A passage from Athenaeus, cited by Oribasius, is very explicit on this point: those who intend to beget children must have body and soul in the best possible condition. In other words, the soul must be tranquil and completely free of pain, of worries accompanied by fatigue, and of any other affliction; and the body must be healthy and not spoiled in any way.[6] An immediate preparation is necessary as well: a period of restraint during which the sperm accumulates and gathers strength, while the urge acquires the necessary intensity (too-frequent sexual relations prevent the sperm from reaching the degree of elaboration at which it becomes fully potent). A rather strict alimentary diet is recommended: no food that is too hot or too moist, just "a light meal which will give the impetus towards coitus, and which should not be overloaded with too many ingredients"; no indigestion, no drunkenness; in short, a general purification of the body that will ensure the quietude necessary to the sexual function. It is in this way that "the farmer sows only after having first cleansed the soil and removed any foreign material."[7] Soranus, who gives this advice, puts no trust in those who prescribe, for a good conception, waiting until the period of the full moon; the essential thing is to choose "a time in which the body is neither in want nor overburdened, but in a satisfactory state in every respect" —both for physiological reasons (the harmful humors that rise up in the body may prevent the seed from adhering to the fundus of the uterus) and for ethical reasons (the embryo will be imbued with the condition of the procreators).

There is, of course, a time more favorable than others in the woman's cycle. According to a metaphor that is already quite ancient and that will still do long service in Christianity, "every season is not propitious for sewing seed upon the land for the purpose of bringing forth fruit, so in humans too not every time is suitable for conception of the seed discharged in intercourse."[8] Soranus places this favorable time immediately after menstruation. His argumentation rests on the metaphor —which is not personal to him, moreover—of the appetite.[9] The uterus is avid; it consumes, it loads itself with nutriment, sometimes with blood (the normal case), sometimes with seed (and fertilization occurs). To be procreative, the sexual act must take place at a favorable time in this alimentary rhythm. Not before menstruation, for "just as the stomach when overburdened with some kind of material and turned to nausea is disposed to vomit what oppresses it and is averse to receiving food, so according to the same principle, the uterus, being congested at the time of menstruation, is well adapted for the evacuation of the blood which has flowed into it, but is unfitted for the reception and retention of the seed." Not during menstrual evacuation, which constitutes a kind of natural vomiting, when the semen runs the risk of being swept out as well. Nor when the flow has completely stopped: the uterus, desiccated and chilled, is then no longer in a condition to receive the seed. The favorable time is when "the flow is ceasing," so that the uterus is still moist with blood and permeated with warmth, "and hence turgescent with a craving to receive the sperm."[10] This craving, which reappears in the body after purgation, is manifested in the woman by a desire that disposes her to sexual intercourse.[11]

But there is more still. For conception to occur in suitable conditions and for the offspring to have every possible quality, the sexual act itself must be performed with the observance of certain precautions. Soranus says nothing precise on this subject. He simply indicates the necessity of a prudent and calm behavior, one that avoids all the disturbances, all the intoxications that might be reflected in the embryo, since the latter would be a kind of mirror and witness of these excesses: "Thus, in order that the offspring may not be rendered misshapen, women must be sober during coitus because in drunkenness the soul becomes the victim of strange phantasies; this furthermore, because the offspring bears some resemblance to the mother as well, not only in body but in soul. Therefore it is good that the offspring be made to resemble the soul when it is stable and not deranged by drunkenness."[12] Finally, during pregnancy sexual relations must be extremely limited: completely discontinued in the first period, because intercourse "causes movement in the whole body in general and especially in the various parts about the uterus which need rest. For just as the stomach when quiet retains the food, but when shaken often ejects through vomiting what it has received, so also the uterus when not shaken holds fast the seed; when agitated, however, discharges it."[13] Yet some physicians, such as Galen, consider it advisable to resume intercourse and practice it during pregnancy: "It is not good for pregnant women either to abstain from coitus or to return to it continually: for in women who are abstinent childbirth becomes more difficult, whereas in those who constantly indulge in coitus the infant will be weak; there may even be a miscarriage."[14]

Hence there is a whole government of the *aphrodisia*, whose principle and whose justification are in this preparation of

offspring. It is not that there is an obligation to practice sexual
intercourse only in order to have children: if the conditions of
probable conception are carefully laid down, this is not for the
purpose of setting the limits of the legitimate act by means of
them, but is meant to serve as useful advice for anyone who
cares about their offspring. And if the latter are an important
concern, this is in the form of a duty that the parents can
assume with respect to them. It is also an obligation vis-à-vis
themselves since it is advantageous for them to have offspring
endowed with the best qualities. These obligations that surround procreation define a whole set of possible errors, which
are at the same time faults. And they are so numerous, they
bring in so many different factors, that few procreations would
be successful were it not for Nature's ability to compensate for
these failings and to prevent disasters. At least this is how
Galen justifies both the necessity of taking a large number of
precautions and the fact that in spite of everything many
births come off well: "How frequently in the fathers that beget
and the mothers that bear us it must be not error that is rare
but right-doing. For drunkards consort with drunkards, and
men do not know their own whereabouts from repletion with
women in the same state. Hence in this way the very beginning
of our procreation is faulty; and then come the unspeakable
errors of the pregnant woman, her indifference to proper exercise, her gluttony, passions, drunkenness, bathing, and untimely indulgence in love [akariōn aphrodisiōn]. Nevertheless,
to such outrages Nature opposes many acts and performs
them successfully." Peasants are careful when they sow their
fields; but, Galen notes, taking up the Socratic themes of the
care of the self, humans who "take little heed of themselves"
in their own lives are no longer concerned about their progeny
either.[15]

2. *The age of the subject.* The practice of the *aphrodisia*
must neither be continued too long nor begun too early. Sexual
intercourse when one is old is dangerous: it exhausts a body
no longer capable of reconstituting the elements that were

withdrawn from it.[16] But it is also harmful when one is too young. It arrests growth and disturbs the development of the signs of puberty—which are the result of the body's development of the seminal elements. "Nothing hinders the progress of the soul and the body as does a premature and excessive practice of sexual intercourse."[17] And Galen: "Many young people are attacked by incurable diseases due to sexual relations because they insisted on violating the time prescribed by Nature."[18] What is this "prescribed time"? Is it the appearance or confirmation of the signs of puberty? All the physicians are in agreement that puberty for boys is situated at about the age of fourteen. But all are in agreement as well that access to the *aphrodisia* should not be had so early. One finds scarcely any exact indication concerning the age at which one may begin sexual intercourse. In any case several years should pass during which the body is forming the seminal liquids without it being advisable to evacuate them. Whence the necessity of a specific regimen designed to ensure the self-control of adolescents. The physicians prescribe, in keeping with tradition, a life of intense physical exercise. Thus Athenaeus: "Since the production of sperm begins at that age [fourteen] and since young people have very strong cravings which incite them to sexual intercourse, physical exercises should be very numerous, so that tiring the body and the soul very quickly, they may repress their desires from the beginning."[19]

The problem for girls is a little different. The practice of early marriage doubtless caused people to concede that the first sexual relations and childbearing could occur as soon as menstruation was regularly established.[20] This is the opinion of Soranus, who advises reliance on organic criteria in setting the age for marriage and not on the desires of the girls themselves. Depending on education, these desires can awaken before the body is ready; "since the female conceives seed into the substance of a living being," there is a danger when the body of the woman has not reached the maturity necessary to this function; so it is good that she remain a virgin until menstruation has been established spontaneously.[21] Other physicians envisage a much later date. Thus Rufus of Ephesus considers that a pregnancy before the age of eighteen risks being unfavorable to mother and child alike. He recalls that this is the age recommended long ago by Hesiod; and he points out that this age—quite late in the eyes of some—did not have, in a former time, the drawbacks that it may have subsequently assumed. In those days, women led a life just as active as men; it is overeating and idleness that cause problems in unmarried girls, making it desirable for them to have sexual relations, which may facilitate the menstrual flow. The solution Rufus suggests, then, is a relatively late marriage (at about eighteen), but a marriage prepared for by a whole regimen that ought to accompany the life of the young girl even before puberty. During childhood let girls be mixed with boys; then when the age comes for separating them from boys, place them under a very careful regimen: no meat, no overly rich dishes, no or very little wine, long walks, exercises. It must be kept in mind that idleness "is for them the most harmful thing of all," and that it is "advantageous to have the exercises be a means of putting warmth into movement and of reheating the habit of the body, but in such a manner that they remain women and do not take on a masculine character." Participation in choruses in which one sings and dances seems to be Rufus' idea of the best form of exercise: "Choruses were not invented just for honoring the deity, but also in view of health."[22]

3. The "favorable time." The kairos of the sexual act is the topic of many discussions. As concerns the larger time frame, the traditional calendar is taken more or less for granted: winter and spring are the best seasons; autumn is accepted by some, rejected by others; in a general way, it is thought that one should abstain, as much as possible, during the summer.[23] On the other hand, determining the right hour of the day requires that a variety of factors be taken into account. In addition to the religious considerations that Plutarch mentions in one of his table-talks,[24] the question of the right time

is linked to that of exercise, eating, and digestion. It is best not to let sexual intercourse be preceded by exercises that are too strenuous, which divert to other parts of the body the resources it needs. Inversely, baths and rubdowns are recommended after lovemaking. It is not good to practice the *aphrodisia* before meals, when one is hungry, because under these conditions the act is not tiring but it loses some of its force.[25] But, on the other hand, one must avoid copious meals and excessive quantities of drink. The time of digestion is always harmful: "That is why coitus in the middle of the night is deceptive, because then the food is not yet elaborated; the same is true of coitus that one has early in the morning, because there still may be ill-digested food in the stomach and because all the superfluities have not yet been evacuated through the urine and the feces."[26] So that, all things considered, it is after a moderate meal and before sleep—or possibly before the afternoon nap—that the time will be most favorable for sexual intercourse. According to Rufus, Nature herself indicated her preference for this time by giving the body its strongest excitation then. Furthermore, if one wishes to have children, it is appropriate that the man "engage in sexual intercourse after having eaten and drunk to satisfaction, whereas the woman ought to follow a less invigorating diet"; indeed, it is necessary that "the one give and the other receive."[27] Galen is of the same opinion: he recommends that time when one is going to sleep, after having enjoyed "a solid meal but one that does not cause discomfort." In this way the food is sufficient to nourish and strengthen the body, and sleep allows one to repair the fatigue; further, this is the best moment for conceiving children "because the woman retains the sperm better while sleeping"; finally, this is in fact the hour for which Nature herself indicates her preference by giving rise then to desire.[28]*

---

*It may be added that for Celsus, night is preferable "but care should be taken that by day it not be immediately followed by a meal, and at night not immediately followed by work and wakefulness."[29]

4. Individual temperaments. Rufus posits as a general principle that the natures most suited for coition are those which are "more or less hot and moist"; in return, sexual activity is rather unfavorable for constitutions that are cold and dry. Thus, in order to maintain or restore the warm moisture needed in the *aphrodisia,* it is good to adopt an entire complex and continuous regimen of suitable exercise and proper nourishment. Around sexual activity, and in order to preserve the balance it risks upsetting, one must keep to a whole mode of living. It is helpful to drink pale red wine, to eat oven bread made from bran (its moisture is useful for preparation and regulation); to consume, in the meat category, young goat, lamb, hen, grouse, partridge, goose, duck; in the seafood category, octopus and mollusks—together with turnips, broad beans, green beans, chick peas (for their heat), and grapes (for their moisture). As for the activities to which one should resort, they include excursions, on foot or horseback, and running, but neither too fast nor too slow; but no violent exercises, no gesticulation as in javelin throwing (which diverts the nutritive material to other parts of the body), no excessively hot baths, no heating and cooling off; no strenuous work. One should also avoid anything that would contribute to tiring the body—anger, joy that is too great, and pain.[30]

THE WORK OF
THE SOUL

The regimen recommended for the sexual pleasures seems to be centered entirely on the body. Its condition, its balances, its ailments, the general or transitory dispositions in which it finds itself, function as the principal variables that ought to determine behavior. It is as if the body dictated to the body. And yet the soul has its part to play as well, and the physicians bring it into the scheme of things. For it is the soul that constantly risks carrying the body beyond its own mechanics and its elementary needs; it is the soul that prompts one to choose the times that are not suitable, to act in questionable circumstances, to contravene natural dispositions. If humans need a regimen that takes into account, with such meticulousness, all the elements of physiology, this is because they always tend to be led astray by their imaginings, their passions, and their loves. Even the proper age for beginning sexual intercourse gets confused in girls and boys alike; education and habits can cause desire to appear at the wrong time.[1]

The reasonable soul thus has a dual role to play: it needs to assign a regimen for the body that is actually determined by the latter's nature, its tensions, the condition and circumstances in which it finds itself. But it will be able to assign this regimen correctly only provided it has done a good deal of work on itself: eliminated the errors, reduced the imaginings, mastered the desires, that cause it to misconstrue the sober law of the body. Athenaeus—on whom the Stoic influence is considerable—defines very clearly this labor of the soul on itself as a requisite condition of the good physical regimen. "What adults need is a complete regimen of the soul and the body . . . to try and calm its impulses [*hormai*], and to achieve a condition in which our desires [*prothumiai*] do not exceed our own particular powers."[2] This regimen does not require that one institute a struggle of the soul against the body, nor even that one establish means by which the soul might defend itself from the body. Rather, it is a matter of the soul's correcting itself in order to be able to guide the body according to a law which is that of the body itself.

This work is described by the physicians in reference to three elements by which the subject risks being carried beyond the actual necessities of the organism: the movement of desire, the presence of images, the attachment to pleasure.

   a. In the medical regimen it is not a question of eliminating desire. Nature herself placed it in all the animal species as a spur for exciting both sexes and for attracting them to one another. Nothing would be more unnatural, therefore, nothing more harmful than to seek to have the *aphrodisia* escape the natural force of desire; one must never—out of a spirit of debauchery or in order to circumvent the lost vigor of age—try to force nature. One must not have sexual relations *aneu epithumein,* without feeling desire: such is the advice of Rufus in the treatise *On Satyriasis.* But this desire is twofold: it appears in the body and it appears in the soul. The problem of regimen consists in bringing about an exact correlation of the two manifestations. One must take care that, in the body and in the soul, its movements are coordinated and adjusted as precisely as possible. Rufus makes a noteworthy pronouncement in this regard: "It is best that the man indulge in sexual intercourse when he is pressed at the same time by the soul's desire and the body's need."[3]

It sometimes happens that this natural correlation is jeopardized through the action of the body itself. The body loses control of itself, as it were. Nothing in the soul corresponds

CHAPTER FOUR

====

to its excitation. It gives way to a kind of pure convulsion. The sexual act then becomes altogether "paroxysmal," as Rufus says.[4] It is to this purely physical excitation that Rufus seems to allude when he speaks of the *hormai* that accompany the warning signs of mania or epilepsy.[5] The same phenomenon occurs, but in a different form, in satyriasis or gonorrhea: the sexual organs become inflamed by themselves, in the first of these diseases; and in the other, "without an act, without a nocturnal image, a profusion of semen is discharged in abundance"; the patient, transported by the crazed mechanics of his body, becomes exhausted and "dies of consumption after a certain time."[6]

But the soul, conversely, can escape the forms and limits of the desire manifested in the body. The term Rufus and Galen use to designate this excess is significant: it is the word *doxa*. The soul, instead of attending only to the wants and needs of the body, allows itself to be enticed by representations that are peculiar to it and have no counterpart in the organism: representations that are vain and empty *(kenai)*. Just as the body must not let itself be carried away without the correlative of a desire in the soul, the latter must not go beyond what the body demands and what its needs dictate. But in the first case, what is involved is an illness, which remedies may be able to cure; in the second, what is involved above all is an ethical regimen, which ought to be applied to oneself. Rufus proposes a formula for this: "subdue the soul and make it obey the body."[7]

A paradoxical proposition, if one thinks of the eminently traditional theme of the soul that must not be seduced by the entreaties of the body. But it has to be grasped in its precise theoretical and medical context, which was inspired perhaps by Stoicism. The voluntary submission of the soul to the body should be understood as obedience to a rationality that has presided over the natural order and has designed, for its own purposes, the mechanics of the body. It is from this natural reason that the *doxai* risk leading the soul astray by creating extraneous desires; it is to this reason that the reasonable

medical regimen, based on the true knowledge of living creatures, must be attuned. In this context the animal example,
which so often served to disqualify the appetites of man, can
on the contrary constitute a model for conduct. This is because in their sexual regimen animals follow the dictates of the
body, but never anything more or anything else. What directs
them, explains Rufus, and hence what ought also to guide
humans, are not the *doxai,* but the "preludes of a nature that
needs evacuation." For Galen, similarly, animals are not led
to seek sexual union by the "belief"—*doxa*—that "pleasure is
a good thing"; they are prompted to desire sexual relations
"for the sake of the discharge, since the retention of semen is
a burden to them." For them, there is no difference between
that which brings them to sexual intercourse and that which
"makes them regard the elimination of stool and urine as a
natural act."[8]

The medical regimen proposes, then, a sort of animalization
of the *epithumia;* that is, a subordination, as strict as possible,
of the soul's desire to the body's needs; an ethics of desire that
is modeled on a natural philosophy of excretions; and the
tendency toward an ideal point where the soul, purified of all
its vain representations, no longer gives its attention to anything but the austere economy of organic functions.

b. Hence the physicians' general distrust of "images"
(phantasiai). The theme recurs again and again in the treatments they recommend. Thus, on the subject of satyriasis,
Rufus suggests a cure that has two aspects; the first concerns
diet, from which all warming foods should be excluded; the
second concerns the stimulations of the soul: "One should
avoid conversations, thoughts, erotic cravings, and above all
one should protect oneself from that which the eyes see, knowing very well that all these things, even in dreams, . . . incite
to copulation if one has abstained from intercourse after having eaten rich food in abundance."[9] Galen, in the same spirit,
recommends a doubly cathartic cure to one of his friends who
has given up sexual activity but finds that he is in a state of

constant excitation. Galen advises him first to relieve himself physically by excreting the accumulated semen; then—once the body is purified—to let nothing enter the mind that might deposit images there: "to refrain completely from spectacles, not to tell stories or recall memories which could stimulate his sexual desire."[10]

These dangerous images, which also give rise in the soul to "empty" desires, having no correlation with the needs of the body, are of several types. There are of course the dream images, which the physicians seem especially concerned about when these images are accompanied by emissions—whence the often repeated advice not to sleep on one's back, not to drink too much or eat before sleeping, and to keep the mind at rest when one is going to go to bed. In any case Rufus of Ephesus makes this an important item in the regimen of those suffering from satyriasis: "Sleep on your side rather than on your back."[11]* Among the images to be avoided are those which can be seen at the theater; those which are suggested by reading, singing, music, and dancing, and which insinuate themselves into the mind without there being anything that corresponds to them in the needs of the body. Galen thus claims to have observed symptoms of satyriasis in subjects "who fail to get rid of an excess of blood, particularly when they do not refrain from erotic ideas. Likewise do persons suffer who are chaste by nature and accustomed to self-control over a long time but who indulge in imaginings in order to stimulate themselves by such spectacles and memories. The condition of the genital organs of these patients is quite contrary to that of others who never indulge in erotic ideas."[13]

But visual perceptions must also be included under this term *phantasia,* in keeping with a philosophical usage. There is a danger not just in imagining or remembering the *aphrodisia,* but also in perceiving them. It is a very old theme of traditional modesty that the *aphrodisia* ought to take place at night and in darkness rather than in broad daylight. But this

*One very often encounters the idea that to sleep on one's back heats up the sexual parts and causes nocturnal emissions.[12]

same precept is also emphasized as an element of regimen: by not seeing, one is protected from the images that might be engraved in the soul, remain there, and return in an untimely manner. Plutarch alludes to this problem in connection with the *kairos*, the right time for sexual acts. Among the reasons for shunning the light there is, for him, the concern to avoid "the images of pleasure" that constantly "renew" our desire; "but night blots out the insatiate and wildest of the deeds of love-making and thus diverts and calms one's own constitution, which visual stimuli do not shipwreck on the shores of lust."[14]

We may recall here that the question of "images" was much discussed in the literature of love. The gaze was thought to be the surest vehicle of passion; it was the path by which passion entered the heart and the means by which passion was maintained. Propertius finds that the play of Venus loses its charm in darkness: "why make love in the dark . . . naked Endymion won the love of Phoebus' sister and held in his arms the goddess naked."[15] By the same token, the gaze, light, and image were considered dangerous. Dangerous as far as strict morals were concerned: the same Propertius believes that immodesty spread when images were introduced into people's houses.[16] Dangerous as well for love itself, which could be wounded by the unloveliness of the images. Ovid recommends prudence to anyone who wishes to preserve their love: "Don't let the light pour in, with all the windows wide open—it is more fitting to keep much of your body concealed."[17] And for the same reason, the cruel image can be an excellent means of protecting oneself against passion or even a means of ridding oneself of it. When one wishes to free oneself of a love there is nothing so effective, says Ovid in *The Remedies for Love*, as to let the light in when it is time for sex: the body's defects, together with the stains and the mess, will be imprinted on the mind, giving rise to disgust. It is also good, when one is trying to get free of one's mistress, to surprise her early in the morning amid the disorder of the dressing table.[18] There is a whole technique of the image, which can be organized for and against love. Moreover, the struggle against internal or external images will be one of the most constant aspects of sexual ethics from the end of antiquity onward.

c. There remains the pleasure inscribed by Nature in the process of the *aphrodisia*. Can one eliminate it, or arrange not to feel it? This is out of the question, seeing that pleasure is tied directly to the movements of the body and the mechanisms of retention and erection. However, Galen believes that one can prevent this pleasure from becoming an element of excess in the economy of the *aphrodisia*. The approach he recommends is clearly Stoic: it is a matter of considering pleasure as nothing more than the accompaniment of the act; it must never be taken as a reason to accomplish the act. "That pleasure is a good thing" is, as we have seen, for Galen, a *doxa* that animals do not have (which ensures that their behavior will have a natural limit). On the other hand, those humans who have such an opinion run the risk of pursuing the *aphrodisia* for the pleasure they provide; consequently, they are liable to become attached to them and always to want to repeat them.

For a reasonable regimen, the task therefore is to elide pleasure as a sought-after object: to indulge in the *aphrodisia* independently of the attraction of pleasure and as if it did not exist. The only goal that reason should set itself is the one indicated by the state of the body, according to its own purgative requirements. "It is evident that chaste persons [*tous sōphronas*] do not indulge in sexual intercourse for pleasure, but with the intention to relieve this urge, as if this were not associated with pleasure." This is precisely the lesson that Galen derives from the famous gesture of Diogenes: without even waiting for the prostitute whom he had asked to come, the philosopher rid himself of the humor that inconvenienced him. In doing this, he wished, according to Galen, to discharge his sperm "without seeking the pleasure that accompanies that emission."[19]

We may note in passing the very modest place that masturbation and the solitary pleasures occupied in these medical regimens—as was generally the case in all the moral reflections of the Greeks and the Romans concerning sexual activity. When masturbation appears, which is rather rare, it is in a positive form: an act of natural elimination, which has the value both of a philosophical lesson and a necessary remedy. One thinks of Dio of Prusa reporting how Diogenes jokingly praised the act he performed in public: an act that, done in time, would have made the Trojan War unnecessary; an act Nature herself recommends to us through the example of the fish; a reasonable act, for it depends on us alone, just as we have no need of anyone to scratch our leg for us; an act, finally, for which we are indebted to the gods, for it was they who showed us how—Hermes in particular, who taught the trick to Pan, hopelessly in love with the inaccessible Echo. And the shepherds seem to have learned it subsequently from Pan.[20] It is an act of Nature herself, one that, without recourse to passions and artifices and in complete independence, corresponds strictly to need. In Western literature—beginning with Christian monasticism—masturbation remains associated with the chimera of the imagination and its dangers. It is the very form of unnatural pleasure that humans invented in order to exceed the limits assigned to them. In a medical ethics anxious, like that of the first centuries of our era, to gear sexual activity to the basic needs of the body, the act of solitary purgation constitutes the barest form of the uselessness of desire, images, and pleasure.

1. However meticulous and complex these regimens of activity may be, we must not exaggerate their relative importance. The place they are allocated is limited in comparison with the other regimens—particularly in comparison with the dietary regimen. When, in the fifth century, Oribasius comes to edit his great collection of medical texts, he will devote four entire books to the qualities, disadvantages, dangers, and virtues of the different possible foods and to the conditions in

which one should and should not consume them. He will give
only two paragraphs to sexual regimen, citing a text by Rufus,
another by Galen. One may think that this limitation reflects,
more than anything else, an attitude characteristic of Oribasius and his epoch. But it is a trait manifested by all Greek and
Roman medicine to accord much more space to the dietetics
of alimentation than to that of sex. For this medicine, the
thing that matters is eating and drinking. A whole development—evident in Christian monasticism—will be necessary
before the preoccupation with sex will begin to match the
preoccupation with food. But alimentary abstentions and fasts
will long remain fundamental. And it will be an important
moment for the history of ethics in European societies when
apprehension about sex and its regimen will significantly out-
weigh the rigor of alimentary prescriptions. In the Roman
epoch, at all events, the regimen of sexual pleasures holds a
relatively limited place next to the great alimentary regimen,
just as, moreover, these pleasures themselves are associated in
moral thought and social ritual with the delights of eating and
drinking. The banquet, an occasion shared by gluttony,
drunkenness, and love, is a direct testimony of this association; the latter is attested indirectly by the inverse ritual of the
philosophical symposium, where the food is always measured,
the drunkenness is still capable of truth, and the love is an
object of reasonable discourses.

2. In these medical regimens, one sees a certain "pathologization" of the sexual act take shape. But there must be no
misunderstanding on this point: the development in question
is in no way similar to the one that occurred much later in
Western societies, when sexual behavior was perceived as a
bearer of unhealthy deviations. In the latter case, it was to be
organized as a domain that would have its normal forms and
its morbid forms, its specific pathology, its nosography and
etiology—to say nothing of its therapeutics. Greco-Roman
medicine operates differently. It inscribes the sexual act within
a field where it constantly risks being affected and disturbed

by alterations in the organism—and where, conversely, it always risks inducing diseases of various kinds, proximate and distant.

We may speak of pathologization in two senses. First, because the disturbing effects are attributed not only to the great excesses in the practice of sex but also to the very nature of the process—to the expenditures, tremors, perturbations, that it provokes in the organism; but, above all, because these medical analyses tend to overturn the representations of the sexual act as an activity, as an energy whose violence is the only thing to be feared. They describe it rather as a process in which the individual is passively overcome by the mechanisms of the body and the movements of the soul, so that he must reestablish his mastery by means of a precise adjustment to the needs of nature alone. It is important to understand that this medicine of the *chrēsis aphrodisiōn* did not aim to delimit the "pathological" forms of sexual behavior: rather, it uncovered, at the root of sexual acts, an element of passivity that was also a source of illness, according to the double meaning of the word *pathos*. The sexual act is not an evil; it manifests a permanent focus of possible ills.

3. A medical science of this sort requires an extreme vigilance toward sexual activity. But this attention does not lead to a decipherment of that activity in its origin and unfolding; it is not a matter of the subject's knowing precisely how things are with his own desire, with the movements that lead him to the sexual act, with the choices he makes, with the forms of acts he commits or the modes of pleasure he experiences. The attention he must give is that which keeps him mindful of the rules to which he must refer his sexual activity. He is not expected to rediscover the obscure processes of desire working within him; he needs to recognize the numerous complex conditions that must be jointly present if one is to perform the acts of pleasure in an appropriate manner, without danger or harm. He must address a discourse of "truth" to himself. But this discourse does not have the function of telling the subject

the truth about himself; it should teach him, given what sexual acts are by nature, how to resort to them in a way that conforms as closely, as strictly as possible to that nature. Georges Canguilhem said that "the cause of the cure" for Aristotle "was the form of health in one's medical activity"; that it was not the physician but rather "health that cured the patient"; and that, broadly speaking, "the responsibility for a technical production did not belong to the artisan but to the art . . . ; the Art, which is to say, the nondeliberative finality of a natural logos."[21] Similarly, one might say that the regimen of the *aphrodisia,* the regimen of their distribution, as proposed by medicine, needed to be nothing more nor less than the form of their nature present to thought, their truth dwelling in conduct as its constant prescription.

4. Between these dietetic recommendations and the precepts that are to be found later, in Christian ethics and medical thought, the analogies are numerous: the principle of a strict economy aiming at scarcity; a dread of individual misfortunes or collective ills that can be caused by disorderly sexual behavior; the need for a rigorous mastery of desires, for a struggle against images and a disallowance of pleasure as the goal of sexual intercourse. These analogies are not distant resemblances. Several continuities can be identified. Certain of them are indirect, relayed through philosophical doctrines: the rule according to which pleasure must not be a goal was doubtless conveyed into Christianity more by philosophers than by physicians. But there are also direct continuities. The treatise by Basil of Ancyra on virginity—its author is thought to have been a physician—refers to considerations that are clearly medical. Saint Augustine makes use of Soranus in his polemic against Julian of Eclana. One must not forget, either, the explicit references to Roman and Greek medicine that were made in the eighteenth century and the first half of the nineteenth, during the time of a major new development in the pathology of sex.

By focusing only on these common traits, one may get the impression that the sexual ethics attributed to Christianity or even to the modern West was already in place, at least with respect to its basic principles, at the time when Greco-Roman culture reached its culmination. But this would be to disregard fundamental differences concerning the type of relation to the self and hence the forms of integration of these precepts in the subject's experience of himself.[22]

PART FIVE

THE WIFE

The great classical texts that dealt with the question of marriage—Xenophon's *Oeconomicus,* Plato's *Republic* and *Laws,* Aristotle's *Politics* and *Nicomachean Ethics,* the Aristotelian *Economics*—inscribed their reflection on marital relations within a broad context: the city, with the laws or customs necessary to its survival and its prosperity; the household, with the organization that made possible its maintenance or enrichment. From this subordination of marriage to civic or familial utilities one should not infer that marriage itself was considered an unimportant tie that had no value other than that of producing descendants for the benefit of families and states. We have seen how demanding were the precepts that Xenophon, Isocrates, Plato, or Aristotle imposed on spouses so that they might conduct themselves properly in marriage; the privilege to which the wife was entitled, the justice owed to her, the care taken to set an example for her, to train her: all this would suggest a mode of relations that went far beyond generative functions alone. But marriage required a particular style of conduct, especially insofar as the married man was the head of the family, an honorable citizen, or a man who aspired to exercise over others an authority that was both political and moral; and in this art of being married it was the requisite self-mastery that was expected to give its particular form to the behavior of the reasonable, moderate, and just man.

The ethics of matrimonial behavior appears in a rather

different light in a series of texts that spread out from the first
two centuries B.C. to the second century of our era, over the
length of that period in which one notes a certain change in
the practice of marriage. We thus have the *Peri gamou* by
Antipater, the Latin translation of a Greek text that was for
a long time held to be the last part of the *Economics* attributed
to Aristotle, the different passages Musonius devotes to marriage, the *Marriage Precepts* by Plutarch and his *Dialogue on
Love,* the treatise on marriage by Hierocles, without counting
the indications that one can find in Seneca, Epictetus, and
certain Pythagorean texts.[1]

Must it be said that marriage became a more insistent and
more often debated question than in the past? Should one
suppose that the choice of the matrimonial life and the way
one was expected to conduct oneself in it occasioned in this
period more apprehension and that they were more carefully
problematized? It is doubtless not possible to give an answer
in quantitative terms. It does seem, however, that the art of
leading the married life was considered and defined in several
important texts in a relatively new way. The first change
appears to consist in the fact that the art of matrimonial
existence, while continuing to be concerned with the household, its management, the birth and procreation of children,
places an increasing value on a particular element in the midst
of this ensemble: the personal relationship between husband
and wife, the tie that joins them, their behavior toward each
other. And this relationship, rather than borrowing its importance from the other exigencies of the life of a master of a
household, seems to be regarded as a primary and fundamental element around which all the others are organized, from
which they derive, and to which they owe their strength. In
sum, the art of conducting oneself in marriage would appear
to be defined less by a technique of government and more by
a stylistics of the individual bond.

The second change resides in the fact that the principle of
moderate conduct in a married man is placed more in the
duties of reciprocity than in mastery over others; or rather, in

the fact that the dominion of oneself over oneself is increasingly manifested in the practice of obligations with regard to others and above all in showing a certain respect for one's wife. The intensification of the concern for the self goes hand in hand with a valorization of the other. The new way in which the question of sexual "fidelity" is sometimes formulated attests to this change. Finally, and this is the most important point in the present context, this art of marriage—in the form of a symmetrical relationship—accords a comparatively greater place to the problems of sexual relations between spouses. These problems are still treated in a rather discreet and allusive manner, but the fact remains that one finds, in authors like Plutarch, a concern with defining a certain way for marriage partners to act, to conduct themselves in pleasure relations. Here the interest in procreation is combined with other significations and values, which have to do with love, affection, understanding, and mutual sympathy.

Once again, I am not claiming that such behaviors or sentiments were unknown in the classical period and that they appeared subsequently: to establish changes of that order would demand an entirely different documentation and very different analyses as well. But it does appear—if we are to believe the texts we possess—that these attitudes, these ways of behaving, of acting and feeling, became themes of problematization, objects of philosophical discussion, and elements of a deliberative art of self-conduct.[2] A stylistics of living as a couple emerges from the traditional precepts of matrimonial management: it can be observed rather clearly in an art of conjugal relationship, in a doctrine of sexual monopoly, and in an aesthetics of shared pleasures.

CHAPTER ONE

===

THE MARRIAGE TIE

In several of these reflections on marriage, and particularly in the Stoic texts of the first two centuries, one discerns the elaboration of a certain model of relationship between spouses. Not that there is any notion of imposing new institutional forms on marriage, or any suggestion of fitting it into a different legal framework. But, without calling the traditional structures into question, there is an attempt to define a mode of coexistence between husband and wife, a modality of relations between them, and a way of living together that are rather different from what was proposed in the classical texts. Schematizing a good deal, perhaps, and employing a somewhat anachronistic vocabulary, we may say that marriage is no longer conceived simply as a "matrimonial form" fixing the complementarity of roles in the management of the household, but also and above all as a "marriage tie" and a personal relationship between the man and the woman. This art of married living defines a relation that is *dual* in its form, *universal* in its value, and *specific* in its intensity and its strength.

1. A dual relation. If there is one thing that is in conformity with nature *(kata physin)* it is marrying, says Musonius Rufus.[i] And in order to explain that nothing could be more essential than the discourse he is undertaking on the subject of marriage, Hierocles declares that it is Nature who causes our species to prefer that form of community.[2]

150

These principles merely restated a lesson that was entirely traditional. The naturalness of marriage, though it was disputed by certain philosophical schools, and by the Cynics in particular, had been broadly founded on a series of reasons: the indispensable joining of male and female for procreation; the necessity of prolonging this conjunction, of transforming it into a stable union in order to ensure the education of offspring; the combination of assistance, comforts, and pleasures that married life can provide, with its services and its obligations; and lastly, the forming of the family as the basic unit of the city. As for the first of these functions, the union of man and woman was sanctioned by a principle common to all animals. In regard to the others, this union manifested the forms of an existence that was generally considered to be properly human and reasonable.

This classical theme of marriage as something natural by virtue of its twofold contribution to procreation and community life was taken up by the Stoics of the imperial epoch, but they transformed it in a significant way.

Musonius first of all. One notes in his formulations a certain shift of emphasis from the "procreative" aim to the "communal" finality. A passage from the treatise *On the Purpose of Marriage* is revealing in this connection.[3] It begins with the duality of the goals of marriage: descendants to beget, a life to share. But Musonius immediately adds that while procreation may very well be an important thing, it could not in itself justify marriage. Recalling an objection made often by the Cynics, he points out that if it were only a matter of begetting offspring, humans could very well behave like the animals: join together and immediately separate. If they do not do so, it is because the essential thing for them is community: a companionship in which they exchange mutual care, in which they compete in attentiveness and kindness for one another, and in which the two partners can be compared to two beasts in a yoke, which make no progress if each one looks off to its side. It would be incorrect to say that Musonius gives preference to relations of help and comfort over the objective goal of descendants. But these goals have to fit into a single form, which is that of a common life; the mutual solicitude that is shown by the partners and the progeny they rear together are two aspects of this essential form.

Musonius indicates in another passage how this form of unity has been inscribed by Nature in each individual. The treatise *Is Marriage a Handicap for the Pursuit of Philosophy?* evokes the original division brought about in the human species between men and women.⁴ Musonius reflects on the fact that after having separated the two sexes, the Creator wished to bring them back together. Now, Musonius notes, he brought them together again by implanting in each of them a "strong desire," a desire that was both for "association" and for "union"—*homilia* and *koinōnia.* Of the two terms, the first seems in fact to refer to sexual intercourse, the second to community life. What should be understood, then, is that there is a certain fundamental and original desire in human beings, and that this desire is directed toward physical intimacy as well as toward the sharing of existence. A thesis that has this double consequence: that the extreme intensity of desire is not characterized simply by the movement that leads to the conjoining of the sexes, but also by the movement that conduces to the sharing of lives; conversely, that the relationship between the sexes belongs to the same rational scheme as the relations that bind two individuals to one another through interest, affection, and community of souls. It is the same natural inclination that leads, with an equal intensity and a rationality of the same type, to the coupling of existences and to the joining of bodies.

For Musonius, then, what founds marriage is not that it is situated at the point of intersection of two heterogeneous predilections, one of which is physical, the other rational and social. It is rooted in a single, primitive tendency that aims directly toward it as an essential goal and hence, through it, toward its two intrinsic effects: the formation of a common progeny and companionship in life. One understands how Musonius can say that nothing is more desirable *(prosphilo-*

steron) than marriage. The naturalness of the latter is not due merely to the consequences that one can derive from its practice; its naturalness is already declared by the existence of an original predilection, which establishes it as a desirable objective.

Hierocles, in a rather similar way, founds marriage on the "binary" nature of man. For him, humans are "conjugal" animals *(syndyastikoi)*.⁵ The notion was already present in the Naturalists: they distinguished between animals that herd together *(synagelastikoi)* and those that live in pairs *(syndyastikoi)*. Moreover, Plato had referred to this distinction in a passage of the *Laws*. He recommended to humans the example of those animals that are chaste so long as they are living in a band but pair off and become "conjugal" when the mating season arrives. Aristotle had likewise spoken of the "syndastic" character of human beings, in order to define the relations of the master with the slave as well as relations between spouses.⁶

Hierocles uses the notion for different ends. He applies it exclusively to the conjugal relation, of which, in his view, it is the founding principle and natural basis. Humans are binary by nature; they are made to live in pairs, in a relation that at the same time gives them descendants and enables them to live their lives with a partner. For Hierocles and Musonius alike, Nature is not content to make allowance for marriage; she incites individuals to marry through a primordial inclination; she urges each of them to do so, including the philosopher himself. Nature and reason coincide in the movement that conduces to marriage. But it should further be noted that Hierocles does not oppose, as if it were a matter of two incompatible possibilities, the syndastic character of human beings, which causes them to live in pairs, and their "synagelastic" character, which causes them to live in groups. Humans are made to live in twos and also to live in a multiplicity. Mankind is at once conjugal and social; the dual relation and the plural relation are linked together. Hierocles explains that a city is made up of households that constitute its basic units, but in each one it is the couple that constitutes both its founding principle and its finished form, so that a household is not complete unless it is organized around a couple. One thus finds this conjugal duality over the entire course of human existence and in all of its aspects: in the original constitution that Nature has given it; in the obligations that man is under insofar as he is a creature endowed with reason; in the form of social life that ties him to the human community of which he is a part. As an animal, as a reasonable creature, and as an individual whose reason connects him to the human race, man is, in every respect, a conjugal being.

2. *A universal relation.* For a long time, the question of knowing whether or not one should marry had been, in philosophical reflection on ways of living, a subject of discussion. The advantages and disadvantages of marriage; the usefulness of having a lawful wife and, through her, of providing oneself with honorable descendants; the cares and troubles, on the other hand, when one had to support one's wife, look after one's children, supply their needs, and at times face their illness or their death—these were the inexhaustible themes of a debate that was sometimes serious, sometimes ironic, and always repetitious. The echoes of it will be heard very late in antiquity. Epictetus and Clement of Alexandria, Pseudo-Lucian, the author of *Affairs of the Heart,* or Libanius in the treatise *Ei gamēteon (Whether One Should Marry),* will draw from this stock of arguments, which scarcely changed over the centuries. The Epicureans and the Cynics were theoretically opposed to marriage. It seems that the Stoics were, on the contrary, favorable toward it from the start.[7] In any case, the thesis that one ought to marry seems to have become very common in Stoicism and entirely characteristic of its individual and social ethics. But what makes the Stoic position important for the history of ethics is the fact that it was not formulated as a simple preference for marriage by reason of the latter's advantages and in spite of its disadvantages; marrying, for Musonius, Epictetus, or Hierocles, is something one

does, not because it is "better," but because it is a duty. The
marital tie derives from a universal rule. This general principle
is supported by two types of reflection. For the Stoics, the
obligation to marry is first of all the direct consequence of the
principle that marriage was ordained by Nature and that
human beings are led to it by an impulse which, being at once
natural and rational, is the same in everyone. But it is also
implied as an element in a set of tasks and duties that must
not be evaded by any human being who acknowledges himself
to be a member of a community and a part of the human race.
Marriage is one of those duties by which private existence
acquires a value for all.

Epictetus' discussion with an Epicurean shows clearly this
recognition of marriage as a universal duty for every human
being who wishes to live in harmony with nature, and as a
function for the individual who aims to lead a life that is useful
to those around him and to humanity in general. The Epicurean whom Epictetus refutes in Discourse Seven of Book III
is a leading citizen; he exercises responsibilities; he is an "inspector of cities." But, out of faithfulness to his philosophical
principles, he rejects marriage. To which Epictetus retorts
with three arguments. The first refers to immediate utility and
to the impossibility of universalizing the renunciation of marriage: if everyone refuses to get married, "what is to happen
then? Where will our citizens come from? Who will educate
them? Who will be governor of the ephebes? Who will manage
the gymnasia? Yes, and what will be their education?" The
second argument refers to the social obligations that no man
must shirk and of which marriage forms a part, alongside the
duties that pertain to political life, religion, and the family:
"citizenship, marriage, procreation of children, worship of
God, care of parents." The final argument concerns the naturalness of a behavior that reason prescribes: "We must subor-
dinate pleasure to these principles, to minister to them as a
servant, to evoke our interests, and to keep us in the way of
our natural activities."[8]

We see then that the principle of having to marry has become detached from the comparative interplay between the advantages and drawbacks of marriage. It is expressed as the need for everyone to make a choice of a life that assumes the form of a universal, in that it conforms to nature and is useful to all. Marriage joins man to himself insofar as he is a natural being and a member of the human race. Epictetus says as much to his Epicurean interlocutor, in taking leave of him: by not doing what Zeus prescribes, "you will suffer penalty and harm. What kind of harm? No harm but that of failing to do your duty; you will destroy the trustworthy, self-respecting, well-behaved man in you. Look not for any greater harm than this!"[9]

And yet, it was the same with marriage as with all the other practices that the Stoics classed among the *proēgoumena*, the things that are preferable. There may be circumstances in which it is not obligatory. This is what Hierocles says: "Marrying is preferable [*proēgoumenon*]; hence it is an imperative for us provided that no circumstance opposes it."[10] It is precisely in this relationship between the obligation to marry and the conjuncture of circumstances that the difference between the Stoics and the Epicureans was most pronounced. For the Epicureans, no one was obliged to marry, unless there existed a circumstance that could make this form of union desirable. For the Stoics, only particular circumstances could lift an obligation that in theory one could not escape.

Among these circumstances, there was one that was long an object of discussion: the choice of the philosophical life. That the marriage of philosophers had been, since the classical age, a theme of debate can be explained by several factors: the heterogeneity of this type of life compared with other forms of existence; the incompatibility between the goal of philosophy (the care of one's own soul, the mastery of one's passion, the search for peace of mind) and what was traditionally described as the agitation and troubles of married life. In short, it seemed difficult to reconcile the style characteristic of the philosophical life with the demands of a marriage defined, above all, by its responsibilities. Two important texts show, however, an entirely different way not only of resolving the difficulty but of posing the very elements of the problem.

Musonius is the author of the oldest. In his text he takes up the question of the practical incompatibility between the married life and the philosophical life, turning it into the affirmation of an essential connection between the two.[11] Anyone who would be a philosopher, he says, should marry. He should do so because the primary function of philosophy is to enable one to live in accord with nature and to fulfill all the obligations that follow from nature. He will take as his "teacher and guide" that which is fitting for a human being who conforms to nature. But, further, he is under a greater obligation to marry than anyone else, for the philosopher's role is not simply to live according to reason; he must be for everyone else an example of that reasonable life as well as a master who shows the way to it. The philosopher cannot be inferior to those he must advise and lead. If he were to refuse marriage, he would be showing himself inferior to all those who, obeying reason and following nature, practice, out of concern for themselves and for others, matrimonial life. The latter, far from being incompatible with philosophy, constitutes for it a double obligation. In relation to oneself, it is the duty of giving one's existence a universally valuable form, and in relation to others, it is the necessity of offering them a model of living.

One might be tempted to oppose to this analysis the one that Epictetus submits when he draws the ideal portrait of the Cynic, of the man who makes a profession of philosophizing, who must be the common pedagogue, the herald of truth, Zeus' messenger to humans, who goes on stage to challenge men and to reproach them for the way they live. Such a man rightly "has nothing, is naked, without home or hearth; he lives in squalor, without a slave, without a city." Nor does he have "a wife or children," but "only earth and sky and one poor cloak."[12] Moreover, Epictetus presents a familiar picture of marriage and its disadvantages. In its banal verve, it conforms to what had been said for a very long time concerning the "annoyances of housekeeping," which disturb the soul and interfere with reflection. Married, a man is bound by "private duties." He has to heat the water for the cooking pot, accompany the children to school, render service to his father-in-law, provide his wife with wool, oil, a bed, and a cup.[13] At first glance, this looks like nothing more than the long list of obligations that burden the sage and prevent him from attending to himself. But the reason for which the ideal Cynic should, according to Epictetus, forgo marriage is not the desire to reserve his attentions for himself and no one else. On the contrary, it is because he has the mission of caring for humans, of looking after them, of being their "benefactor." It is because, like a doctor, he must "make his rounds" and "feel men's pulses."[14] Kept occupied by the responsibilities of a household (and perhaps especially by the household Epictetus describes), he would not have the leisure to go about a task that takes in the whole of humanity. His renunciation of all these private ties is but the consequence of the ties he establishes, *qua* philosopher, with the human race. He has no family because his family is mankind; he has no children because, in a sense, he has fathered all men and all women. It is important to understand, therefore, that the responsibility for the universal family is what prevents the Cynic from devoting himself to a particular household.

But Epictetus does not stop there. He fixes a limit to this incompatibility. It is limited by the present situation, by what he calls the current "catastasis" of the world. If in fact we lived in a city of wise men, there would be no further need of these men who are sent by the gods and who, unburdening themselves of everything, rise up to awaken others to truth. Everyone would be a philosopher. The Cynic and his rude profession would be unnecessary. Furthermore, marriage, in this state of things, would not present the same kind of difficulties as it does today, in the present form of humanity. Each philosopher would be able to find in his wife, in his father-in-law, in his children, people like him and brought up in the same manner as he.[15] The conjugal relation would bring the sage face to face with an alter ego. Hence it must be borne in mind that the militant philosopher's refusal of marriage does not bespeak an essential condemnation. It answers only to a circumstantial necessity. The philosopher's celibacy could just as well be abandoned if all humans were in a condition to lead an existence conforming to their essential nature.

3. A singular relation.　The philosophers of the imperial epoch obviously did not invent the affective dimension of the conjugal relationship, just as they did not efface the useful purposes it might serve in individual, familial, or civic life. But to that relationship and to the way in which it established a bond between husband and wife, they proposed to give a form and particular qualities.

Aristotle ascribed considerable importance and strength to the relationship between spouses. But when he analyzed the ties that attach humans to one another, it was blood relations that he seemed to favor. According to him, no tie was more intense than the attachment of parents to their children, in whom they could recognize a part of themselves.[16] The hierarchy Musonius posits in the treatise *Is Marriage a Handicap for the Pursuit of Philosophy?* is different. Of all the communities that can be established among humans, Musonius designates marriage as the highest, the most important, and the most venerable *(presbytatē)*. It is greater in strength than that which can join a friend to a friend, a brother to a brother, a son to his parents. It even surpasses—this is the decisive point—the bond that attaches parents to their offspring. No father, no mother, writes Musonius, will feel greater friendship for their child than for their marriage partner, and he cites the example of Admetus: Who was willing to die for him? Not his old parents, but his wife, Alcestis, in spite of her youth.[17]

Conceived in this way, as a closer and more fundamental relationship than any other, the marriage tie serves to define a whole mode of existence. Married life had been characterized by an allocation of tasks and behaviors that were complementary in form. The man was expected to do those things which the wife could not do, and she, for her part, did the work that was not within the competence of the husband. It was the fact of having the same goal (the prosperity of the household) that gave a unity to these activities and to modes of life that were different by definition. This adjustment of specific roles did not disappear from the set of precepts for living that could be given to married people. Hierocles refers, in his *Economics,* to rules that are identical to those found in Xenophon.[18] But behind this distribution of behaviors relating to the house, the possessions, and the estate, one sees a shared life and a common existence being affirmed as an exigency. The art of marriage is not simply a rational way for the spouses to act, each on his or her own account, in view of a purpose both partners recognize and in which they are united. It is a way of living together and of being as one person. Marriage calls for a certain style of conduct in which each of the two partners leads his or her life with the other, and in which, together, they form a common existence.

This style of existence is characterized first of all by a certain art of being together. For his business affairs, the husband must be away from home, while the wife must remain at home. But good spouses will want to rejoin one another and remain separated as little as possible. Closeness, the other's presence, living side by side, are presented not simply as duties, but as an aspiration characteristic of the relationship that should join husband and wife. They may each have their roles; there is no question of their doing without each other. Musonius underscores the need felt by spouses in a good marriage to be together. He even makes the difficulty of being apart the criterion of their singular friendship. No absence, he says, is as difficult to endure as, for the wife, that of the husband and, for the husband, that of the wife. No presence has such a power to lighten grief, to increase joy, to remedy misfortune.[19] The presence of the spouse is at the heart of married life. One thinks of Pliny describing to his absent wife the nights and days he spends looking for her in vain, and recalling her face in order to evoke a quasi-presence in his mind.[20]

An art of being together, and an art of dialogue as well. To be sure, the *Oeconomicus* of Xenophon described a certain model of exchange between the two spouses. The husband was supposed above all to guide, to give advice, to instruct, and, when required, to direct her in her activity as mistress of the house. For her part, the wife needed to ask questions about those things she did not know and to give an account of what she had been able to accomplish. The later texts suggest another kind of dialogue, with different ends. Each of the two spouses, according to Hierocles, should report to the other concerning what they have done. The wife will tell the husband what is going on at home, but she will also need to ask him about what is happening on the outside.[21] Pliny likes Calpurnia to keep informed of his public activity, to encourage him, and to rejoice in his successes—a custom that had long been traditional in aristocratic Roman families. But he associates it directly with his work; and in return, the taste his wife has for belles-lettres is inspired by the tenderness she feels for her husband. She must be the witness and judge of his literary endeavors. She reads his works, listens to his speeches, and receives with pleasure the compliments she may hear. Pliny trusts that in this way mutual affection, *concordia,* will endure and grow stronger day by day.[22]

Whence the idea that married life must also be the art of collaborating to form a new unity. One recalls how Xenophon had distinguished the different qualities with which nature had endowed the man and the woman so that they might carry out their respective responsibilities in the household, or how Aristotle bestowed on men the possibility of developing, to the point of perfection, virtues which in women would always remain inferior, justifying their subordination. The Stoics, on the other hand, granted both sexes, if not identical aptitudes, at least an equal capability for virtue. The good marriage, according to Musonius, depends on *homonoia.* What is meant by this word is not just likemindedness between the partners; rather, it denotes an identity in their way of being reasonable, in their moral attitude, and in their virtue. The couple is expected to form a veritable ethical unity in marital life. This unity is compared by Musonius to the fitting of two pieces of wood in a frame: they must both be straight in order to constitute a solid whole.[23] But in order to characterize the substantial unity the couple must form, writers occasionally resort to another metaphor, stronger than that of pieces fitted together: *di'holōn krasis*, complete fusion, according to a notion borrowed from Stoic physics.

The treatise by Antipater had already appealed to this model in order to contrast conjugal affection with the other forms of friendship.[24] He described the latter as combinations in which the elements remain independent of each other, like the seeds that one mixes and that can be separated again. The term *mixis* denotes this type of blending by juxtaposition. By contrast, marriage should be in the nature of a total fusion, like that observed between water and wine, which form by their mixture a new liquid. This same notion of matrimonial "crasis" is reencountered in Plutarch, in the thirty-fourth of the *Marriage Precepts*. It is used to distinguish between three types of marriage and to rank them in relation to one another. There are marriages that are contracted solely for the pleasures of the bed. They belong in the category of those mixtures that juxtapose separate elements, each of which retains its individuality. There are marriages that are concluded for reasons of self-interest. They are like those combinations in which the elements form a new, solid unity, but can always be dissociated from one another: e.g., the unity constituted by the parts of a frame. As for total fusion—the "crasis" that ensures the formation of a new unity that nothing can undo—only marriages in which the spouses are bound together by love can achieve it.[25]*

By themselves these few texts cannot represent the actual

---

*Precept 20 also compares the good marriage to a rope that is strengthened by the intertwining of strands.[26]

practice of marriage in the first centuries of our era, or even sum up the theoretical debates to which it may have given rise. They have to be taken in their partiality, for what they present that was characteristic of certain doctrines and no doubt peculiar to a few limited milieus. But they reveal, albeit in fragments, the outlines of a "strong model" of conjugal existence. In this model, the relationship to the other that appears as the most fundamental of all is neither the blood relationship nor that of friendship; it is the relationship between a man and a woman when it is organized in the institutional form of marriage and in the common life that is superimposed on the latter. The familial system and the friendship network have doubtless retained a large part of their social importance. However, in the art of existence they lose some of their value in comparison with the tie that attaches two persons of different sexes. A natural privilege, at once ontological and ethical, is granted to this dual, heterosexual relationship at the expense of all others.

In light of the above, one understands what was no doubt one of the most characteristic features of this art of being married—that attention to oneself and devotion to conjugal life could be closely associated. If relationship with a woman who is "the wife," "the spouse," is essential to existence, if human beings are conjugal individuals whose nature is fulfilled in the practice of shared life, then there could not be an essential and primary incompatibility between the relationship one establishes with oneself and the rapport one forms with the other. The art of conjugality is an integral part of the cultivation of the self.

But the individual who is concerned about himself does not simply have to marry; he must give his married life a deliberate form and a particular style. This style, with the moderation it requires, is not defined by self-mastery alone and by the principle that one must govern oneself in order to be able to rule others. It is also defined by the elaboration of a certain form of reciprocity. In the conjugal bond that so strongly marks the existence of each person, the spouse, as privileged partner, must be treated as a being identical to oneself and as an element with whom one forms a substantial unity. Such is the paradox of this thematics of marriage in the cultivation of the self, as it was developed by an entire philosophy. The woman as spouse is valorized within it as the other par excellence. But the husband must also recognize her as forming a unity with himself. Compared with the traditional forms of matrimonial relations, the change was considerable.

CHAPTER TWO

THE QUESTION OF MONOPOLY

One might expect that the treatises on matrimonial life would assign an important role to the regimen of sexual relations that must be established between husband and wife. In actual fact, the place reserved for them is relatively limited. It is as if the objectivation of the conjugal relation had preceded, and by far, the objectivation of the sexual relations that developed within it. As if all the effort and attention that needed to be devoted to living together continued to leave the question of conjugal sex in the shadows.

A discretion that was traditional, no doubt. Plato, at the point where he is nevertheless about to legislate on these matters—determining the precautions to take in order to produce healthy children, prescribing the physical and moral state of future parents, even instituting female inspectors who will need to look into the lives of young married couples—underscores the difficulty people probably would have in accepting legislation concerned with such things.[1] Opposing this Greek discretion, there will be the meticulous attentiveness of the Christian pastoral ministry, starting in the Middle Ages. One will then attempt to regulate everything—positions, frequency, gestures, each partner's state of mind, knowledge by the one of the intentions of the other, signs of desire on one side, tokens of acceptance on the other, and so on. For its part, Hellenistic and Roman moral philosophy says little on this subject.

165

Yet several important principles bearing on the relations between the use of pleasure and married life are formulated in certain of these texts.

We have seen that traditionally the connection between the sexual act and marriage was established on the basis and in terms of the need to have descendants. This procreative aim figured among the reasons for marrying. It was what made sexual relations within marriage necessary. Its absence, moreover, was what could dissolve the conjugal union. It was in order to take account of the best possible conditions for procreation that certain recommendations were made to married people regarding the proper way to perform the conjugal act (the time one should choose, the regimen that ought to precede the act). It was also in order to avoid the disadvantages of illegitimate offspring that extramarital liaisons were discouraged (for women, certainly, but also for men). Let us say schematically that in the classical texts the synthesis of the marriage tie and sexual relations was granted mainly for reasons pertaining to procreation. For men at least, it was neither the very nature of sexual acts nor the essence of marriage itself that implied that there should be pleasure only in conjugality. Apart from the question of illegitimate births, and allowing for the ethical requirement of self-mastery, there was no reason to expect a man, even a married man, to reserve all his sexual pleasures for his wife, and for her alone.

Now in the ethics of strict marriage that we see being formulated in the first centuries of our era, it is easy to ascertain something that might be called a "conjugalization" of sexual relations—a conjugalization at once direct and reciprocal. Direct: it is the nature of sexual intercourse that must prevent one from resorting to it outside marriage. Reciprocal, for it is the nature of marriage and of the bond formed between spouses that must rule out the sexual pleasures one might find elsewhere. The state of marriage and sexual activity must therefore coincide, and for good reasons, rather than for the sole aim of a legitimate progeny. This coincidence—or rather the movement that tends to make them coincide, not without a certain number of possible gaps and margins—is manifested in the elaboration of two principles. First, given its nature, sexual pleasure cannot be allowed outside marriage, which implies practically that it should not even be tolerated in an unmarried individual. Second, the marriage bond is such that the wife risks being hurt not just by the loss of her status but by the fact that her husband might take his pleasure with someone other than her.

1. It is doubtless rare to see formulated the principle that all sexual relations are culpable if they do not take place in a relationship of marriage that makes them legitimate. Provided that he exhibits personal moderation and respect for customs, laws, and the rights of others, an unmarried man may very well enjoy his pleasure as he sees fit. It would be very difficult, even within this austere ethics, to oblige him to abstain completely so long as he has not contracted a marriage. It was owing to a great personal virtue that the son of Marcia, by Seneca's account, rejected the advances of the women who desired him, even going so far as to blush at the thought of pleasing them, as if this were a fault *(quasi peccasset).* [2] We may also remark that Dio of Prusa shows himself to be very severe with regard to prostitution and the way it is organized: first, because he sees it as a form of "loveless love," and a kind of union that is foreign to Aphrodite; second, because its victims are nonconsenting human beings. Though he hopes that a truly well-governed city will abolish these institutions, he does not expect such an inveterate evil to be eliminated at once. [3] Marcus Aurelius expresses pride in his own sobriety in matters of sexual pleasure: he has "preserved [his] adolescence," he "did not become a man before the proper time," he "even took a little longer." Now these statements show very clearly that the point of virtue is not in the fact that he has reserved his pleasures only for marriage, but that he has managed to master himself well enough to wait, longer than men usually do, for the right time to taste the pleasures of sex. [4] Epictetus also evokes the ideal of sexual intercourse not taking place prior to the marriage tie, but he makes it the object of a piece of advice that one gives. This advice is to be followed if one can, but there is no reason to make an arrogant precept of this sort of chastity: "Before marriage guard yourself with all your ability from illicit intercourse with women; yet be not uncharitable or severe to those who are led into this, nor boast frequently that you yourself do otherwise."[5] Epictetus does not justify the extreme reserve that he demands in the sexual relationship by the form of marriage, by the rights and duties it establishes and which must be rendered to the wife; he explains it by saying that one owes it to oneself since one is a fragment of God, that one must honor this principle which dwells for a time in the body, and that one must respect it over the entire course of one's everyday existence. Mindfulness of one's own nature, rather than consciousness of one's ties with others, should serve as the permanent basis of austerity: "Will you not remember, when you eat, who you are that eat, and whom you are feeding, and the same in your relations with women? When you take part in society, or training, or conversation, do you not know that it is God you are nourishing and training? ... Yet when God himself is present within you and sees and hears all things, you are not ashamed of thinking and acting thus: so slow to understand your nature, and estranged from God!"[6]

On the other hand, it seems that Musonius Rufus undertakes a thorough conjugalization of sexual activity since he condemns all sexual intercourse that does not take place within marriage and with a view to the latter's particular objectives. The passage of the treatise on the *aphrodisia* that is preserved in Stobaeus opens with a customary criticism of the life of debauchery: a life that, being incapable of exercising the necessary mastery over itself, gets caught up in the pursuit of rare and affected pleasures and "shameful intimacies." Now, to this banal condemnation, Musonius adds as a positive prescription a definition of what must be considered as *aphrodisia dikaia,* legitimate pleasures: these, he says, are pleasures that the partners enjoy together in marriage and for the purpose of begetting children *(ta en gamōi kai epi genesei paidōn synteloumena)*. And Musonius then states precisely the two hypotheses that can emerge: either extramarital relations are sought in adultery *(moicheia),* and nothing could be more unlawful *(paranomōtatai);* or one obtains them without any adultery. Yet from the moment they are "without that which makes them lawful," they are themselves shameful and have their origin in self-indulgence.[7] Conjugality is for sexual activity the condition of its legitimate exercise.

Between the ancient theme that the overly intense pursuit of pleasure goes against the necessary self-mastery and the principle that there can be legitimate pleasure only in the context of the matrimonial institution, there is an important threshold that Musonius crosses. He draws the consequence this necessarily implies, even if it may have seemed paradoxical to many of his contemporaries. Moreover, he himself presents the inference in connection with a possible objection: Should one regard as culpable, sexual relations that would occur between two free persons not bound by the ties of marriage? "The man who has relations with a courtesan or a woman who has no husband wrongs no one for he does not destroy anyone's hope of children." Even in these circumstances, one commits an offense—just as a man can commit an offense and an injustice without doing wrong to anyone around him: he defiles himself, and "like swine, rejoices in his own vileness."[8] One must also count among the implications of this conception of the essential relationship between marriage and sexual activity the objection raised by Musonius to contraceptive practices. These practices, he says, in a text devoted to the question of whether all children must be raised, transgress the laws of cities that take care to maintain their population. They are harmful to individuals as well since it is useful to have descendants. They also violate the universal order that was willed by the gods: "How could we not be sinning against our ancestral gods and against Zeus, protector

of the family, when we do such things? For just as he who
mistreats a guest sins against Zeus, the protector of the rights
of hospitality, and he who acts unrighteously to a friend,
against Zeus, the god of friendship, even so whoever acts
unrighteously toward his family line sins against his ancestral
gods and against Zeus, protector of the family."[9]

Here one might be tempted to see the anticipation of the
Christian idea that sexual pleasure is in itself a defilement,
which only the lawful form of marriage, with the possibility
of procreation, could render acceptable. It is a fact that this
passage from Musonius was utilized by Clement of Alexandria
in the second book of the *Pedagogue*.[10] However, although
Musonius—like most of the ancient moral philosophers, with
the exception of the Cynics—does consider the public practice
of this type of relation to be reprehensible, it would undoubtedly be a falsification of his doctrine to attribute to him the
idea that sexual pleasure is an evil, and that marriage was
instituted in order to redeem and regulate the necessary experience of it within a strict framework. If Musonius regards as
shameful any sexual intercourse outside marriage, it is not
that the latter has been superimposed on the former so as to
rid it of its intrinsically wrongful character. It is that, for the
reasonable and social human being, the very nature of the
sexual act demands that it be inscribed within the matrimonial
relation, where it may produce a legitimate progeny. The
sexual act, the conjugal tie, offspring, the family, the city, and
beyond it, the human community—all this constitutes a series
whose elements are connected and in which man's existence
achieves its rational form. To withdraw pleasure from this
form, to detach pleasure from the conjugal relation in order
to propose other ends for it, is in fact to debase the essential
composition of the human being. The defilement is not in the
sexual act itself, but in the "debauchery" that would dissociate
it from marriage, where it has its natural form and its rational
purpose. From this perspective, marriage constitutes for
human beings the only legitimate context for sexual union and
the experience of the *aphrodisia*.

2. Given this essential association of sexual relations and sexual pleasure with lawful conjugality, one can understand the new problematization of adultery and the incipient requirement of double sexual fidelity.

We know that adultery was juridically condemned and morally reproved on account of the injustice done by a man to the one whose wife he led astray. What constituted adultery, therefore, in an extramarital sexual relation was the fact that the woman was married and that fact alone: the marital status of the man was not relevant. The deceit and injury were a matter between the two men—the one who had possessed himself of the woman and the one who had the legitimate rights to her.[11] This definition of adultery, solely in terms of the derogation of the husband's rights, was common enough to be found even in an ethics as exacting as that of Epictetus.[12] In the middle of a lecture on the theme "man is born for mutual trust" *(pistis),* there enters a man of letters *(philologos)* who had been discovered committing adultery and who defends himself by appealing to the doctrine of Archedemus on women as common property. The remonstrances that Epictetus addresses to him relate to two points. By the practice of adultery the man has transgressed "the principle of trust for which we were born." But Epictetus does not localize this "trust" in the matrimonial institution. What is more, he does not even cite the marriage bond as one of its essential forms. He characterizes it by the ties that join a man to his neighborhood, his friends, his city. And what constitutes in his eyes adultery as a transgression is the rent it effects in this fabric of relations between men, where each is called upon not only to respect others but to recognize himself. "If we put away this trust, for which we are born, and plot against our neighbor's wife, what are we doing? Are we not pulling down and destroying? Whom? The man of trust, of honor, of piety. Is this all? Are we not overthrowing neighborly feeling, friendship, the city itself?"[13] It is to himself and to other men, as human beings, that adultery is injurious.

Yet, contrary to and alongside of this traditional characterization of adultery, one finds, in certain reflections on married life, exigencies that are much more rigorous, in the double sense that they tend to bring more and more into play a principle of symmetry between the man and the woman, and that they justify this principle by referring to the respect owed to the personal bond between the two spouses. Concerning those "salutary truths," which one knows at a distance but which, not having been sufficiently dwelled upon, are not really capable of governing conduct, Seneca evokes the obligations of friendship together with those of a strictly symmetrical conjugal fidelity: "You know that friendship should be scrupulously honored, and yet you do not hold it in honor. You know that a man does wrong in requiring chastity of his wife while he himself is intriguing with the wives of other men; you know that, as your wife should have no dealings with a lover, neither should you yourself with a mistress."[14]

It is in Musonius that one finds the most detailed statement of the principle of a symmetrical conjugality.[15] The argument is set forth in the long passage of the treatise *On the Aphrodisia* where it is demonstrated that only marriage can constitute the naturally legitimate tie for sexual relations. Musonius focuses on what might be called "the problem of the servant." The slave was so taken for granted as a household sexual object that it might seem impossible to forbid a married man to use her; yet this is precisely what Musonius would prohibit, even, he notes, if the slave is not married (which implies that a married slave couple in a house was entitled to a certain respect). And to justify this prohibition, Musonius posits a principle of symmetry, or rather a relatively complex interplay between a symmetry with respect to rights and a superiority concerning obligations. In the first place, how could one accept that the husband might have relations with a maidservant, whereas one does not recognize the right of a wife to have relations with her manservant? The right that is disputed on the one hand cannot be granted on the other. And while Musonius finds it both natural and lawful for the husband, as head of the family, to have more rights than the wife, in the domain of sexual relations and pleasures he demands an exact symmetry. But, second, this symmetry of rights is completed by the need to accentuate, in the sphere of self-mastery, the superiority of the husband. If in fact one allowed the husband to do with the servant girl that which one expects a wife not to do with a slave, one would be supposing that the wife were more able than the husband to master herself and govern her desires. The one who in the house should be led would then be stronger than the one who leads her. For the husband to be the one who actually prevails, he must forgo doing that which is forbidden a wife. In this Stoic art of marriage, for which Musonius proposes such a strict model, a form of fidelity is required. It obligates the man and the woman alike. It does not merely prohibit anything that might compromise the rights of other men. Nor is it content just to protect the wife against the threats that could compromise her privileged status as mistress of the house and as a mother. It interprets the marriage relationship as a system that establishes an exact balance of obligations in the practice of pleasure.

This integral conjugalization of sexual practice that one finds in Musonius and the principle of a strict monopoly of the *aphrodisia* reserved for marriage are no doubt exceptional. A point has been reached where the art of married life seems to be organized around the formal principle of double prohibition. But in the authors who are careful not to formulate such rigid rules, one also notes the emergence of a requirement of fidelity calling for slightly different modes of conduct and ways of acting. These authors do not assert an explicit prohibition, but rather a concern with preserving the conjugal bond with all that it may entail in the way of individual relationship, attachment, affection, and personal respect between the marriage partners. This fidelity is defined less by a law than by a style of relating to the wife, by a way of being and of behaving with respect to her. The renunciation, as complete as possible, of extramarital relations must stem, on the part of the husband, from a pursuit of refinement in marital relations. It must be the result of conduct that is both skillful and affectionate, while a certain subtlety is expected of the wife in the *de facto* tolerance that she is fully obliged to concede and that she would be unwise not to show.

The rather belated Latin text that was long considered to be a translation of the *Economics* attributed to Aristotle thus places a traditional perspective on the dignity of the wife side by side with advice to be prudent and accommodating. On the one hand, the author instructs the husband to take proper care of a wife who will become the mother of the children he hopes for. He also enjoins him not to deprive the woman he has married of the honor she is due.[16] But he also demands that the two spouses prevent one another from doing anything base and dishonest. He counsels the husband to "approach his wife in an honorable way, full of self-restraint and awe" *(cum honestate, et cum multa modestia et timore)*. He hopes that the husband will be "neither indifferent nor harsh" *(nec negligens nec severus)*: "Between a courtesan and her lover, such tempers are allowed their course." With his wife, on the contrary, the good husband should be attentive but also restrained, and the wife will respond with modesty and tact, and by showing affection and fear "in equal parts."[17] And while he stresses the value of this fidelity, the author makes it clear to the wife that she will need to have a relatively accommodating attitude toward her husband's faults: "and let her forget any wrong her husband may have done her through distress of mind" *(si quid vir animae passione ad ipsam peccaverit)*; "let her refrain from all complaint nor charge him with the wrong, but rather attribute everything of this kind to sickness or ignorance or accidental errors." In this way the husband in return will be ready to show her his gratitude after his cure.

In a similar fashion, the *Marriage Precepts* affirm the principle of a reciprocal fidelity. They do not, however, formulate it as a rigorously and formally symmetrical requirement. While the text assumes, without even having to recall the fact, that the wife owes her husband fidelity, it implies that although the pursuit of other pleasures may be for the husband a rather frequent offense, it is also a rather minor one. At all

events, it is within the marriage relationship, according to the
affective relations obtaining between the two spouses, and not
according to rights and prerogatives, that the question must
be resolved. Plutarch expects the husband not to have sexual
relations with other women, not just because to do so would
pose a threat to the prestige of the lawful wife, but because it
would inflict a wound—a natural wound that causes suffering.
He calls to mind the behavior of cats, which are excited to
frenzy by the odor of perfume. In the same way, women are
infuriated when the husband has intercourse with other
women. It is therefore unjust *(adikon)* to make them suffer
such a violent vexation for a pleasure that is "trivial." And he
advises the husband to follow, with his wife, the example of
the beekeeper, who does not go near his bees if he has had
intercourse with a woman.[18] Conversely, Plutarch counsels
wives to show a certain tolerance; not only would it be better
for them to shut their eyes—a little like the wives of Persian
kings who take part in banquets with their husbands but return to their apartments when, with the onset of drunkenness,
the musicians and courtesans are summoned. But they ought
to tell themselves that if their husbands are going to seek
pleasure with a hetaera or a maidservant, this is out of respect
for them, and because he would not want them to share his
debauchery, his licentiousness, and his excess.[19] Thus marriage, as a bond of affection and a relation of respect, much
more than as a statutory structure, draws all sexual activities
to it and condemns all those that might take place outside it.
And while it tends to demand a symmetrical fidelity of the two
partners, it also constitutes a locus of conciliation, where the
husband's attachment to the wife and the wife's prudence
vis-à-vis the husband will manage to correspond. The external
pleasures of the husband will no longer be the recognized
consequence of his statutory superiority, but the consequence
of a certain weakness, which he is all the more obliged to limit
seeing that the wife tolerates it through a concession that,
while possibly saving her honor, also proves her affection.

CHAPTER THREE

THE PLEASURES OF MARRIAGE

This definition of marriage as a relationship that is as exclusive as possible regarding the practice of the *aphrodisia* raises (or could raise) a number of questions pertaining to the integration, the role, the form, and the finality of acts of pleasure in the interplay of affective or statutory relations between husband and wife.

In actual fact, one has to admit that even in the forms of reflection in which marriage occupies an important place, the economy of pleasures in the conjugal relationship is treated with a great deal of reserve. Marriage, in this rigorous ethics advocated by some, demands a monopoly of pleasure. But as to which pleasures will be allowed within marriage and which others excluded, little is said.

However, two general principles are often evoked. First, it is made clear that the conjugal relation must not be foreign to Eros, to that love which some philosophers wished to reserve for boys; but neither must it ignore or exclude Aphrodite. Musonius, in the text where he shows that marriage, far from being a hindrance, is an obligation for the philosopher, affirms the greatness and value of the marital state. He invokes the three great deities who watch over it: Hera, whom "we address as the patroness of wedlock"; Aphrodite, since people have called "*Aphrodision ergon* the joining of wife and husband"; and Eros (to what indeed could the name be better applied "than to the lawful union of man and wife"?). Together, these three powers have the function of "bringing together man and woman for the procreation of children."[1] It is in the same manner that Plutarch will affirm the role of Aphrodite and Eros in that which properly constitutes the conjugal relationship.[2]

In correlation with this presence of amorous passion and physical pleasures in marriage, another principle, opposite to the first one but also quite general, is brought into play; namely, that one must not treat one's wife as a mistress and one should behave as a husband rather than as a lover.[3] It is only logical that the old principle of conjugal decency will become all the more important as marriage tends to constitute the only licit context for the pleasures of sex. Aphrodite and Eros must be present in marriage and nowhere else. Moreover, the conjugal relationship needs to be different from the relationship of lovers. One encounters the principle in several forms. In the form of a (doubtless quite traditional) counsel of prudence: by introducing one's wife to overly intense pleasures one risks giving her lessons she will put to bad use and which one will regret having taught her.[4] Or in the form of advice given to both spouses: let them find a middle way between an excessive austerity and a conduct too close to that of profligates, and let the husband always remind himself that "I cannot have the society of the same woman as wife and paramour" *(hōs gametē kai hōs hetaira)*.[5] Or, further, in the form of a general thesis: behaving too ardently with one's wife amounts to treating her as an adulteress.[6] The theme is important, for it will be reencountered in the Christian tradition, where it will appear very early (Clement of Alexandria refers to it in the *Stromateis*), and where it will persist for a very long time (Saint Francis of Sales works out its implications in the *Introduction to the Devout Life*).[7] It is no doubt necessary, if we are to understand its meaning for the Stoics who formulate it, to bear in mind that the natural and rational principle of marriage ordains that it combine two existences, that it produce descendants, that it be useful to the city and beneficial to the entire human race. To make the enjoyment of pleasur-

able sensations the most important thing in marriage would
be to violate the law, reverse the order of ends, and transgress
the principle that should join a man and a woman into a
couple.

More concretely, though, one faces the problem of determining what status and what forms the practice of pleasure
ought to assume in marital relations, and on what principles
the precepts of its internal limitation can be based. Given that
marriage demands a conjugal tie that must be at the same time
a highly valued personal relationship and the exclusive locus
of relations of pleasure, relations a man was heretofore rather
freely permitted on the fringes of his marriage, how is this
matrimonial structure to play its role as a principle of regulation? What austerity will be exacted in this marriage, if it must
be at once the strongest of individual ties and the only place
for lawful pleasures? The formulations are, more often than
not, rather vague, a little like those one finds in the Latin text
that is supposed to be Book III of the *Economics* attributed
to Aristotle. The author asks the husband to approach his wife
"in an honorable way" *(cum honestate)*, "full of self-restraint
and awe" *(cum multa modestia et timore)*. He recommends
that "in his conversation with her, he should use the words of
a right-minded man, suggesting only such acts as are themselves lawful and honorable." He advises him to treat his
spouse with "respect and modesty" *(verecundia et pudore)*. [8]

In a more precise way, intraconjugal austerity will be justified by the two great natural and rational finalities that will
be ascribed to marriage. The first, of course, is procreation.
One must not—Seneca stresses this, but we have also seen that
there were physicians who called attention to it—make pleasure the goal of an act that Nature has designed for procreation. If the desires of love were given to men, this was not in
order that they might enjoy sensual pleasure, but that they
might propagate their kind *(non voluptatis causa, sed propa-
gandi generis)*. [9] From this general principle, Musonius draws
the conclusion that sexual relations can rightfully take place
only if they have propagation as their goal. As for those rela-

tions which only seek pleasure as an end, they are "unjust and unlawful, even in marriage."[10] This rule, which one also finds in the neo-Pythagoreans, seems to have served to justify certain traditional prohibitions forbidding sexual intercourse during menstruation (which, according to physicians, might carry away the semen) and during the time of pregnancy (not only because it would be unproductive, but above all because it might endanger the life of the embryo). But, apart from these general recommendations, it does not seem that there was, despite the identity of principle, the kind of interrogation that will be encountered in Christian teaching concerning the lawfulness of sexual relations in case of recognized sterility or after the age of menopause, and concerning the intentions that both partners may have before or even during the act. The exclusion of pleasure as an end does seem, in the most rigorous of the moral philosophers, to have been an exigency. But this exigency was more a statement of principle than a schema enabling a regulation of behaviors and a precise codification of their permitted or forbidden forms.

The second great finality of marriage—making a life together, a life entirely shared—constitutes the other principle that calls for austerity in conjugal relations. Like the procreative finality, this principle does not trace a clear dividing line between what is permitted and what is forbidden. But certain authors—and foremost among them Plutarch—have it play, in the linking of pleasure relations to the conjugal relationship, a more subtle and complex role. Thus, on the one hand, the obligation to make the wife a companion to whom one opens one's soul requires that one have a respect for her directed not just to her rank and status, but to her personal dignity. The regimen of the *aphrodisia* must therefore take this obligation as a principle of internal limitation. On the other hand, if married life must have the purpose of forming a perfect community—a true "fusion of existences"—it is also clear that sexual relations and pleasures, if they are shared and enjoyed in common, constitute a factor of rapprochement between husband and wife. The formation and strengthening of a solid bond are, in the practice of the *aphrodisia*, not only a guarantee, but also an element in favor of the *aphrodisia*. Hence there is a valorization of sexual pleasures (provided they are incorporated into the matrimonial relationship and well integrated within it), combined with the recommendation of an austerity in their practice, which enables them actually to play this positive role in the conjugal union.

This spiraling process of necessary austerity and desirable intensity is clearly apparent in the *Marriage Precepts;* in fact it constitutes one of that work's guiding threads. The text reiterates some of the old familiar principles concerning the modesty and secrecy that should surround not only the procreative act but also the simple acts of pleasure such as kissing and caressing.[11] It also recalls to mind, transforming a well-known saying of Herodotus, that a woman's modesty should not fall along with the gown that she lays aside,[12] nor should darkness cover any licentiousness whatever. Recalling the example of a woman who tried to get away from Philip by pointing out to him that all women are the same once the lights are out, Plutarch notes that the wife, on the contrary, does not have to be like the others. Hidden by the night, without one's being able to see her body, she must cause what is virtuous in her *(to sophrōn autēs)* to shine forth. Now, what is virtuous in her is also what attaches her exclusively to her husband and makes her his own; it is "her constancy and her affection."[13]

Around this principle of gracious reserve, a modesty that signifies the exclusiveness of an attachment, Plutarch extends a number of recommendations that exclude both a supercilious austerity and an unrestrained facility, and this on the part of the husband and the wife alike. No doubt, like the young Spartan whose example he cites, a good wife must not herself make advances to her husband;[14] but neither must she show annoyance at his advances. The first attitude would have something brash about it that smacks of the courtesan, but there would be an unfriendly disdain in the second.[15] Here we have, still in a very nebulous way, the outline of those rules

fixing the forms of the respective initiatives and the signs to be exchanged on which the pastoral ministry will later set such a high value. Plutarch attaches a good deal of importance to the dangers that can compromise, in a married couple's first sexual relations, subsequent mutual understanding and the solidity of the bond to be formed. He draws attention to the risk of bad experiences that the bride may have. He advises her not to dwell on them, for the benefits of marriage may appear later: not to behave like those who "submit to the bees' stings, but abandon the honeycomb."[16] But he also fears that too intense a physical pleasure experienced at the outset of marriage may cause the affection to be lost when this pleasure disappears. It is better for the love to owe its vitality to the spouses' character and disposition.[17] It is also necessary, throughout married life, to bring into play anything that might benefit conjugal friendship in sexual relations between husband and wife. Specific examples of this function of affective reactivation—to which one of the interlocutors of the *Dialogue on Love* explicitly refers[18]—are given in the *Marriage Precepts*: avoid quarrels, especially those that might take place in the bedroom, because "the disagreements, recriminations, and angry passions which the bed generates are not easily settled in another place and at another time";[19] or, further, when you are in the habit of occupying the same bed, don't go to a separate bedroom because of an angry disagreement. On the contrary, this is the right time to invoke Aphrodite, "who is the best physician for such disorders."[20]

The theme holds a relatively important place in Plutarch himself. We will encounter it again in the *Dialogue on Love*, where it will serve as a basic discriminant between the love of women, in which pleasure is integrable with a positive role in the spiritual relation, and the love of boys, in which physical pleasure (assumed to be nonreciprocal) can figure only as a favorable factor within the relationship. This theme is also evoked in the *Dinner of the Seven Wise Men*, where it is a question of sexual pleasures in connection with the two other physical pleasures with which they are often associated: intoxication and music. The interlocutor—Mnesiphilus—observes that in every art or craft the work is not in the manipulation of tools or materials but in what one aims to make: the *ergon* of the architect does not consist of the mortar he mixes but of the temple he constructs; the Muses, when they employ themselves with the lyre or the flute, have no other task than "the development of characters and the soothing of the emotions."[21] In the same way, and just as the task of Dionysus is not in the fact of drinking intoxicating wine, the task of Aphrodite *(ergon Aphroditēs)* is not in the mere relating and conjoining of bodies *(synousia, meixis);* it is in the feeling of friendship *(philosophrosynē),* the longing *(pothos),* the association *(homilia),* and the intimacy *(synētheia)* between two people. Sexual intercourse, in married life, ought to serve as an instrument for the formation and development of symmetrical and reciprocal affective relations. "Aphrodite," says Plutarch, "is the artisan who creates concord and friendship [*homophrosynēs kai philias dēmiourgos*] between men and women, for through their bodies, under the influence of pleasure, she at the same time unites and welds together their souls."[22]*

This advice may appear rather crude. Nevertheless, it figures among the preliminaries of a long history: that of the codification of moral relations between spouses, in the dual form of a general recommendation of reserve and a complex lesson of affective communication through sexual pleasure.

A "monopolistic" principle: no sexual relations outside marriage. A requirement of "dehedonization": sexual intercourse between spouses should not be governed by an economy of pleasure. A procreative finalization: its goal should be the birth of offspring. These are three fundamental traits marking the ethics of conjugal existence that certain moralists

---

*Babut points out that Antipater, Musonius, and Hierocles "are more interested in marriage than love; they seem to want above all to establish that marriage does not prevent one from leading the philosophical life; in them one finds no trace of one of the important ideas of the *Amatorius,* namely, that the woman is just as capable as the man of inspiring amorous passion."[23]

developed at the beginning of the imperial epoch, an ethics whose elaboration owes a great deal to late Stoicism. But these traits are not peculiar to it. We have found similar exigencies in the rules enjoined by Plato on the citizens of his Republic. We shall find them again in a later period, in what the Church demanded of a good Christian married couple. Much more than an innovation of Stoic rigor, much more than a project specific to the moral philosophy of that epoch, these three principles did not cease, for centuries, to characterize the role that marriage was expected to play as a focus of sexual austerity.

But the constancy of these three phenomena should not be taken as evidence of a pure and simple identity. A certain more or less Stoicizing ethics of the imperial epoch did not merely carry forward, from the Platonic utopia to Christianity, the code of a "monopolistic" marriage dedicated to procreation and distrustful of pleasure. It contributed a number of particular inflections that derived from the forms taken at the time by the development of the cultivation of the self.

It should be noted first that in Plato the obligation to integrate all sexual pleasure into the matrimonial structure had for one of its chief justifications the need to supply the city with the children it required to survive and maintain its strength. In Christianity, on the other hand, the link between sexual intercourse and marriage will be justified by the fact that the former bears the marks of sin, the Fall, and evil, and that only the latter can give it a legitimacy that still may not exculpate it entirely. Now, in Musonius, Seneca, Plutarch, or Hierocles, although utility has its part to play, although distrust of the transports of pleasure is very strong, the link between marriage and the *aphrodisia* is not really established by positing the primacy of the social and political objectives of marriage, or by postulating an original evil intrinsic to pleasure, but by affirming a natural, rational, and essential relationship between them. In order to make allowance for the differences of position and doctrinal variants, let us say that the sexual monopoly that tends to be claimed for marriage in this form of ethics centers less on the "external" utilities of marriage or the "internal" negativity of pleasure than on an attempt to bring a certain number of relations into coincidence: the union of two sexual partners, the dual tie of husband and wife, and the social role of the family—while achieving as perfect a congruence as possible with the relation to the self.

Here we touch on an important difference. The obligation to keep the use of pleasure within the bounds of marriage was also, for Plato's guardian, Isocrates' leader, or Aristotle's citizen, a way of exercising self-mastery, a mastery made necessary by one's status or by the authority one had to exercise in the city. The principle of a perfect conjugal fidelity will be, in the pastoral ministry, an unconditional duty for anyone concerned about his salvation. By contrast, in this ethics inspired by Stoicism, it is in order to satisfy the specific requirements of the relation to oneself, not to violate one's natural and essential being, and to honor oneself as a reasonable being that one must keep one's practice of sexual pleasure within marriage and in conformity with its objectives. Doubtless this principle, which tends to exclude, even for men, sexual intercourse outside marriage, and to authorize it only for certain definite purposes, will be one of the anchor points for a subsequent "juridification" of marital relations and sexual practices. Like that of women, the sexual activity of married men will, in theory at least, risk coming within the provisions of the law. Even within marriage, a precise code will say what one is permitted or forbidden to do, to want, or even to think. But this juridification—which will be so pronounced in later times —is tied to Christian pastoral practice, to its own peculiar structure. Even in the most detailed texts on the life of the couple, such as those of Plutarch, what is proposed is not a regulation that would draw a division between permitted and forbidden acts. It is instead a mode of being, a style of relations. The ethics of marriage and the advice on conjugal life are at the same time universally valid principles and rules for those who wish to give their existence an honorable and noble form. It is the lawless universality of an aesthetics of existence that in any case is practiced only by a few.

The conjugalization of sexual activities that tends to localize legitimacy within marriage alone obviously results in their manifest limitation (at least for the husband, since this limitation has long been required of the married woman). Moreover, the insistence on a dissociation between the practice of pleasure and the hedonic finality will tend toward an internal disqualification of this activity itself. But it needs to be understood as well that these restrictions and this disqualification are accompanied by another process: an intensification of the value and meaning of sexual relations within marriage. On the one hand, in fact, intramarital sexual relations are no longer simply the consequence and manifestation of a right. They must be placed within a cluster of relations characterized by affection, attachment, and reciprocity. And on the other hand, while pleasure must be eliminated as a goal, it is, at least in certain of the most subtle formulations of this ethics, to be used as an element (at once an instrument and a guarantee) in the interplay of affective expressions between spouses.

And it is precisely on behalf of this intensification of the value of the *aphrodisia* in marital relations, by reason of the role it is assigned in the communication between husband and wife, that one begins to question, in an increasingly doubtful mode, the privileges that used to be granted to the love of boys.

PART SIX

===

BOYS

In the first centuries of our era, compared with the lofty formulations of the classical period, reflection on the love of boys lost some of its intensity, its seriousness, its vitality, if not its topicality. Where it appears, it has a facile, repetitive sound. Playing on ancient themes, often those of Platonism, it participates in the reactivation of classical culture, but in a dull way. Even when philosophy tries to restore to the figure of Socrates some of its former prestige, the love of boys, with the problems it poses, does not constitute an active and vital focus of reflection (the four speeches of Maximus of Tyre cannot furnish an argument to the contrary).

This does not mean that the practice disappeared or that it became the object of a disqualification. All the texts plainly show that it was still common and still regarded as a natural thing. What seems to have changed is not the taste for boys, or the value judgment that was brought to bear on those who had this partiality, but the way in which one questioned oneself about it. An obsolescence not of the thing itself, but of the problem; a decline in the interest one took in it; a fading of the importance it was granted in philosophical and moral debate. There are no doubt many reasons for this "deproblematization." Certain of them can be traced to the influence of Roman culture. It is not that the Romans were more insensitive than the Greeks to this sort of pleasure; but the difficult question of boys as objects of pleasure was posed, in the context of their institutions, with less acuity than in the Greek city. In the first place, children of good birth were well "protected" by parental right and by public laws. Fathers were determined that the power they exercised over their sons would be respected; and the famous *Lex Scantinia,* which, as Boswell has shown, did not prohibit homosexuality, defended the free adolescent from abuse and violence.[1] Second, and doubtless by way of a consequence, love for boys was practiced for the most part with young slaves, about whose status there was no reason to worry. "In Rome the freeborn ephebe was replaced by the slave," says Paul Veyne.[2] Hellenized though it was, and saturated with philosophy, Rome, whose poets were so fond of singing of adolescents, offered few echoes of the great speculation of the Greeks on the love of boys.

Further, the forms taken by pedagogical practice and its modes of institutionalization made it much more difficult to valorize the relationship with adolescents in terms of educational efficacy. When Quintilian speaks of the moment when a boy should be entrusted to the rhetoric teacher, he emphasizes the need to make sure of the latter's "morals": "Pupils are transferred to the school of rhetoric when they are practically grown up, and they continue there when they are young men; accordingly, we must at this stage exercise even greater care that the stainless character of the teacher may preserve their more tender years from harm and that the weight of his authority may deter their bolder age from excess." The teacher must therefore "adopt the attitude of a parent toward his pupils and consider that he is taking the place of those who entrust their children to him."[3] In a more general way, a certain lessening of the importance of personal relations of *philia,* together with the valorization of marriage, no doubt had much to do with the fact that the love relation between men ceased to be the focus of an intense theoretical and moral discussion.

Three important texts remain nevertheless: Plutarch's dialogue on love, the later dialogue attributed to Lucian, and the four lectures by Maximus of Tyre on Socratic love. We can leave aside this last text: not because of its rhetorical and artificial character—Pseudo-Lucian's *Affairs of the Heart* are scarcely less so, and the reactivation of ancient themes in academic exercises was a feature characteristic of the epoch. But the text by Maximus of Tyre is essentially devoted—this is what constitutes its traditionalism—to the distinction and comparison, in male relations, between two sorts of love: the love that is fine and just and the love that is not.[4] Conforming to the Socratic tradition, Maximus of Tyre has this distinction coincide with the opposition between true love and the love that is only a simulation. Starting from this point, he develops a systematic and traditional comparison of the two loves. In terms of the qualities that belong to each: the first comprises virtue, friendship, modesty, candor, stability; the second comprises excess, hatred, immodesty, infidelity. In terms of the ways of being that characterize them: the one is Hellenic and virile; the other is effeminate and barbaric. And lastly, in terms of the behaviors in which they are manifested: with the first, the lover takes care of the beloved, accompanies him to the gymnasium, goes hunting with him, into battle with him; he will be with him in death; and it is not in darkness or solitude that he seeks his company; with the second, on the other hand, the lover flees the sun, seeks darkness and solitude, and avoids being seen with the one he loves.[5]

Plutarch's and Pseudo-Lucian's dialogues on love are constructed quite differently. Their erotics is also binary and comparative: it is still a matter of distinguishing two forms of love and of contrasting their value. But this time, instead of operating within an Eros that is dominated, if not entirely represented, by masculine love, in order to isolate two morally unequal forms of the latter, the comparison starts from two forms of relations that are naturally distinct: the relation with boys and the relation with women (and more specifically the relation that one may have with one's lawful wife in the context of marriage). It is to these two distinct forms that the question of value, beauty, and moral superiority will be directed. This will have various consequences, which will modify the question of erotics considerably: love for women and, particularly, marriage will belong indisputably to the domain of Eros and its problematization. The latter will rest on the natural opposition between love for one's own sex and love for the other sex. Finally, the ethical valorization of love will no longer be able to be carried out through the elision of physical pleasure.

This is the paradox: it was around the question of pleasure that reflection on pederasty developed in Greek antiquity; it is around this same question that it will go into decline. Marriage, as an individual tie capable of integrating relations of pleasure and of giving them a positive value, will constitute the most active focus for defining a stylistics of moral life. The love of boys will not become a doomed figure for all that. It will find many other ways of expressing itself in poetry and art. But it will undergo a kind of philosophical "disinvestment." When it is examined, instead of asking it to reveal one of the highest possible forms of love, one will criticize it for a radical inadequacy, for its inability to accommodate relations of pleasure. The difficulty of accounting for the relations between this form of love and the use of the *aphrodisia* had long been the cause of its philosophical valorization. Now the difficulty becomes the reason for seeing it as a taste, a practice, a preference, which may have their tradition, but which are incapable of defining a style of living, an aesthetics of behavior, and a whole modality of relation to oneself, to others, and to truth.

Plutarch's dialogue and that of Pseudo-Lucian attest both to the legitimacy that is still granted to the love of boys and to its increasing decline as a vital theme of a stylistics of existence.

CHAPTER ONE

PLUTARCH

Plutarch's *Dialogue on Love* opens and closes under the sign of marriage. Shortly after their wedding, Plutarch has come with his wife on a pilgrimage to Thespiae. They wish to offer a sacrifice to the god and to ask him to bless this union, which a quarrel between their families has placed under unfavorable auspices. On arriving at their host's, they find themselves in the midst of a minor commotion: Should the young Bacchon, a coveted ephebe, marry the woman who is pursuing him? Debate, turn of events, abduction. The dialogue ends with everyone preparing to form a procession for this new married couple and to offer a sacrifice to the benevolent god. The dialogue unfolds between one marriage and the other.*

It also unfolds under the sign of Eros, during the time of the *Erotidia*, the holidays that were celebrated at Thespiae every four years, "in honor of Eros as well as the Muses." He is the god whom Plutarch was anxious to ask for protection for his marriage. He is also the god who will be invoked for the contested marriage of Bacchon with Ismenodora, for it seems that he "approves and is graciously present at this affair."[2] Meanwhile, Plutarch will have had time to sing a long eulogy of Eros, of his divinity, of his antiquity, of his power, of his

---

*H. Martin remarks that the dialogue does not explicitly differentiate between heterosexual love and marriage. Comparing the *Dialogue on Love* and the *Marriage Precepts*, L. Goessler calls attention to the connection, emphasized by Plutarch, between *gamos* and *eros*, and to what is new about this in the traditional question of marriage.[1]

193

good works, of the force by which he elevates and attracts souls. In this way Plutarch will have contributed to the worship of the god who is being celebrated throughout the festive city. Eros and Gamos, the strength of love and the marriage bond in their mutual relations: such is the theme of the dialogue. The purpose of the religious rites that serve as its background is clear: that the power of Eros, invoked for the protection of the couple, may triumph over the misunderstanding of families; that he may appease dissensions between friends and ensure the happiness of conjugal lives. The theoretical aim of the debate is in harmony with this devotional practice. It will provide the rational justification for the latter: to show that the conjugal relationship, more than any other, is capable of accommodating the force of love, and that, among humans, love has its privileged place in the couple.

The pretext for the conversation and the external peripeteia that give rise to its successive developments are recounted in a solemn and ironic fashion. A "pathetic" situation has arisen, which "merely wants a chorus to sympathize and lacks a stage, for no other element of drama is wanting." In reality, what has transpired is a little comic episode. Bacchon, the desirable adolescent—he is handsome and virtuous—is pursued by an *erastes,* but also by a widow, who is much older than he. She had been commissioned to find a suitable wife for him, but she didn't find anyone better than herself. She tries to seduce the boy, chases after him, abducts him, already organizes the wedding under the nose of his male lover, who is furious, then resigned. The dialogue begins when the plans of the formidable widow are already known, but before she has carried out her *coup de force.* The boy is therefore still torn between the two suitors. He doesn't know which path to choose. As he has entrusted the decision to his elders, the latter will deliberate on the matter. The debate thus takes place between the advocates of the love of boys, Protogenes and Pisias, and two advocates of the love of women, Anthemion and Daphnaeus. It unfolds in front of Plutarch, who soon abandons the role of witness, takes charge of the discussion, and leads it in the direction of a general theory of love. The first champions of the two loves having disappeared by then, his interlocutors and adversaries will be Pemptides and especially Zeuxippus, who have a materialistic conception of marriage and an aggressively critical idea which Plutarch will need to answer.

Here we touch on one of the notable features of the dialogue. It starts from the traditional schema—be it in the mythical figures or in the moral casuistry—of the crossroads. There are two paths: Which does one choose, that of love for boys or that of love for women? Now, in actual fact the debate does not exactly raise this problem. Whereas in the Platonic texts the noble, masculine Eros is contrasted with the facile, multiple, physical, "pandemian" Eros (which, clearly, is the love that can be practiced with boys and with girls outside marriage), in Plutarch the choice is between boys on the one hand and marriage on the other, as if it were in the latter that the relationship with women is fulfilled.

Another distinctive element in Plutarch's dialogue is the personage of the woman who is pursuing the boy. All the traits that characterize her are significant. She is older than the boy, while being still young; she is richer than he; she has a more important social status; her past life has already given her experience.[4] This kind of situation was not unusual in Greece —both because of the scarcity of women and because of the strategy of marriages. But people nevertheless felt a certain reticence with regard to this kind of union. The younger and poorer husband was in a somewhat awkward position with respect to his wife, seeing that the preeminence of the husband was statutory in marital relations. Moreover, one finds numerous remarks concerning these drawbacks. Plutarch, in the *Life of Solon,* advises the magistrate who discovers a young man zealously attending an old woman, "like a cock-partridge in her service," to have him removed to the house of a young woman in need of a husband.[5] Nor will Pisias fail to recall these habitual fears to the advocates of Bacchon's marriage.[6] Without being totally exceptional, this was a paradoxical and dangerous union, where the interests of one party and the appetites of the other were too salient for it to hold the promise of a happy and reasonable existence. What Bacchon sees himself being offered—in opposition to pederastic love—is therefore not the best but the least good of all possible marriages. The value of the discussion that will justify it and of the outcome that will see it triumph will be only increased by this fact.

But still another paradoxical trait should be noted. Ismenodora, the passionate widow, is a woman full of good qualities: she is virtuous, she leads a "life of decorum." She commands the respect of public opinion. There has never been "a word of censure" concerning her. Never "did any hint of wrongdoing leave a stain on her house."[7] Yet she has shamelessly set out in pursuit of the boy. He had been entrusted to her so that she might promote his marriage; but after hearing so many good things said about him, after seeing his beauty and his qualities with her own eyes, she loves him in turn. What is more, she chases after him. Being unable to accompany him to the gymnasium, she watches for him when he returns. And with the collusion of some friends, she "kidnaps" him. We know that such "kidnappings"—in part "real," in part arranged also—were a frequent element if not in reality itself, at least, certainly, in pederastic literature. Many mythical and historical narratives revolve around one of these episodes of violence. The *Love Stories* attributed to Plutarch and those *Lectures* of Maximus of Tyre that are devoted to Socratic love make reference to them.[8] If a person as virtuous as Ismenodora gives way to such an assault, this is because she has been possessed by "some divine impulse, more powerful than human reason." Now all these traits (the age difference, the acknowledged merit, the interest taken in the moral qualities and good reputation of the beloved, the initiative of the pursuit, the violence of divine inspiration) are easily recognizable. They are those which characterize the lover of boys in the traditional pederastic model. Ismenodora, in Plutarch's description, is exactly in the position of the *erastes*. So that, in essence, Bacchon does not really have to choose between two fundamentally different forms of love—the love that can develop between a gifted young man and an older man who is interested in the beauty of his friend, and the love that can be established between a husband and a wife with a view to managing an estate and rearing children—but between two forms of the same love, the only difference being that in one case it is love of a man and in the other, love of a woman. Plutarch makes it quite clear, in one of his statements in favor of the marriage with Ismenodora, that the same type of relationship is involved. No one, he says, can do without authority, or be perfect by himself; "the ephebe is ruled by the gymnasiarch, the young man by the erastes, the adult by the law and by the strategus. . . . Since this is so, what is there dreadful about a sensible older woman piloting the life of her young husband? She will be useful because of her superior understanding [*tōi phronein mallon*]; she will be sweet and affectionate [*tōi philein*] because she loves him."[9]

One sees two movements running beneath Plutarch's dialogue. First, there is the shift resulting from the discussion itself; the question of the choice the beloved must make between his two lovers surreptitiously becomes the question of love in its two possible forms—for boys and for girls. And second, the shift, made possible by the paradoxical situation of the intrigue, which confers on the relationship with a woman the same ethical potential as the relationship with a man. The objective of the entire debate is clearly visible in the little drama that underlies the vicissitudes of the dialogue: what is wanted is to form a conception of a single love. This conception will not reject the characteristic values of pederastic love. Instead, it will include them in a broader, more complete form, which ultimately only the relationship with women, and more precisely with the wife, will be able to put into practice.

One is tempted to see in this dialogue by Plutarch one of the numerous rhetorical contests that staged an encounter, with a winner declared at the end, between the love of women and

the love of boys. Viewed in this way, it can pass for one of
the most fervent pleas in favor of conjugal affection and the
pleasures of marriage. It is legitimate to place it alongside the
Stoic treatises on marriage. It has many themes and formulations in common with them. But we are dealing, in this text,
with something quite different from an argumentation in favor
of marriage and against pederasty. We can see in it the first
shape of an important change in the old erotics. This transformation can be summed up briefly: whereas scarcely any dis-
continuity, impassable boundary, or important difference of
values was recognized in the practice of the *aphrodisia*, in
return the elaboration of the erotics was clearly dualistic. This
dualism was, moreover, double and, in itself, rather complex.
On the one hand, common love (that love in which sensual
acts are preponderant) was opposed to noble, pure, elevated,
heavenly love (in which the presence of these same acts are,
if not disallowed, at least veiled). On the other hand, the
specificity of the love for boys was stressed, the aspiration,
form, goals, and effects of which were supposed—at least
provided one acted in conformity with its true nature—to be
different from those found in the other loves. Furthermore,
these two dualisms tended to overlap, since it was held that
"true" love for boys could only be a pure love, a love free of
the vulgar pursuit of the *aphrodisia* (which actuates the desire
for women or the corrupt appetite for boys). A continuous
domain of the *aphrodisia*, and an erotics with a binary structure: it is this configuration that begins to be reversed here.
Plutarch's *Dialogue* may bear witness to a movement that will
not actually be completed until much later, when an absolutely unitary conception of love will be constructed, while the
practice of pleasure will be divided by a strict boundary: the
one that separates the conjoinings of one sex with the other
and relations within the same sex. It is roughly this order of
things which is still ours today, solidified as it is by a unitary
conception of sexuality, which enables one to delimit strictly
the dimorphism of relations and the differential structure of
desire.

In Plutarch's *Dialogue,* one sees the effort to constitute a unitary erotics, very clearly organized on the model of the man-woman, and even husband-wife, relationship. In comparison with this single love (it is supposed to be the same, whether it is directed to women or to boys), the pederastic attachment will in fact be disqualified, but without a rigid line of demarcation being drawn, as it will be later, between "homo-" and "heterosexual" acts. The whole burden of the text bears on this unification of erotics. The latter is carried out through a critical discussion (that of "dualism"), through the working out of a unitary theory (that of love), and through the bringing into play of a fundamental concept (that of *charis,* grace).

1. The exposition and criticism of the traditional "dualism" can be quickly summarized. This dualism is of course defended by the partisans of the love of boys. Moreover, Protogenes and Pisias will very soon leave the stage—as soon as one learns of Bacchon's abduction. They were there long enough to celebrate differential erotics one last time. According to this erotics, the love of boys is both different from the attraction to women and superior to it, for two reasons: one has to do with their respective positions relative to nature, and the other concerns the role played, in each of them, by pleasure.

The advocates of the love of boys do refer briefly to the frequent argument that contrasts everything that is artificial about women (adornments and perfumes for some; razors, philters, and makeup for the most shameless) with the naturalness of the boys one sees at the palestrae.[10] But their main argument against love for women is that it is nothing more than a natural inclination. In reality, it is nature, says Protogenes, that has placed an appetite *(orexis)* in us that draws the two sexes to each other. Indeed, it was necessary that we be induced to procreate, just as we are prompted to feed ourselves. But it is clear that this same type of appetite is found in flies for milk and in bees for honey. It will be found, too,

in cooks for their fowls and their calves. Protogenes would not
think to give the name "Love" to all these appetites.[11] The
naturalness of the attraction to the other sex obviously does
not condemn the indispensable practice that brings men into
union with women. But it restricts the value of this practice
to that of a behavior found everywhere in the animal world,
a behavior whose reason for being is basic necessity. The
natural character of relations with women is put forward by
Protogenes in order to underscore its defectiveness and to
show how it differs from a love of boys, which scorns such
necessities and aims much higher. Actually he does not explain what he understands by this love that is beyond nature.
It is Plutarch who will take up these Platonic themes, but only
to integrate them, against the apologists of boys, into a unitary
conception of love.

The other difference is marked by the role of pleasure. The
fondness for women cannot be detached from pleasure. The
love for boys, on the contrary, does not truly accord with its
own essence unless it frees itself of pleasure. The argumentation used by Protogenes and Pisias in support of this principle
is Stoic, if anything. They observe that intercourse with
women was indeed designed by nature for the conservation of
the species. But things were arranged in such a way that
pleasure is associated with this act. For this reason, the appetite and the impulse *(orexis, hormē)* that induce us to perform
it are always apt to become violent and unrestrained; in this
case, they are transformed into desire *(epithumia)*. Thus we
are led in two ways toward that natural object which a woman
constitutes: by the appetite, a natural movement, which looks
to the survival of the generations as its reasonable goal and
uses pleasure as a means; and by desire, a violent movement,
with no internal regulation, which has "pleasure and enjoyment as its goal."[12] It is clear that neither the one nor the other
can be love in its true form: not the first, because it is common
to all the animals; not the second, because it exceeds reasonable limits and attaches the soul to sensual pleasures.

It is only logical, then, to rule out the very possibility of

Eros in relations between men and women. "True love has nothing to do with the women's quarters," says Protogenes in a turn of phrase that is given two meanings by the adherents of boys: first, the nature of desire, which attaches a man to a woman "by their sexual parts," like a dog to his female, excludes love; second, it would not be proper for a sober-minded and chaste woman to feel "love" for her husband and to accept "being loved" by him *(eran, erastai).* [13] Hence there is only one true love, the love of boys, because unworthy pleasures are absent from it and because it necessarily implies a friendship that is indissociable from virtue. If, moreover, the *erastes* finds that his love does not give rise to friendship and virtue in the other, then he abjures his attention and his fidelity. [14]

To this traditional line of argument, there will be an expected reply: Daphnaeus' denunciation of pederastic hypocrisy. As if a tearful Achilles had not evoked the thighs of Patroclus, as if Solon, apropos of boys in the flower of their youth, had not praised "the sweetness of their thighs and their lips," the fancier of boys likes to pose as a philosopher and a sage. But undoubtedly he waits only for an opportunity. At night when all is quiet, "sweet is the harvest when the guard is away." One sees the dilemma: either the *aphrodisia* are incompatible with friendship and love, and in this case the lovers of boys who enjoy in secret the bodies they desire have fallen from the heights of love; or one admits that sensual pleasures have a place in friendship and love, and so there is no reason to exclude from the latter relationships with women. But Daphnaeus does not stop there. He also recalls the other great disjunction, which was often cited as an objection to the conduct of lovers and to the pleasure they tried to take: if the *eromenos* is virtuous, one cannot obtain this pleasure except by subjecting him to violence; and if he consents, one has to recognize that one is consorting with an effeminate. [15] Hence the primary model of all love is not to be sought in the fondness for boys. The latter should be thought of, rather, as "one come late and untimely to the world, illegitimate and ill-favored, [who] drives out the legitimate and older love"; unless, as Daphnaeus suggests, the fondness for boys and the fondness for women are basically one and the same thing.[16]

But the real working out of the general theory of love is done after the departure of the first adversaries and outside their presence—as if it were necessary, in order to reach the main object of the debate, to take leave of this familiar confrontation. Up to this point, remarks Pemptides, the debate has focused on personal questions; it needs to be directed toward general themes.

2. The central part of the dialogue consists of a eulogy of Love in the traditional manner of praising a god; his truly divine nature is thereby established. Here Plutarch opposes the Epicurean-inspired argument outlined by Pemptides, according to which the gods are nothing more than our passions; and he shows that the Love that takes possession of us is the effect of a necessarily divine power. This power is compared to that of the other gods, an important passage because it shows how Eros is a necessary complement of Aphrodite. Without him, the work of Aphrodite would be nothing more than the pleasure of the senses and could be bought for a drachma. Contrary to what people say, he is also stronger and more courageous than Ares: it is out of mutual love that lovers, in battle, throw themselves on the enemy, fighting boldly to their death rather than fleeing in shame. Plutarch describes his action on men's souls, which he renders "generous, compassionate, and liberal, and which he pervades through and through, as in a divine possession." Finally, the eulogy ends with a reference to Egyptian myths and an exposition of the Platonic theory.

The remarkable thing about this eulogy is that all the elements stem from the traditional erotics of pederasty. Most of the cases are borrowed from the love of boys or from the example of Sappho (Alcestis and Admetus form almost the only exception). And in fact it is as the god of boy love that Eros appears in the praises addressed to him. Yet these praises are sung by Plutarch, who calls himself at the same time "a

chorist of feminine love." He intends to illustrate the general
proposition advanced by Daphnaeus: "if we have regard for
the truth, the liking for boys and the liking for women originate in one and the same Love."[17]

This seems to be the essential business of the dialogue. The
little drama of the "pederastic" kidnapping of Bacchon by
Ismenodora merely serves as its immediate context and illus-
tration. Everything that the erotics of boys was able to claim
as properly belonging to that form of love (in opposition to the
false love for women) will be reutilized here, without anything
from the great pederastic tradition being overlooked—on the
contrary. But it will be used as a general form capable of
subsuming both loves. In particular, it will be applied not only
to the fondness for women, but to the conjugal relationship
itself.

After a speech by Zeuxippus—which the manuscripts have
not passed down to us and which is supposed to have criticized
conjugal love, not on behalf of pederasty, but in Epicurean
terms—Plutarch speaks again in order to establish three essential points. First, he observes that if Love is indeed what
he is said to be, he will make his presence, his power, and his
actions felt in relations between the two sexes as well as in
relations with boys. Let us assume for a moment that the
Epicurean argument is correct: the images which emanate
from the loved body, which are conveyed to the eyes of the one
who loves, which enter into his body, fill it with emotion and
agitate it to the point where sperm is formed—there is no
reason why this mechanism should be set in motion by boys
and not by women.[18] On the other hand, suppose that we
accept the Platonic argument toward which Plutarch inclines:
if "through the freshness and grace of a body" one perceives
the beauty of a soul, and the latter, recalling the heavenly
spectacle, gives wings to our soul, why would the difference
between the sexes matter here, where it is only a question of
"beauty" and "natural excellence"?[19] Plutarch shows that this
element of virtue, *aretē,* by which the traditional erotics of
boys marked one of its important differences from the fond-

ness for women, transcends any difference of sex: "They say that beauty is the flower of virtue; yet it would be absurd to deny that the female produces that flower or gives it a presentation of a natural bent for virtue . . . all these characteristics belong to both sexes alike."[20]

As for the friendship that the pederasts wish to reserve exclusively for the love of boys, Plutarch shows that it can also characterize the relationship of a man with a woman, or at least with his wife (this specification is obviously crucial). It is conjugality and it alone that engenders the form of friendship in the relationship between the sexes. Plutarch evokes this conjugality briefly here, in a few strokes reminiscent of the *Marriage Precepts*. It involves sharing a common life (Plutarch plays on the words *stergein* and *stegein*, "to shelter," "to keep at home"); it calls for mutual kindness *(eunoia);* it implies perfect community and a oneness of souls in separate bodies, a unity so strong that the spouses "no longer wish to be separate entities, or believe that that are so"[21]; lastly, it requires reciprocal moderation, a *sophrosyne* that abjures any other liaison. It is concerning this last point that the transposition of the theory of Eros to the practice of married life is most interesting, for it suggests an idea of the high value of marriage very different from that found in the Stoics. As a matter of fact, against the moderation that "comes from without," which is nothing but obedience to laws and is imposed by shame and fear, Plutarch opposes the moderation that is the effect of Eros: it is Eros in fact, when he inflames the two spouses for one another, who teaches "self-control, decorum, and mutual trust." Into the amorous soul of the husband and the wife, he introduces "modesty, silence, calm"; he bestows "a reserved manner" on them and makes them "attentive to a single being." It is easy to recognize in this sketch the characteristics of the pederastic Eros, the bringer of virtue and measure to the souls of lovers, the source, in the more perfect beings like Socrates, of that self-restraint which made him hold his silence and keep control of his desires in the presence of those he loved. Plutarch transposes to the married couple the traits that had long been reserved for the *philia* of lovers of the same sex.

However, the elaboration of a general theory of love, equally valid for the relationship with women and the relationship with boys, is skewed: Plutarch has not gone, as Anthemion asked him to do and as he claimed to be doing, from a particular love to a more general love. He has borrowed from the erotics of boys its fundamental and traditional features in order to demonstrate that they can be applied, not to all forms of love, but to the conjugal relationship alone.

3. Such is in fact the ultimate goal of the dialogue: to show that this single chain of love, which can find its perfect realization in marriage, cannot be accommodated, at least not in its complete form, in the relationship with boys. While this relationship, with its traditional values, has been able to serve as a support and model for the general conception of love, it finds itself, in the last analysis, invalidated and fallen into disfavor: an imperfect love when one compares it with that of husband and wife.

Where does Plutarch have this imperfection reside? So long as one had a dualistic erotics that distinguished true love (true because it was pure) from false, delusive love (false because it was physical), the absence of the *aphrodisia* was not merely possible, it was necessary if this was to be made the love relation par excellence. But the elaboration of a general erotics, linking Eros and Aphrodite closely together, changes the terms of the problem. The elision of the *aphrodisia,* ceasing to be a precondition, becomes an obstacle. Plutarch says this explicitly: if Aphrodite without Eros offers only a momentary pleasure that can be purchased for a few drachmas, Eros without Aphrodite, when physical pleasure is lacking, is no less imperfect. A love without Aphrodite is "like drunkenness without wine, brought on by a brew of figs and barley. No fruit [*akarpon*], no fulfillment [*ateles*] comes of the passion; it is cloying and quickly wearied of."[22]

Now, can the love of a boy find a place for the *aphrodisia*?

We know the argument.* Either sexual relations will be imposed through violence and the individual who undergoes them will feel only anger, hatred, and desire for revenge. Or they will be consented to by an individual who, because of his "softness," his "femininity," "enjoys being passive" *(hēdomenos tōi paschein),* which is a "shameful," "unnatural" thing, and which reduces him to the lowest condition.[24] Plutarch has gone back to the "dilemma of the *eromenos*": compelled, he feels hatred, and consenting, he becomes an object of contempt. The traditional adversaries of pederasty let it go at that. But Plutarch's analysis goes further, attempting to define what is lacking in the love of boys, what prevents it from being, like conjugal love, a harmonious mixture of Eros and Aphrodite, in which the bond between souls is associated with physical pleasure. Plutarch designates this deficiency with one word: the love of boys is *acharistos.*

The word *charis,* which appears several times in the course of the dialogue, seems to be one of the keys to Plutarch's reflection. It is introduced with a good deal of solemnity at the beginning of the text, before the formulation of the great theory of a single love. Daphnaeus is the first to use it, as an "overpowering" argument in favor of his thesis: the love of women is special, he says, in that through the practice of such sexual relations as nature has established, it can lead to friendship *(eis philian)* by way of *charis.* [25] And Daphnaeus attaches so much importance to this term that he immediately undertakes to define it and to give it a few great poetic sponsors: *charis* is the consent that a woman willingly grants to a man, a consent that can appear only with nubility, according to Sappho, and the absence of which can result, according to Pindar, in ungraceful births; thus Hephaestus was born from Hera *"aneu chariton."*[26] The role that is assigned to this acquiescence is clear: to integrate sexual relations, with their two naturally defined poles of activity and passivity, into recipro-

*Here Plutarch repeats the argument put forward by Daphnaeus.[21]

cal relations of kindness and to bring physical pleasure into friendship.

After this preliminary presentation, and once the unitary doctrine of love is established, the question of *charis* becomes preponderant at the end of the dialogue. It will serve as a discriminant between the love of women and the love of boys, only the former being able to engender that complete form in which are joined, owing to the gentleness of consent, the pleasure of Aphrodite and the virtue of friendship. Now Plutarch does not conceive of this junction simply as a tolerance that could concede, in the conjugal relationship, a more or less utilitarian place (e.g., for procreation) to sexual acts. On the contrary, he makes the latter the starting point of the whole relation of affection that should animate the relationship. Physical pleasure, precisely insofar as the gentleness of consent excludes everything in the way of violence, deceit, or base compliance, can be at the very origin of the affectionate reciprocities that marriage requires: "Physical union with a lawful wife is the beginning of friendship, a sharing, as it were, in great mysteries." Sensual pleasure is a small matter (this is even a traditional expression among the enemies of physical pleasure); but, Plutarch immediately adds, "it is like the seed out of which mutual respect [*timē*], kindness [*charis*], affection [*agapēsis*], and loyalty [*pistis*] daily grow between husband and wife."[27]

To this fundamental role and this germinative function of physical pleasure, Plutarch gives a solemn historical sanction. He finds it in the legislation by Solon, which prescribed that husbands must have intercourse with their wives "not less than three times a month." In the *Life of Solon,* he also referred to this law, pointing out that it applied only to the marriage of heiress girls. The reason for it was the need for offspring to whom one could leave the estate. But, Plutarch added, this was not the only reason: for this regular intercourse, even when "it does not result in children," "is a mark of esteem and affection which a man should pay to a chaste wife; it always removes the many annoyances which develop, and prevents their being altogether estranged by their differences."[28] To this role of sexual intercourse as an inducement to regular intimacy and a guarantee of good understanding, Plutarch, in the *Dialogue on Love,* lends an even more solemn formulation. He makes it a way to put new life into the conjugal relationship, similar to the way in which one renews an agreement: "As cities renew their mutual agreements from time to time, just so he [Solon] must have wished this to be a renewal of marriage and with such an act of tenderness to wipe out the complaints that accumulate in everyday living."[29] Sexual pleasure is therefore at the heart of the matrimonial relation as a source and a token of the relationship of love and friendship. It founds the relationship, or in any case, reaffirms it as a covenant of existence. And if Plutarch acknowledges that the sexual relations at the beginning of marriage may be "wounding" to the wife, he also explains how this very "bite" is necessary for the formation of a vital, solid, and durable conjugal unity. He resorts to three metaphors: that of a plant that is grafted and must be well incised if it is to form, with the graft, a tree that will bear the desired fruit; that of a child or young man in whom one must inculcate, not without pain for him, the rudiments of a knowledge he will later turn to advantage and profit; that, lastly, of one liquid that is poured into another—after a period of effervescence and agitation, a mixture is produced, resulting in that *di' holōn krasis* to which the *Marriage Precepts* also made reference,[30] and together they form a new liquid whose two components can no longer be separated. A certain suffering, agitation, and disorder are inevitable at the beginning of conjugal relations; but this is the necessary condition for a new, stable unity to be formed.

And Plutarch thus arrives at the basic formulation: "To love is a greater boon than to be loved."[31] The statement is important given that in every love relation, the traditional erotics laid strong emphasis on the polarity of the lover and the beloved and on the necessary dissymmetry between them. Here it is the double activity of loving, by the husband and the wife, that forms the essential element. And for reasons that are easily determined. This double activity of loving is a source of reciprocity. It is because each of the two spouses loves the other that they consent to receive the tokens of the other's love, that they like to be loved. The activity therefore is a source of faithfulness as well, since each of the two can take the love they feel for the other as a guide for their conduct and a reason for limiting their desires. "Love rescues us from all errors that wreck or impair wedlock."[32] This union owes its value and its stability to the schema of a double love in which each partner is, from the standpoint of Eros, always an active subject. Owing to this reciprocity in the act of loving, sexual relations can have their place in the form of mutual affection and consent. In terms of this relational model, pederasty can only be inadequate in view of the strongly marked difference between the *erastes* and the *eromenos,* the dilemma of passivity, and the necessary fragility that is due to the age factor. It lacks the double and symmetrical activity of loving, hence it lacks the internal regulation and the stability of the couple. It is wanting in that "grace" which makes it possible for the *aphrodisia* to be combined with friendship in order to constitute the complete and perfect form of Eros. Pederasty, Plutarch might say, is a love that lacks "grace."

In sum, Plutarch's text testifies to the formation of an erotics that, on certain essential points, differs from the erotics Greek civilization had known and developed. It is not entirely different, since, as the great central passage devoted to the eulogy of Eros shows, the traditional notions continue to play an essential role. But this Platonizing erotics is used by Plutarch to produce effects different from those with which it was usually associated. For a long time it had served to mark the existence of two distinct and antithetical loves (the first one common, oriented toward the *aphrodisia;* the second one elevated, spiritual, oriented toward the care of souls), but also to reestablish between them a kind of unity since only the second was considered genuine, the other being only its earthly shadow and simulacrum. Plutarch brings these same Platonic notions into play in an erotics that seeks to form a single Eros capable of accounting for the love of women and the love of boys, and to integrate the *aphrodisia* into it. But in the interests of such a unity, this erotics ultimately excludes the love of boys, for it lacks *charis*. Starting from a dualistic erotics traversed by the question of truth and semblance, and intended essentially to provide a rational foundation for the love of boys, but at the cost of an elision of the *aphrodisia,* one sees, in Plutarch, a new stylistics of love being formed. It is monistic in that it includes the *aphrodisia,* but it makes this inclusion a criterion allowing it to keep only conjugal love and to exclude relations with boys because of the deficiency that characterizes them. There can no longer be a place for them in this great unitary and integrative chain in which love is revitalized by the reciprocity of pleasure.

CHAPTER TWO

PSEUDO-LUCIAN

The *Affairs of the Heart,* attributed to Lucian, is manifestly a later text.* It is presented in the quite customary form of interlocking dialogues. Theomnestus, whose loves—for women or for boys—reappear more numerous than the heads of Hydra, almost before they have ended, complains of Aphrodite. From the time when as a child he became an ephebe, the wrath of the goddess has been pursuing him. And yet, he is not a child of the Sun, nor does he have the boorish contempt of Hippolytus. He feels equally inclined toward both kinds of love, without managing to decide which of the two is more deserving of his attention. He asks Lycinus—who is not affected by either of these two passions—to serve as an impartial judge and to tell him which is the better choice. Fortunately, Lycinus has preserved, as if engraved in his memory, the dialogue of two men on this very subject. One of them loved only boys, considering the female Aphrodite to be only "an abyss." The other was passionately fond of women. So he will relate their discussion. But Theomnestus should make no mistake—he was able, for his part, to pose the question in jest; Charicles and Callicratidas, whose views are about to be heard, spoke very seriously indeed.

Needless to say, this last piece of information is not to be taken at face value. The two adversaries are certainly serious,

*M. D. MacLeod places it at the beginning of the fourth century; F. Buffière thinks it is from the second century.[1]

211

but Pseudo-Lucian is being ironic when he writes the emphatic and weighty demonstrations he attributes to them. There is an element of pastiche in these pieces of bravura. Taken together, they constitute the typical discourse of the Advocate of Women and the Devotee of Boys. Traditional arguments, obligatory quotations, references to great philosophical ideas, rhetorical flourishes—the author smiles in reporting the speeches of these imperturbable disputants. And, from this point of view, it should be noted that the pederastic discourse is much more ponderous, pretentious, and "baroque" than the one spoken in favor of women, which is plainer, more Stoicizing. The final irony—Theomnestus will observe that what it all comes down to is just a matter of kisses, caresses, and hands that wander beneath tunics—will be mainly at the expense of the eulogy of the love of boys. But this very irony indicates the seriousness of the problem that is raised. And whatever enjoyment Pseudo-Lucian may have had in sketching the "theoretical-discursive" portrait of these two devotees—their rhetorical profile, in rather heavy strokes —one can see in it a contemporary example, displaying the most prominent features, of that "contest of loves" which had such a long career in Hellenic culture.

There is something surprising at the beginning of the dialogue reported by Lycinus in order to enlighten his friend who is undecided between the two loves: this dialogue, which will be concluded (not without some ambiguity) in favor of the love of boys, is not placed under the sign of Eros, who is regarded as the guardian of this form of attachment, but under that of Aphrodite. The scene that Lycinus is supposed to recall in its smallest details unfolds at Cnidus, near the temple of the goddess, where the famous statue sculpted by Praxiteles stands. This does not, however, prevent the advocate of boys from invoking Eros, as tradition demands, in the course of the dialogue: Eros, "the heavenly spirit," "hierophant of the mysteries of Love." As for the one who speaks for female pleasures, it is naturally to Aphrodite that he will appeal for support. The fact that the goddess of Cnidus may be said to preside over this debate where she is made to vie with Eros, her traditional partner-adversary, is easily explained. The reason is that the problem of physical pleasure traverses the entire dialogue. This is what the perplexity expressed by Theomnestus, equally susceptible to the charm of girls and the beauty of boys, is about; it is a question of the *aphrodisia*. It is physical pleasure that will have the last word and dismiss the prudish speeches with a peal of laughter. And it is physical pleasure that serves as a pretext for the debate between Charicles and Callicratidas—in the form of a meaningful anecdote: a young man, enamored of the marble by Praxiteles, had let himself be locked in the temple at night, and he had sullied the statue, but as if it had been a boy.[2] The telling of this story —a very traditional one—occasions the debate. Since the sacrilegious act was addressed to Aphrodite, was it an homage to the goddess who presides over female pleasures? But given the form in which it was carried out, was it not a testimonial against that particular Aphrodite? An ambiguous act. Should this impious homage, this profanatory reverence, be accounted to the love of women, or of boys?

And the question that runs through the whole dialogue, even if it appears forgotten in the most ethereal statements, will be this: What place, what form, should be given to sexual pleasure in the two loves? The answer to this question will serve as a discriminant, offering to the love of boys, in the heaven of philosophy, a moment's victory, which the irony of reality will soon compromise.

The debate has a rigid composition. Each of the two orators speaks in turn, and pleads, in a continuous discourse, the cause of the love he prefers. A silent witness (Lycinus) will judge the contest and determine the winner. Although the "boy-favoring" discourse of Callicratidas is longer and more ornate than that of Charicles, the two speeches have the same structure. The arguments are arranged in the same order and in such a way that one corresponds exactly to the other. Both discourses comprise two parts. The first replies to the question: What of the nature of the love being considered, what of its origin and its place in the natural order? The second replies to the question: What of the pleasure that one enjoys in this love, or in the other? What should its form be, and what value might it have? Rather than follow each of the two expositions in its continuity, we shall examine these two questions in turn in order to see how the partisan of the love of women and the advocate of the love of boys reply to them, each in his own way.

1. The "pro-women" discourse of Charicles is based on a conception of the world that is doubtless Stoic in tone.[3]* Nature is defined as the power that, by blending the elements, brought life to everything by giving it a soul. It was she as well, Charicles continues, repeating a familiar lesson in well-known words, who provided for the succession of the generations.[5] Knowing very well that living beings were made "from perishable matter," and since the time allotted to each being was brief, she contrived *(emēchanēsato)* things in such a way that the death of one would be the birth of another. Thus, through the process of succession, we can live forever. To accomplish this, she also contrived the division of the sexes, one being designed to ejaculate semen, the other to receive it. And she imbued each with an appetite *(pothos)* for the other. From the intercourse of these two sexes can come the succession of the generations, but never from the intercourse between two individuals of the same sex. In this way Charicles anchors the proper nature of each sex, and the pleasure that befits each, firmly in the order of the universe, where death, generation, and eternity are interconnected. The "female" must not become unnaturally male, nor "the male be unbecomingly soft." By defying this determination, one not only transgresses the proper attributes of the individual, one interferes with the concatenation of universal necessity.

The second criterion of naturalness used in Charicles' discourse is the state of mankind at its beginnings.[6] A closeness

*In his study on Hierocles, K. Praechter emphasizes the Stoic character of the passage. R. Bloch notes the presence of neo-Pythagorean themes in it.[4]

to the gods through virtue, a desire to behave heroically, marriage at a suitable age, and a noble progeny: these were the four traits that characterized that lofty existence and ensured its accord with nature. Then came the fall, which was gradual. It seems that Charicles distinguishes, as stages in this degeneration, the time when, pleasure leading humans to the depths, people sought "strange and extraordinary paths to enjoyment" (Should this be taken to mean nonprocreative forms of sexual relations or pleasures alien to marriage?), then the time when they came to "transgress the laws of Nature herself," a bold development whose basic form—the only one in any case which is mentioned in the text—consists in treating a man like a woman. Now, in order for an act so alien to Nature to be possible, it was necessary that what enables one to do violence and to deceive—tyrannical power and the art of persuasion— be brought into relations between men.

Charicles finds the third mark of naturalness in the animal world[7]—"the laws of nature" rule over them without restriction or division: neither lions, nor bulls, nor rams, nor boars, nor wolves, nor fish seek out their own sex. For them, "the decisions of Providence are unchangeable." To this chaste animality, Pseudo-Lucian's orator opposes the "perverse bestiality" of men, which makes them lower than other creatures whereas they were meant to be superior to the highest of them. Several significant terms are employed in Charicles' speech to characterize this "bestiality" on the part of men: passion, but also "strange infection," "blind insensibility" *(anaisthēsia),* inability to hit the mark, so that they neglect what should be pursued and pursue what should be left alone. In contrast to the conduct of the animals, who obey the law and aim for the goal that is assigned to them, men who have sex with men evince all the signs traditionally ascribed to the passional state: uncontrolled violence, a sickly condition, blindness to the reality of things, an incapacity for attaining the goals set for human nature.

In sum, the love of boys is placed in turn on the three axes of nature, as the general order of the world, the original state of mankind, and a behavior that is reasonably adapted to natural ends. It disturbs the orderly progression of things; it gives rise to violent and deceitful conduct. Finally, it is pernicious from the standpoint of human objectives. Cosmologically, "politically," and morally, this type of relation transgresses nature.

In the part of his discourse that replies to these assertions, Callicratidas does not so much advance arguments that refute his adversary, as put forward a different conception of the world, the human race, its history, and the noblest ties that can connect men to each other. To the idea of nature as a provident "mechanic" who, by means of sex, arranged for procreation and the succession of generations so as to give the human race an eternity that individuals are denied, he opposes the vision of a world formed out of chaos. It was the demiurgic Eros who conquered this primeval disorder by creating all things that have a soul and all that do not, by instilling the principle of harmony in the body of men, and by attaching them to one another through "the holy sentiment of friendship." Charicles saw, in relations between men and woman, an artful Nature who established temporal succession in order to circumvent death. Callicratidas recognizes, in the love of boys, the strength of the bond that, by attaching and combining, triumphs over chaos.[8]

From this perspective, the history of the world should not be read as an early disregard for the laws of nature and a plunge into "the depths of pleasure," but rather as a gradual release from the primary necessities.[9] In the beginning, man was pressed by needs. The arts and skills (technai and epistēmai) made it possible for him to escape from these pressures and to provide for himself in a better fashion. People learned to weave garments and build houses. Now, as the weaver's art is to the use of animal skins, and as the builder's art is to caves for shelter, the love of boys is to intercourse with women. The latter, in early times, was necessary in order that the race might not disappear. The love of boys, on the other hand, came into existence very late, not, as Charicles maintained, because there was a degeneration, but because, on the contrary, there was an elevation toward more curiosity and knowledge. Indeed, when men, after having learned so many useful skills, began to "leave nothing unexplored," philosophy appeared and with it pederasty. Pseudo-Lucian's orator does not really explain this twin birth, but his speech contains enough familiar references so that it would have been readily understandable to any reader. It rests implicitly on the opposition between the imparting of life through intercourse with the other sex and the imparting of "techniques" and "knowledges" through teaching, learning, and the relationship of disciple with master. When, emerging from the particular arts, philosophy began to inquire concerning all things, it found, as a means of transmitting the wisdom it obtains, the love of boys —which is also the love of noble souls, capable of virtue. One understands, then, how Callicratidas can reply with laughter to the animal lesson presented by his adversary:[10] What exactly is proved by the fact that lions do not love the males of their species, and that he-bears are not enamored of he-bears? Not that men have corrupted a nature that remains intact among the animals, but that animals do not know what it means to "philosophize," and they are ignorant of the beauty that friendship can produce.

The arguments of Callicratidas are evidently no more original than those of Charicles. Commonplaces of a vulgarized Stoicism, on the one hand, and a mixture of Platonic and Epicurean elements on the other?* No doubt. One cannot help but recognize, in this comparison of the two loves, an excuse for oratorical variations on the texture of traditional arguments. The banality (nicely embellished in places) of Charicles' and Callicratidas' explanations shows rather clearly that they were meant to function as philosophical escutcheons: the enthusiast of boys, on the Platonizing side, under the colors of Eros; and the defender of women, on the Stoic side, under

---

*K. Praechter singles out the Epicurean aspects of Callicratidas' speech, but R. Bloch observes that the cosmogony that opens the discourse is not specifically Epicurean. Moreover, there are clear references to Plato (e.g., in paragraph 49).[11]

the exacting sign of Nature. Which does not mean, obviously, that the Stoics condemned a pederasty that Platonism justified while rejecting marriage. We know that, from the viewpoint of doctrines, this is not the way things were—or in any case, things were far from being so simple. But one cannot fail to notice, in the documents we have, the presence of what might be called "a privileged association." We have seen in the preceding part that the art of conjugal life was understood largely in terms of a Stoic mode of reflection, and in reference to a certain conception of nature, of its basic necessities, of the place and function ordained by it for all beings, of a general scheme of successive procreations, and of a state of original perfection from which the human race was estranged owing to a perverse decadence. Moreover, it is from a similar conception that Christianity will amply draw when it decides to construct an ethics of the marital relationship. In the same way, the love of boys, practiced as a way of life, consolidated and reproduced for centuries a rather different theoretical landscape: a cosmic and individual force of love, an upward movement that enables man to escape from immediate necessities, the acquisition and transmission of knowledge through the intense forms and secret ties of friendship. The debate between the love of women and the love of boys is more than a literary joust. It is not, however, the conflict of two forms of sexual desire struggling for supremacy or for their respective right to expression. It is the confrontation of two forms of life, of two ways of stylizing one's pleasure, and of the two philosophical discourses that accompany these choices.

2.   After the theme of "nature," both of these discourses—that of Charicles and that of Callicratidas—develop the question of pleasure. A question that, as we have seen, always constitutes a difficult point for a pederastic practice that is reflected in the form of friendship, affection, and the beneficial action of one soul on another. To speak of "pleasure" to the lover of boys is already to raise an objection. This is clearly how Charicles understands the matter. He begins the debate

on this theme with a traditional denunciation of pederastic hypocrisy: You pretend to be disciples of Socrates who are not enamored of bodies but of souls. How is it then that you do not pursue old men full of wisdom, but rather children, who are unable to reason? If it's a matter of virtue, why love, as Plato did, a Phaedrus who betrayed Lysias, or, as Socrates did, an impious Alcibiades, an enemy of his country, eager to become a tyrant? One would do well, therefore, despite the claims of this love of souls, "to descend," along with Charicles, to the question of pleasure, and to compare "the practice of boys" with the "practice of women."

Among the arguments that Charicles employs to differentiate between these two "practices" and the place that pleasure occupies in each, the first is that of age and transience.[12] Until the threshold of old age, a woman preserves her charms—even if she must lend them the support of her long experience. A boy, for his part, is agreeable only for a moment. And Charicles contrasts the body of a woman—who, with her ringlets of hair, her skin always smooth and "not a hair growing on it," remains an object of desire—with the body of a boy, which very soon becomes hairy and muscled. But from this difference, Charicles does not conclude, as is often done, that one can love a boy only for a very short time, and that one is very soon led to abandon him. Rather, he evokes the man who goes on loving a boy past twenty. What he pursues in this case is an "equivocal Aphrodite," a love in which he plays the passive part. The physical modification of boys is here invoked as a cause not of the transience of feelings but of an inversion of sexual roles.

A second reason in favor of the "female practice" is reciprocity.[13] This is doubtless the most interesting part of Charicles' discourse. He first refers to the princple that man, a rational being, is not made to live alone. From this he does not, however, deduce the necessity of having a family or of belonging to a city, but the impossibility of "passing one's time" all alone and the need for a "community of affection" *(philetairos koinōnia),* which makes good things more pleasant and painful things more bearable. That the shared life has this role is an idea that is regularly found in the Stoic treatises on marriage. Here it is applied to the specific domain of physical pleasures. Charicles first evokes the meals and banquets that one enjoys with others, because, according to him, shared pleasures are made more intense. Then he speaks of the sexual pleasures. According to the traditional assertion, the boy who is passive, hence more or less violated *(hubrismenos),* cannot experience pleasure; no one "could be so mad" as to state the contrary. When he no longer cries and suffers, the other becomes a nuisance to him. The lover of a boy takes his pleasure and leaves; he gives none in return. With women, things are completely different. Charicles first states the fact, then the rule. In sexual intercourse with a woman, there is, he affirms, "an equal exchange of enjoyment"; and the two partners separate after having given each other an equal amount of pleasure. To this fact of nature corresponds a principle of conduct: it is good not to seek a selfish enjoyment *(philautōs apolausai),* not to try and have all the pleasure oneself, but to share it by supplying the other with as much of it as one experiences. To be sure, this reciprocity of pleasure is already a well-known theme, which amatory or erotic literature has used quite often. But it is interesting to see it used here at the same time to give a "natural" characterization of intercourse with women, to define a rule of behavior in the practice of the *aphrodisia,* and to designate what there might be that is nonnatural, violent, hence unjust and bad, in the intercourse of a man with a boy. Reciprocity of pleasure in an exchange where one shows concern for the other's enjoyment, while observing as strict an equality as possible of the two partners, inscribes within sexual practice an ethics that extends the ethics of communal existence.

To this serious bit of reasoning, Charicles adds two arguments that are less so, although they both relate to the exchange of pleasures. One refers to a theme that was common in erotic literature: women, for anyone who knows how to use them, are capable of offering all the pleasures that boys can give, but the latter cannot provide the pleasure that is held exclusively by the female sex.[14] Women are thus capable of giving all the forms of sensual delight, including those most pleasing to the lovers of boys. According to the other argument, if one finds love between men acceptable, one should also accept intercourse between women.[15] This polemical symmetry invoked here between intermale relations and interfemale relations is interesting: first, because it denies, as does the second part of Charicles' discourse, the cultural, moral, affective, and sexual specificity of the love of boys, bringing it back into the general category of relations between male individuals; second, because, in order to compromise the latter, it uses the traditionally more scandalous love—one is "ashamed" even to talk about it—between women; and third, because Charicles, reversing this hierarchy, suggests that it is even more shameful for a man to be passive like a woman than for a woman to take the male role.*

The part of Callicratidas' discourse that replies to this criticism is by far the longest. Even more so than in the rest of the debate, the characteristic features of a "piece of rhetoric" are visible here. Engaging, apropos of sexual pleasure, the most problematic element of the love of boys, the pederastic argumentarium is fully deployed, with all its resources and its most noble references. But they are brought into play in response to the question that Charicles has stated very clearly: the reciprocity of pleasure. On this point both adversaries refer to a simple and coherent conception: for Charicles, and the "adherents of female love," it is the fact of being able to occasion the other's pleasure, to be attentive to it, and to take pleasure in it oneself—it is this *charis,* as Plutarch says,† that legitimates pleasure in intercourse between a man and a woman, and allows it to be integrated into Eros; it is the absence of *charis,* on the other hand, that marks and disqualifies intercourse with boys. As the tradition of this other

*Is it not better that a woman should play the role of a man "than that the nobility of the male sex should become effeminate and play the part of a woman"?[16]
†Charicles does not himself use this word.

love prescribes, Callicratidas cites as its keystone not *charis* but *aretē*—virtue. It is virtue that should ensure between partners both an honorable, wisely apportioned pleasure and the commonality that is indispensable to the relationship between two individuals. Let us say, to be brief, that to the "gracious reciprocity" that only pleasure with women is capable of providing, according to its proponents, its adversaries oppose the "virtuous commonality" that is the exclusive privilege of the love of boys. Callicratidas'. demonstration consists first of all in criticizing, as illusory, that reciprocity of pleasure which the love of women claims as its specific trait, and in setting against it, as the only relationship capable of truth, the virtuous relationship with boys. Thus, in a single stroke, the privilege of reciprocal pleasure attributed to male-female relations will be contested, and the theme that the love of boys is unnatural will be turned around.

In a display of rancor, Callicratidas reels off a series of commonplaces against women.[17] One only has to look closely to see that women are intrinsically "ugly," "truly" *(alēthōs)* so: their bodies are "unshapely" and their faces are as ill-favored as those of monkeys. They must take great pains to mask this reality: makeup, fancy clothes, coiffures, jewels, adornments. For the benefit of spectators they give themselves a spurious beauty, which a careful gaze suffices to dissipate. And then they have a liking for secret cults, which allow them to envelop their debauches in mystery. There is no need to recall all the satirical themes that are echoed, rather flatly, by this passage. One could find many other examples, with similar arguments, in the eulogies of pederasty. Thus Achilles Tatius, in *Leucippe and Clitophon,* has one of his characters, a lover of boys, say: "False are the ways of a woman, words and deeds alike; and although she may seem fair to behold, it is all the result of the laborious use of pigments, and her beauty is all of myrrh, hair dye and makeup; and if she is stripped of all these many devices, she is like the jackdaw that was plucked of its feathers in the fable."[18]

A woman's world is deceptive because it is a secret world.

The social separation between the group of men and that of women, their different ways of life, the careful division between female activities and male activities—all this probably did much to heighten, in the experience of Hellenic men, this apprehension of women as mysterious and deceptive objects. One could be deceived about a woman's body, which was hidden by adornments and which might be disappointing when it was uncovered. One was apt to suspect it of cleverly masked imperfections. One was afraid of discovering some repellent defect. The female body, with its secrecy and its particular characteristics, was charged with ambiguous powers. Do you wish, says Ovid, to rid yourself of a passion? Look a little more closely at the body of your mistress.[19]* One could be deceived, too, regarding morals, with that secret life which women led, a life enclosed in disturbing mysteries. In the argumentation that Pseudo-Lucian attributes to Callicratidas, these themes have a precise significance: they enable him to question the principle of reciprocity of pleasure in intercourse with women. How could there be such a reciprocity if women are deceptive, if they have their own pleasure, if, unbeknown to men, they indulge in secret debauchery? How could there be a valid exchange if the pleasures their appearance lets one imagine are nothing but false promises? So that the objection usually made to intercourse with boys—that it does not accord with nature—can just as easily be applied to women, even more seriously in their case, since by choosing to mask the truth of their nature, they deliberately introduce falsehood. The makeup argument may seem to us to carry little force in this debate on the two loves. For the ancients, however, it is based on two serious considerations: the apprehension that derives from the female body, and the philosophical and moral principle that a pleasure is legitimate only if the object that gives rise to it is genuine. In the pederastic argumentation,

*Or these verses: "Open the windows wide, all of them, draw back the curtains, / Let the light make clear parts that are ugly to see." After lovemaking, "note down in your mind her every blemish of body, / Keep your eyes on her faults, memorize every defect."[20]

pleasure with a woman cannot be reciprocal because it is accompanied by too much falseness.

In contrast, pleasure with boys is placed under the sign of truth.[21] The beauty of a young man is real because it is uncontrived. As Achilles Tatius has one of his characters say: "The beauty of a boy is not fostered by the odor of myrrh perfumes, nor yet by cunning and foreign unguents. And the fresh natural odor of a boy has a sweeter smell than all the anointings and perfumery of a woman."[22] Callicratidas contrasts the deceptive enticements of the female dressing table with a description of the boy who gives no thought to any preparations: he jumps out of bed at dawn and washes with pure water. He has no need of a mirror, he doesn't use a comb. He throws his chlamys on his shoulder and hurries off to school. At the palestra he exercises vigorously, works up a sweat, and bathes quickly. And once the lessons of wisdom he is given have been understood, he quickly falls asleep as a result of the day's beneficial exertions.

How could one not wish to share one's whole life with this guileless boy?[23] One would like to "pass one's time sitting opposite this dear friend," enjoying his pleasant conversation, and "sharing every activity with him." A sensible pleasure that will last not just for the fleeting time of youth. Since it does not take as its object the physical grace that fades away, it can endure all through life: old age, sickness, death, the tomb even, everything can be experienced in common; "to unite my bones with his and not to keep even our dumb ashes apart." It was a traditional theme, certainly, that friendships could grow out of youthful love affairs and sustain life, until the moment of death, through a lasting manly affection. This passage from Pseudo-Lucian appears to be a variation on one of the themes developed in Xenophon's *Symposium*. The ideas are the same, presented in an analogous order and expressed in similar words: the pleasure of looking at each other, the conversation, the sharing of feelings in success or failure, the care given when one of the two falls ill—in this way, affection can reign between the two friends through to old age.[24] Pseudo-Lucian's text gives particular emphasis to one important point concerning this affection that continues after adolescence. It is a matter of forming a bond in which the equality is so perfect, or the reversibility so complete, that the role of the *erastes* and that of the *eromenos* can no longer be distinguished. This is how things were, says Callicratidas, between Orestes and Pylades, about whom it was traditional to wonder, as in the case of Achilles and Patroclus, who was the lover and who the beloved. Pylades was the lover, it seems. But as they grew older, and when the time of trial came—the two friends had to decide which one would face death—the beloved behaved as the lover. One should see a model in this. It is in this way, says Callicratidas, that the zealous and serious love one bears for a young boy (the famous *spoudaios erōs*) must be transformed. It must become the manly form *(androusthai)* with the coming of that age when a youth is at last capable of reason. In this masculine affection, the one who had been loved "gives love in return," and to such an extent that it becomes difficult to know "which of the two is the *erastes*"; the affection of the one who loves is returned to him by the beloved the way an image is reflected in a mirror.[25]

The return by the beloved of the affection he has received had always been a part of pederastic ethics, whether this was in the form of help in misfortune, care in old age, companionship in life, or unexpected sacrifice. But Pseudo-Lucian's insistence on the equality of the two lovers and his use of words that characterize conjugal reciprocity seem to show a concern to adapt male love to the descriptive and prescriptive model of marriage. After enumerating everything that is simple, natural, and free of all artifice in the body of a young man, and hence after establishing the "truthfulness" of the pleasure he is capable of providing, the author of the text relates the spiritual bond, not to pedagogical action, or to the formative effect of this attachment, but entirely to the exact reciprocity of an equal exchange. In proportion as the description of the

male and female bodies sets them in contrast, in this speech
by Callicratidas, the ethics of living as a couple seems to draw
manly affection closer to the marriage tie.

But there is still a basic difference. For, while the love of
boys is defined as the only love in which virtue and pleasure
can be combined, pleasure is never designated as sexual pleasure. There is the charm of that juvenile body, without
makeup or deception, of that regular, disciplined life, of the
amical conversation, of the affection that is returned—true.
But the the text makes it quite clear: in his bed, the boy is
"without a companion"; he looks at no one when he is on his
way to school; in the evening, tired from his work, he goes
right to sleep. And Callicratidas gives some unequivocal advice to the lovers of such boys: Remain as chaste as Socrates
when he slept beside Alcibiades. Approach them with temper-
ance *(sōphronōs)*. Don't squander a lasting affection for the
sake of a brief pleasure. And it is this very lesson which will
be drawn, once the debate is concluded, when, with an ironic
solemnity, Lycinus awards the prize; it goes to the speech that
praised the love of boys, insofar as the latter is practiced by
"philosophers" and insofar as it pledges itself to ties of friendship that are "just and undefiled."

The debate between Charicles and Callicratidas thus ends
with a "victory" of the love of boys. A victory conforming to
a traditional schema that reserves for philosophers a pederasty
in which physical pleasure is evaded. A victory, however, that
gives everyone not only the right but also the duty to marry
(according to a formula we have encountered in the Stoics:
pantapasi gamēteon). This is in effect a syncretic conclusion,
which superimposes on the universality of marriage the privilege of a love of boys reserved for those who, being philosophers, are capable of a "perfect virtue." But one should not
forget that this debate, whose traditional and rhetorical character is emphasized in the text itself, is embedded in another
dialogue: that of Lycinus with Theomnestus, who asks his
opinion on which of the two loves he should choose, since he
feels equally drawn to both. So Lycinus has just reported to

Theomnestus the "verdict" he gave to Charicles and Callicratidas. But Theomnestus immediately waxes ironic about
the crucial point of the debate and about the deciding factor
in the victory of pederastic love: the latter won because it was
linked to philosophy, to virtue, and hence to the elimination
of physical pleasure. Is one expected to believe that this is
really the way in which one loves boys? Theomnestus does not
become indignant, as did Charicles, at the hypocrisy of such
a discourse. Whereas, in order to link together pleasure and
virtue, the advocates of boys stressed the absence of any sexual
act, he reinstates the physical contact that one enjoys, the
kisses, the caresses, and the gratification, as the real reason for
the existence of this love. Seriously, he says, they can't make
us believe that the whole pleasure of this relationship is in
looking into each other's eyes and in being enchanted by
friendly conversation. Looking is agreeable, certainly, but it is
only the first stage. After that comes touching, which thrills
the whole body. Then kissing, which is timid at first but soon
becomes eager. The hand does not remain idle during this
time; it glides down under the clothing, squeezes the breasts
for a moment, descends the length of the firm belly, reaches
the "flower of puberty," and finally strikes the target.[26] For
Theomnestus, and doubtless for the author as well, this description does not amount to a rejection of an inadmissible
practice. It is a reminder that it is not possible—without resorting to violence—to keep the *aphrodisia* outside the domain of love and its justifications. Pseudo-Lucian's irony is not
a way of denouncing this pleasure which one can take in boys,
a pleasure he evokes with a smile. It is a fundamental objection
to the very old line of argument of Greek pederasty, which,
in order to conceptualize, formulate, and discourse about the
latter and to supply it with reasons, was obliged to evade the
manifest presence of physical pleasure. He does not say that
the love of women is better. But he demonstrates the essential
weakness of a discourse on love that makes no allowance for
the *aphrodisia* and for the relations they engage.

CHAPTER THREE

A NEW EROTICS

During this period in which one notes that reflection on the love of boys manifests its sterility, one sees some of the elements of a new erotics coming to the fore. Its privileged place is not in philosophical texts, and it does not borrow its major themes from the love of boys. It develops in reference to the relationship between a man and a woman, and it finds expression in romances, of which the chief surviving examples are the adventures of *Chaereas and Callirhoe,* written by Chariton of Aphrodisias; those of *Leucippe and Clitophon,* recounted by Achilles Tatius; and the *Ethiopica,* by Heliodorus. It is true that many uncertainties remain in connection with this literature, relative to the circumstances of its emergence and success, the date of the texts, and their possible allegorical and spiritual significance.[1] But one can nonetheless call attention to the presence, in these long narratives with their countless episodes, of some of the themes that will subsequently characterize erotics, both religious and profane: the existence of a "heterosexual" relation marked by a male-female polarity, the insistence on an abstention that is modeled much more on virginal integrity than on the political and virile domination of desires; and finally, the fulfillment and reward of this purity in a union that has the form and value of a spiritual marriage. In this sense, and whatever may have been the influence of Platonism on this erotics, it is clearly far removed from an erotics that referred essentially to the temperate love of boys and to its perfection in the lasting form of friendship.

It is true that the love of boys is not completely absent from this romantic literature. Not only does it occupy an important place, certainly, in the tales of Petronius or Apuleius, which attests to the frequency and quite general acceptance of the practice. But it is also present in certain tales of virginity, betrothal, and marriage. Thus in *Leucippe and Clitophon,* two characters represent it, and in a completely positive manner: Clinias, who tries to dissuade his own male lover from marriage, nevertheless gives the hero of the tale some excellent advice for making progress in the love of girls.[2] Menelaus, for his part, offers a charming theory of a boy's kiss—not cunning, or soft, or licentious, like that of a woman; a kiss that is the product not of art but of nature: a glaze of nectar become lips, such is the simple kiss of a boy at the gymnasium.[3] But these are only episodic and marginal themes. The love of a boy is never the principal object of the narrative. The whole focus of attention is centered on the relationship of the boy and the girl. This relationship always begins with a revelation that strikes them both and makes them love each other with an equal intensity. Except in the novel by Chariton of Aphrodisias, *Chaereas and Callirhoe,* this love does not immediately result in their union: the novel recounts a long series of adventures, which separate the two young people and prevent both marriage and the consummation of pleasure until the last moment.* These adventures are, insofar as possible, symmetrical. Everything that happens to the one has its counterpart in the changes of fortune the other is made to undergo, which allows them to show the same courage, the same endurance, the same fidelity. This is because the primary significance of these adventures and their ability to sustain one's interest until the denouement have to do with the fact that in the midst of

---

*In *Chaereas and Callirhoe,* the separation occurs immediately after marriage; but the two spouses preserve their love, their purity, and their faithfulness throughout their adventures.

them the two characters hold strictly to a reciprocal sexual fidelity. A fidelity where the protagonists are married, as in the case of Chaereas and Callirhoe; a virginity in other tales, where the adventures and misfortunes come after the discovery of love and before marriage. Now it must be understood that this virginity is not simply an abstention resulting from a pledge. It is a choice of lives, which in the *Ethiopica* even appears to be prior to love. Chariclea, carefully schooled by her adoptive father in the quest for "the best of lives," refused even to entertain the idea of marriage. The father had complained of this, moreover, after suggesting an honorable candidate: "Neither by kind attentions, nor by promises, nor by appeals to reason, have I been able to persuade her. Hardest blow of all, she has aimed, as they say, my own shafts against me, and brandishes over me her accomplishment in the arts of speech—the subtleties of which I have imparted to her . . . glorifying the virgin state, which, she declares, is next to the immortal."⁴ Symmetrically, Theagenes had never had relations with a woman: "He affirmed with many oaths that he had never yet had intimacy with a woman. He had spurned all women, and marriage itself, and many love affairs that were mentioned to him, until the beauty of Chariclea had proved to him that he was not by nature obdurate. But up to the previous day he had never beheld a woman worthy of being loved."⁵

We see then that virginity is not simply abstention as a preliminary to sexual practice. It is a choice, a style of life, a lofty form of existence that the hero chooses out of the regard that he has for himself. When the most extraordinary occurrences separate the two protagonists and expose them to the worst dangers, the gravest will of course be that of falling prey to the sexual cupidity of others. The greatest test of their own worth and their mutual love will be that of resisting at all costs and of saving that virginity which is essential to the relationship with themselves and essential to the relationship with each other. Thus the novel by Achilles Tatius unfolds as a kind of odyssey of double virginity. A virginity exposed, assailed, doubted, slandered, safeguarded—except for an honorable, minor lapse that Clitophon allowed himself—and finally justified and certified in a sort of divine ordeal, which makes it possible to proclaim concerning the girl, "she is still the same, up to the present day, as when you sent her away from Byzantium; it is to be put down to her credit that she remained a virgin when surrounded by a gang of pirates, and overcame the worst of them." And speaking of himself, Clitophon can also say, in a symmetrical fashion: "You will find that I have imitated your virginity, if there be any virginity in men."[6]

But if love and sexual abstention thus coincide during the entire adventure, one has to understand that it is not simply a question of defending oneself against outsiders. This preservation of virginity holds within the love relation as well. The lovers save themselves for each other until the time when love and virginity find their fulfillment in marriage. So that premarital chastity, which brings the two fiancés together in spirit so long as they are separated and being put to the test by others, keeps them self-restrained and makes them abstain when they are finally reunited after many twists of fate. Finding themselves alone in a cave, left to themselves, Theagenes and Chariclea "took their fill of ardent embraces and kisses. In a moment they were oblivious of everything else. For a long time they clung to each other as though grown into one person, satiating themselves with a devout, virginal love, communing with one another through the flow of hot tears, and commingling only by the chaste means of their kisses. For Chariclea, when she found Theagenes making some too impulsive advance of manly ardor, restrained him by recalling his oaths, and his attempt was easily checked. It was a light matter for him to be temperate, for although mastered by love he could be master of his pleasures.'" This virginity is not to be understood, then, as an attitude that is set against all sexual relations, even if they take place within marriage. It is much more the test preparatory to that union, the movement that leads to it and in which it will find its fulfillment. Love, virginity, and marriage form a whole: the two lovers have to preserve their physical integrity, but also their purity of heart, until the moment of their union, which is to be understood in the physical but also the spiritual sense.

Thus there begins to develop an erotics different from the one that had taken its starting point in the love of boys, even though abstention from the sexual pleasures plays an important part in both. This new erotics organizes itself around the symmetrical and reciprocal relationship of a man and a woman, around the high value attributed to virginity, and around the complete union in which it finds perfection.

CONCLUSION

A whole corpus of moral reflection on sexual activity and its pleasures seems to mark, in the first centuries of our era, a certain strengthening of austerity themes. Physicians worry about the effects of sexual practice, unhesitatingly recommend abstention, and declare a preference for virginity over the use of pleasure. Philosophers condemn any sexual relation that might take place outside marriage and prescribe a strict fidelity between spouses, admitting no exceptions. Furthermore, a certain doctrinal disqualification seems to bear on the love for boys.

Does this mean that one must recognize, in the schema thus constituted, the lineaments of a future ethics, the ethics that one will find in Christianity, when the sexual act itself will be considered an evil, when it will no longer be granted legitimacy except within the conjugal relationship, and when the love of boys will be condemned as unnatural? Must one suppose that certain thinkers, in the Greco-Roman world, already had a presentiment of this model of sexual austerity which, in Christian societies, will be given a legal framework and an institutional support? One would thus find, formulated by a few austere philosophers isolated in the midst of a world that did not itself appear to be austere, the outline of a new ethics, destined, in the following centuries, to take more stringent forms and to gain a more general validity.

The question is important, and it has a long tradition behind

it. Since the Renaissance, it has laid down, in Catholicism and
Protestantism alike, relatively similar dividing lines. On the
one side, a certain ancient ethics closely related to Christianity
(this is the thesis of the *Manuductio ad stoicam philosophiam*
by Justus Lipsius, which Karl Barth radicalized by making
Epictetus into a true Christian; it is, later, on behalf of the
Catholics, the thesis of J.-P. Camus and, most notably, of the
Epictète chrétien by Jean-Marie de Bordeaux). On the other
side, those for whom Stoicism was just another philosophy,
one that was virtuous, certainly, but indelibly pagan (thus
Salmasius among the Protestants, and Arnauld or Tillemont
among the Catholics). The point at issue, however, was not
just to bring certain of the ancient philosophers within the
bounds of the Christian faith or to preserve the latter from any
pagan contamination; the problem was also to determine what
foundation to give to an ethics whose prescriptive elements
seemed to be shared, up to a point, by Greco-Roman philosophy and the Christian religion. The debate that developed at
the end of the nineteenth century is not unconnected with this
problematic either, even if it sets up an interference with problems of historical method. Zahn, in his famous address, did
not try to make a Christian of Epictetus, but to call attention
to the signs of a knowledge of Christianity and to the traces
of its influence.[1] Bonhöffer's work, which replied to Zahn,
sought to establish the unity of philosophy without there being
the need to appeal to the disparate elements of an external
action in order to explain this or that aspect of it.[2] But it was
also a matter of knowing where to look for the basis of
the moral imperative and whether it was possible to detach
Christianity from a certain type of ethics that had long been
associated with it. Now, in this debate it seems that the partici-
pants granted, in a relatively confused way, three presupposi-
tions: according to the first, the essential component of an
ethics is to be sought in the code elements it contains; according to the second, the philosophical ethics of late antiquity
resembled Christianity in its severe precepts, which represented an almost complete break with the previous tradition;

lastly, according to the third presupposition, it was in terms of loftiness and purity that Christian ethics could best be compared with the ethics that, in certain philosophers of antiquity, prepared the way for it.

It is hardly possible, however, to let the matter remain there. One has to bear in mind, first, that the principles of sexual austerity were not defined for the first time in the philosophy of the imperial epoch. We have encountered in Greek thought of the fourth century B.C. formulations that were not much less demanding. After all, as we have seen, the sexual act appears to have been regarded for a very long time as dangerous, difficult to master, and costly; a precise calculation of its acceptable practice and its inclusion in a careful regimen had been required for quite some time. Plato, Isocrates, and Aristotle recommended, each in his own way, at least some forms of conjugal fidelity. And the love of boys could be held in the highest esteem. But the practice of abstention was demanded of it as well, so that it might preserve the spiritual value expected of it. Hence a very long time had passed during which concern for the body and for health, the relation to wives and to marriage, and the relationship with boys had been motifs for the elaboration of a severe ethics. And in a certain way, the sexual austerity that one encounters in the philosophers of the first centuries of our era has its roots in this ancient tradition. It is true that one should not ignore the carefully maintained continuity and the conscious reactivation evident in this thought of the first centuries, so manifestly haunted by classical culture. Hellenistic philosophy and ethics experienced what Henri Marrou called "a long summer." But the fact remains that several modifications are perceptible: they prevent one from considering the moral philosophy of Musonius or that of Plutarch simply as the accentuation of the lessons of Xenophon, Plato, Isocrates, or Aristotle; they also prevent one from considering the recommendations of Soranus or Rufus of Ephesus as variations on the principles of Hippocrates or Diocles.

As concerns dietetics and the problematization of health,

the change is marked by an increased apprehension, a broader and more detailed definition of the correlations between the sexual act and the body, a closer attention to the ambivalence of its effects and its disturbing consequences. And this is not just a greater preoccupation with the body; it is also a different way of thinking about sexual activity, and of fearing it because of its many connections with disease and with evil. With regard to wives and to the problematization of marriage, the modification mainly concerns the valorization of the conjugal bond and the dual relation that constitutes it; the husband's right conduct and the moderation he needs to enjoin on himself are not justified merely by considerations of status, but by the nature of the relationship, its universal form and the mutual obligations that derive from it. Finally, as regards boys, the need for abstinence is less and less perceived as a way of giving the highest spiritual values to the forms of love, and more and more as the sign of an imperfection that is specific to sexual activity.

Now, in these modifications of preexisting themes one can see the development of an art of existence dominated by self-preoccupation. This art of the self no longer focuses so much on the excesses that one can indulge in and that need to be mastered in order to exercise one's domination over others. It gives increasing emphasis to the frailty of the individual faced with the manifold ills that sexual activity can give rise to. It also underscores the need to subject that activity to a universal form by which one is bound, a form grounded in both nature and reason, and valid for all human beings. It likewise emphasizes the importance of developing all the practices and all the exercises by which one can maintain self-control and eventually arrive at a pure enjoyment of oneself. It is not the accentuation of the forms of prohibition that is behind these modifications in sexual ethics. It is the development of an art of existence that revolves around the question of the self, of its dependence and independence, of its universal form and of the connection it can and should establish with others, of the procedures by which it exerts its control over itself, and of the way in which it can establish a complete supremacy over itself.

And it is in this context that a dual phenomenon, characteristic of this ethics of pleasure, occurs. On the one hand, a more active attention to sexual practice is required, an attention to its effects on the organism, to its place and function within marriage, to its value and its difficulties in the relationship with boys. But at the same time as one dwells on it, and as the interest that one brings to bear on it is intensified, it increasingly appears to be dangerous and capable of compromising the relation with oneself that one is trying to establish. It seems more and more necessary to distrust it, to confine it, insofar as possible, to marital relations—even at the cost of charging it with more intense meanings within that conjugal relationship. Problematization and apprehension go hand in hand; inquiry is joined to vigilance. A certain style of sexual conduct is thus suggested by this whole movement of moral, medical, and philosophical reflection. It is different from the style that had been delineated in the fourth century, but it is also different from the one that will be found in Christianity. Here sexual activity is linked to evil by its form and its effects, but in itself and substantially, it is not an evil. It finds its natural fulfillment in marriage, but—with certain exceptions —marriage is not an express, indispensable condition for it to cease being an evil. It has trouble finding its place in the love of boys, but the latter is not therefore condemned as being contrary to nature.

Thus, as the arts of living and the care of the self are refined, some precepts emerge that seem to be rather similar to those that will be formulated in the later moral systems. But one should not be misled by the analogy. Those moral systems will define other modalities of the relation to self: a characterization of the ethical substance based on finitude, the Fall, and evil; a mode of subjection in the form of obedience to a general law that is at the same time the will of a personal god; a type of work on oneself that implies a decipherment of the soul and a purificatory hermeneutics of the desires; and a mode of ethical fulfillment that tends toward self-renunciation. The code elements that concern the economy of pleasures, conjugal fidelity, and relations between men may well remain analogous, but they will derive from a profoundly altered ethics and from a different way of constituting oneself as the ethical subject of one's sexual behavior.

NOTES

For titles briefly cited here, fuller references are given in the Bibliography. *The Use of Pleasure* is the previous volume of *The History of Sexuality.*

PART ONE: DREAMING OF ONE'S PLEASURES

Chapter 1: The Method of Artemidorus

1. Artemidorus, *The Interpretation of Dreams,* I, 2 (Nicostratus of Ephesus); I, 2; I, 64; II, 35 (Panyasis of Helicarnassus); I, 79 (Apollodorus of Telmessus); I, 2; II, 9; IV, 48; IV, 66 (Phoebus of Antioch); II, 66 (Dionysius of Heliopolis); I, 67; II, 9; II, 66 (Alexander of Myndus).
2. Ibid., I, 31; IV, 23; IV, 24 (Aristander of Telmessus); I, 2; II, 44.
3. See A.-J. Festugière, "Introduction" to French translation of Artemidorus, p. 9; C. A. Behr, *Aelius Aristides and the "Sacred Tales,"* p. 181 ff.
4. Artemidorus, *The Interpretation of Dreams,* II, conclusion.
5. Achilles Tatius, *Leucippe and Clitophon,* I, 3.
6. Synesius, *On Dreams,* 15–16.
7. Artemidorus, *The Interpretation of Dreams,* I, 12; III, conclusion.
8. Ibid., IV, preface.
9. Ibid., I, dedication.
10. Ibid., III, conclusion.
11. Ibid., II, conclusion.
12. Ibid., II, 44.

13. Ibid., dedication.
14. Ibid., II, conclusion.
15. R. J. White, "Introduction" to English translation of Artemidorus; A. H. M. Kessels, "Ancient Systems of Dream Classification," p. 391.
16. Artemidorus, *The Interpretation of Dreams,* I, 1.
17. Ibid., I, 1. See also *Odyssey,* XVIII, 7.
18. Seneca, *Letters to Lucilius,* 56, 6.
19. Plutarch, *Quomodo quis suos in virtute sentiat profectus,* 12.
20. Artemidorus, *The Interpretation of Dreams,* IV, preface.
21. Plato, *Republic,* IX, 572a–b.
22. Chariton of Aphrodisias, *The Adventures of Chaereas and Callirhoe,* V, 5.
23. Artemidorus, *The Interpretation of Dreams,* II, 25.
24. Ibid., II, 12. See also A.-J. Festugière's note, p. 112.
25. Ibid., II, 12.
26. Ibid., II, 49; II, 65.
27. Ibid., II, 65.
28. Ibid., IV, 2.
29. Ibid., I, 5.

Chapter 2: The Analysis

1. Artemidorus, *The Interpretation of Dreams,* I, 77–80.
2. Ibid., I, 78.
3. Ibid., I, 78; I, 79.
4. Ibid., IV, 4.
5. Ibid., I, 78.
6. Ibid., I, 79–80.
7. P. Veyne, "L'Homosexualité à Rome," p. 78.

Chapter 3: Dream and Act

1. For cases in which sexual elements do appear as the dream's signified, see Artemidorus, *The Interpretation of Dreams,* IV, 37, 41, 46, 66; V, 24, 44, 45, 62, 65, 67, 95.
2. Ibid., I, 77. See also IV, 4, on the equivalence between "to possess" (to penetrate) and "to possess" (to have acquired).
3. Ibid., I, 78.
4. Ibid.
5. Ibid., IV, 68.
6. Ibid., I, 79; see also I, 45.
7. Ibid., I, 45.

PART TWO: THE CULTIVATION OF THE SELF

1. Dio Chrysostom, *Discourses*, VII.
2. A. J. Voelcke, *Les Rapports avec autrui dans la philosophie grecque, d'Aristote à Panétius*, pp. 183–189.
3. For an interesting discussion of these themes, see P. Hadot, *Exercices spirituels et philosophie antique*.
4. Xenophon, *Cyropaedia*, VII, 5, 41.
5. Plutarch, *Apophthegmata laconica*, 217a.
6. Plato, *Alcibiades*, 127d–e.
7. Plato, *Apology of Socrates*, 29d–e.
8. Albinus, quoted by A.-J. Festugière, *Études de philosophie grecque*, p. 536.
9. Apuleius, *On the God of Socrates*, XXI, 167–168.
10. Epicurus, *Letter to Menoeceus*, 122.
11. Seneca, *Letters to Lucilius*, 66, 45.
12. Musonius Rufus, *Reliquiae*, 36; quoted by Plutarch, *De cohibenda ira*, 453d.
13. Seneca, *Letters to Lucilius*, 17, 5; *On the Shortness of Life*, 7, 5.
14. Seneca, *On the Shortness of Life*, 24, 1 *(se formare)*; *Letters to Lucilius*, I, 1 *(sibi vindicare)*; ibid., 13, 1, and *On the Happy Life*, 24, 4 *(se facere)*; *On Tranquillity of Mind*, 3, 6 *(se ad studia revocare)*; ibid., 24, 2 *(sibi applicare)*; *Letters to Lucilius*, 75, 118 *(suum fieri)*; *On Tranquillity of Mind*, 17, 3, and *Letters to Lucilius*, 74, 29 *(in se recedere)*; *On the Shortness of Life*, 18, 1 *(ad se recurrere)*; *Letters to Lucilius*, 2, 1 *(secum morari)*.
15. Seneca, *Letters to Lucilius*, 35, 4.
16. Marcus Aurelius, *Meditations*, III, 14.
17. Epictetus, *Discourses*, I, 16, 1–3.
18. Ibid., I, 1, 4.
19. Ibid., II, 8, 18–23.
20. See M. Spanneut, "Epiktet."
21. Pliny the Younger, *Letters*, I, 10.
22. Ibid., I, 9.
23. Epicurus, *Letter to Menoeceus*, 122.
24. On this theme, see, for example, Seneca, *Letters to Lucilius*, 82, 76; 90, 44–45; *On the Constancy of the Wise Man*, IX, 13.
25. Seneca, *Letters to Lucilius*, 76, 1–4. See also A. Grilli, *Il problema della vita contemplative nel mondo greco-romano*, pp. 217–280.

26. Lucian, *Hermotimus*, 1–2.
27. I. Hadot, *Seneca und die griechisch-römische Tradition der Seelenleitung*, p. 160.
28. Xenophon, *Oeconomicus*, V, 1; Dio Chrysostom, *Discourses*, III, 55; Plutarch, *Regum et imperatorum apophthegmata*, 197d; Plato, *Laws*, 717e.
29. Seneca, *On Anger*, III; Epictetus, *Discourses*, II, 21 ff; III, 10, 1–5; Marcus Aurelius, *Meditations*, IV, 3; XII, 19.
30. Musonius Rufus, *Reliquiae*, 60.
31. Pliny the Younger, *Letters*, III, 1.
32. Marcus Aurelius, *Meditations*, IV, 3.
33. See Seneca, *Letters to Lucilius*, 7, 99 and 109.
34. Philodemus, *Works*, ed. A. Olivieri, fragment 36, p. 17.
35. On the practical exercises of the school, see B. L. Hijmans, *Askēsis*, pp. 41–46.
36. F. H. Sandbach, *The Stoics*, p. 144; see also J. H. Liebeschütz, *Continuity and Change in Roman Religion*, pp. 112–113.
37. Galen, *On the Passions and Errors of the Soul*, III, 6–10.
38. Seneca, *Letters to Lucilius*, 109, 2. On Seneca, his relationships, and his activity as a moral director, see P. Grimal, *Sénèque ou la conscience de l'Empire*, pp. 393–410.
39. Plutarch, *De tuenda sanitate praecepta*, 122e.
40. Cf. Cicero, *Tusculan Disputations*, IV, 10; Seneca, *Letters to Lucilius*, 75, 9–15. See also on this point, I. Hadot, *Seneca und die griechisch-römische Tradition der Seelenleitung*, part two, chap. 2.
41. On the comparison between the therapeutics of the body and the medicine of the soul, see, for example, Seneca, *Letters to Lucilius*, 64, 8.
42. Epictetus, *Discourses*, III, 23, 30; III, 21, 20–24. See also Seneca in reference to someone who attends the classes of a philosopher: *Aut sanior domum redeat, aut sanabilior* (*Letters to Lucilius*, 108, 4).
43. Epictetus, *Discourses*, II, 21, 12–22; see also II, 15, 15–20.
44. Galen, "The Diagnosis and Cure of the Soul's Passions," I, 1, in *On the Passions and Errors of the Soul*.
45. Ibid., IV, 16; VI, 28.
46. Epictetus, *Discourses*, I, 9, 12–17; I, 22, 10–12; *Enchiridion*, 41.
47. Seneca, *Letters to Lucilius*, 55, 57, 78.

48. Marcus Aurelius, *Letters*, VI, 6.
49. Epictetus, *Discourses*, I, 26, 15–16; see also II, 11, 1.
50. Plutarch, *Animine an corporis affectiones sint pejores*, 501a.
51. Plutarch, *Socrates' Daemon*, 585a.
52. Seneca mentions this Epicurean peculiarity in the *Letters to Lucilius*, 18, 9.
53. Ibid., 18, 6.
54. Ibid., 20, 13.
55. See also Seneca, *Consolation to Helvia*, 12, 3.
56. Seneca, *Letters to Lucilius*, 18, 1–9.
57. Ibid., 17, 5.
58. See Diogenes Laertius, *Lives of Eminent Philosophers*, VIII, 1, 27; Porphyry, *Life of Pythagoras*, 40.
59. Seneca, *On Anger*, III, 36.
60. Epictetus, *Discourses*, III, 12, 15.
61. Ibid., I, 20, 7–11; see also III, 3, 1–13.
62. Plato, *Apology to Socrates*, 38a.
63. Epictetus, *Discourses*, III, 12, 15.
64. Epictetus, *Discourses*, I, 4, 18; III, 16, 15; III, 22, 39; III, 23, 37; III, 24–106; *Enchiridion*, 41.
65. Seneca, *Letters to Lucilius*, 82, 5.
66. Seneca, *On the Shortness of Life*, II, 4; *On Tranquillity of Mind*, XI, 2; *Letters to Lucilius*, 62, 1; 75, 18.
67. Seneca, *On the Shortness of Life*, V, 3 *(sui juris); Letters to Lucilius*, 75, 8 *(in se habere potestatem);* 32, 5 *(facultas sui).*
68. Seneca, *On the Shortness of Life*, X, 4; XV, 5.
69. Seneca, *Letters to Lucilius*, 13, 1; see also 23, 2–3; Epictetus, *Discourses*, II, 18; Marcus Aurelius, *Meditations*, VI, 16.
70. Seneca, *Letters to Lucilius*, 72, 4.
71. Ibid., 72. See also *On the Happy Life*, III, 4.
72. Seneca, *Letters to Lucilius*, 23, 3–6. See also 124, 24. For Seneca's criticism of *voluptas*, see *On the Happy Life*, XI, 1–2.

PART THREE: SELF AND OTHERS

Chapter 1: The Marital Role

1. J.-P. Broudehoux, *Marriage et famille chez Clément d'Alexandrie*, pp. 16–17.
2. C. Vatin, *Recherches sur le mariage et la condition de la femme mariée à l'époque hellénistique*, p. 4.

3. J. A. Crook, *Law and Life of Rome*, p. 99 ff. P. Veyne, "L'Amour à Rome," pp. 39–40.
4. Vatin, *Recherches*, pp. 177–178.
5. Veyne, "L'Amour à Rome."
6. Ibid.
7. J. Boswell, *Christianity, Social Tolerance, and Homosexuality*, p. 62.
8. S. B. Pomeroy, *Goddesses, Whores, Wives and Slaves*, p. 133.
9. Ibid., p. 209.
10. Veyne, "L'Amour à Rome," p. 40; Pomeroy, *Goddesses*, p. 193.
11. Pomeroy, *Goddesses*, p. 129.
12. Vatin, *Recherches*, pp. 203–206.
13. Ibid., p. 274.
14. Veyne, "L'Amour à Rome."
15. Pliny the Younger, *Letters*, VII, 5.
16. Statius, *Silvae*, III, 5, v. 23–26 and 106–107.

Chapter 2: The Political Game

1. J. Ferguson, *Moral Values in the Ancient World*, pp. 135–137.
2. F. H. Sandbach, *The Stoics*, p. 23.
3. M. Rostovtzeff, *The Social and Economic History of the Hellenistic World*, II, pp. 1305–1306.
4. J. Gagé, *Les Classes sociales dans l'empire romain*, pp. 155 ff.
5. Dio Cassius, *Dio's Roman History*, LII, 19.
6. R. MacMullen, *Roman Social Relations*, pp. 125–126.
7. Dio Cassius, *Dio's Roman History*, LII, 19.
8. C. G. Starr, *The Roman Empire*, p. 64.
9. R. Syme, *Roman Papers*, II, p. 1576.
10. MacMullen, *Roman Social Relations*, p. 93.
11. Ibid., p. 110, with references to Seneca, *Letters*, 31, 11; Epictetus, *Discourses*, III, 14, 11; IV, 6, 4.
12. Seneca, *Letters to Lucilius*, 31, 11; 47, 16; *On Benefits*, III, 18.
13. Epictetus, *Discourses*, IV, 7, 37–39.
14. Plutarch, *Praecepta gerendae reipublicae*, 798c–d.
15. Ibid., 823c.
16. Ibid., 798c–d.
17. Aristotle, *Politics*, I, 12, 1259b.
18. Aristides, *Roman Oration*, 29–39.
19. Seneca, *Natural Questions*, IV, preface.
20. Plutarch, *Praecepta gerendae reipublicae*, 814c.

21. Ibid., 811a–813a.
22. Dio Chrysostom, *Discourses,* III.
23. Plutarch, *Ad principem ineruditum,* 780c–d.
24. Marcus Aurelius, *Meditations,* VI, 30.
25. Epictetus, *Discourses,* III, 24, 36.
26. Ibid., III, 7, 33–36.
27. Plutarch, *Ad principem ineruditum,* 780b.
28. Seneca, *Letters to Lucilius,* 14, 4.
29. Seneca, *On Tranquillity of Mind,* XI, 11.
30. Ibid., X, 6.
31. Plutarch, *On Exile,* 602c–e.
32. Seneca, *Letters to Lucilius,* 22, 1–12.
33. Ibid., 31, 11.
34. Ibid., 47, 15.

PART FOUR: THE BODY

Introduction

1. G. W. Bowersock, *Greek Sophists in the Roman Empire;* see also C. Allbut, *Greek Medicine in Rome,* and J. Scarborough, *Roman Medicine.*
2. Bowersock, *Greek Sophists,* p. 67.
3. Celsus, *De Medicina,* "Proemium," p. 4.
4. Plutarch, *De tuenda sanitate praecepta,* 122d–e.
5. Celsus, *De Medicina,* preface, p. 7; I, 1, p. 43.
6. Athenaeus, XXI (doubtful books), in Oribasius, *Collection of Greek and Latin Physicians,* vol. III, p. 164.
7. Antyllus, ibid., vol. II, p. 307.
8. Athenaeus, XXIII (doubtful books), ibid., vol. III, pp. 182 ff.
9. Celsus, *De Medicina,* I, 2, pp. 45, 49.
10. See A. Rousselle's important work on this topic, *Porneia.*

Chapter 1: Galen

1. Galen, *On the Usefulness of the Parts of the Body,* XIV, 2.
2. Ibid., XIV, 2 and 3.
3. Plato, *Laws,* VI, 782e–783a.
4. Galen, *On the Usefulness of the Parts of the Body,* XIV, 2.
5. Ibid., XIV, 6.
6. Ibid., XIV, 9.
7. Ibid.
8. Ibid., XIV, 7.

9. Ibid., XIV, 9.
10. Galen, XXII, in Oribasius, *Collection of Greek and Latin Physicians,* vol. III, pp. 46–47.
11. Galen, *On the Affected Parts,* III, 8.
12. Galen, *On the Usefulness of the Parts of the Body,* XIV, 10.

Chapter 2: Are They Good? Are They Bad?

1. Aretaeus, *On the Causes and Signs of Acute and Chronic Diseases,* II, 5.
2. Rufus of Ephesus, *Fragments,* in Aetius, *Works,* Daremberg ed., p. 320.
3. Aretaeus, *On the Cure of Chronic Diseases,* I, 4.
4. Caelius Aurelianus, *On Chronic Diseases,* I, 4.
5. Aretaeus, *On the Causes and Signs of Acute and Chronic Diseases,* II, 12.
6. Galen, *On the Affected Parts,* VI, 6.
7. Soranus, *Gynecology,* III, 25.
8. Galen, *On the Affected Parts,* VI, 5.
9. Ibid., VI, 6.
10. Aretaeus, *On the Causes and Signs of Acute and Chronic Diseases,* II, 5.
11. Celsus, *De Medicina,* IV, 28.
12. Aretaeus, *On the Cure of Chronic Diseases,* II, 5, 488.
13. Galen, VIII (doubtful books), in Oribasius, *Collection of Greek and Latin Physicians,* vol. III, p. 110.
14. Ibid., vol. III, p. 109
15. Rufus of Ephesus, *Fragments,* in Aetius, *Works,* p. 318.
16. Galen, *On the Affected Parts,* VI, 5.
17. Rufus of Ephesus, *Fragments,* in Aetius, *Works,* pp. 320–321. See also text VI in Oribasius, vol. I, p. 541.
18. Galen, VIII (doubtful books), in Oribasius, vol. III, p. 109.
19. Ibid., vol. III, p. 112.
20. Ibid., X; vol. III, p. 113.
21. Rufus of Ephesus, VI, 38, ibid., vol. I, p. 542.
22. Galen, X, ibid., vol. III, p. 113.
23. Rufus of Ephesus, *Fragments,* in Aetius, *Works,* p. 320.
24. Aretaeus, *On the Cure of Chronic Diseases,* I, 4, p. 473.
25. Galen, *On the Affected Parts,* VI, 5.
26. Ibid.

27. Aretaeus, *On the Causes and Signs of Acute and Chronic Diseases,* II, 5.
28. Soranus, *Gynecology,* I, 7.
29. Rufus of Ephesus, VI, 37, in Oribasius, vol. I, p. 537.

Chapter 3: The Regimen of Pleasures

1. Rufus of Ephesus, VI, 38, in Oribasius, *Collection of Greek and Latin Physicians,* vol. I, pp. 540–541.
2. Ibid., p. 541.
3. Galen, VIII (doubtful books), ibid., vol. III, p. 110.
4. Celsus, *De Medicina,* I, 1, p. 43.
5. See *The Use of Pleasure,* Part Three.
6. Athenaeus, VII (doubtful books), in Oribasius, vol. III, p. 107.
7. Soranus, *Gynecology,* I, 10.
8. Ibid.
9. See, for example, Galen's text XXII, 3, in Oribasius, vol. III, p. 53.
10. Ibid., XXII, 7; vol. III, p. 70.
11. Soranus, *Gynecology,* I, 10.
12. Ibid., I, 10.
13. Ibid., I, 14.
14. Galen, VI (doubtful books), in Oribasius, vol. III, p. 102.
15. Galen, *On the Usefulness of the Parts of the Body,* XI, 10.
16. Galen, VIII (doubtful books), in Oribasius, vol. III, p. 110.
17. Athenaeus, XXI (doubtful books), ibid., vol. III, p. 165.
18. Galen, VIII (doubtful books), ibid., vol. III, p. 111.
19. Athenaeus (doubtful books), ibid., vol. III, pp. 164–165.
20. On these relationships between the age of marriage and the problematization of women's health, see A. Rousselle, *Porneia,* pp. 49–52.
21. Soranus, *Gynecology,* I, 8.
22. Rufus of Ephesus, II (doubtful books), in Oribasius, vol. III, pp. 82–85.
23. Celsus, *De Medicina,* I, 3; Rufus of Ephesus, VI, in Oribasius, vol. I, p. 543; Galen, VIII (doubtful books), in idem., vol. III, p. 110. Concerning this seasonal distribution of pleasures, see *The Use of Pleasure,* Part Two.
24. Plutarch, *Table-Talk,* III, 6, 655d.
25. Rufus of Ephesus, VI, 38, in Oribasius, vol. I, p. 540 ff.
26. Ibid., p. 547.

27. Ibid., p. 549.
28. Galen, VIII (doubtful books) in ibid., vol. III, p. 111.
29. Celsus, *De Medicina,* I, 1, p. 45.
30. Rufus of Ephesus, VI, 38, in Oribasius, vol. I, pp. 543–546.

Chapter 4: The Work of the Soul

1. Soranus, *Gynecology,* I, 8.
2. Athenaeus, XXI (doubtful books), in Oribasius, *Collection of Greek and Latin Physicians,* vol. III, p. 165.
3. Rufus of Ephesus, VI, ibid., vol. I, p. 549.
4. Rufus of Ephesus, *Works,* p. 75.
5. Rufus of Ephesus, VI, in Oribasius, vol. I, p. 549.
6. Celsus, *De Medicina,* IV, 28.
7. Rufus of Ephesus, VI, in Oribasius, vol. I, p. 550.
8. Galen, *On the Affected Parts,* VI, 5.
9. Rufus of Ephesus, *Works,* pp. 74–75.
10. Galen, *On the Affected Parts,* VI, 6.
11. Rufus of Ephesus, *Works,* p. 74.
12. Galen, *On the Affected Parts,* VI, 6; Diocles (doubtful books), in Oribasius, vol. III, p. 177.
13. Galen, *On the Affected Parts,* VI, 6.
14. Plutarch, *Table-Talk,* III, 654e.
15. Propertius, *Elegies,* II, 15.
16. Ibid., II, 6.
17. Ovid, *The Art of Love,* III, 808.
18. Ovid, *The Remedies for Love,* v. 399 ff.; v. 345–348. Compare the advice given to women not to let themselves be seen washing and dressing in *The Art of Love,* III, 209.
19. Galen, *On the Affected Parts,* VI, 5.
20. Dio Chrysostom, *Discourses,* VI, 19–20.
21. G. Canguilhem, *Études d'histoire et de philosophie des sciences,* pp. 337–338.
22. For Part Four, I have also made use of J. Pigeaud, *La Maladie de l'âme.*

PART FIVE: THE WIFE

Introduction

1. H. Thesleff, "An Introduction to the Pythagorean Writings of the Hellenistic Period," and "The Pythagorean Texts of the Hellenistic Period."

2. M. Meslin, *L'Homme romain, des origines au 1er siècle de notre ère*, pp. 143–163.

Chapter 1: The Marriage Tie

1. Musonius Rufus, *Reliquiae*, XIV, p. 71. See also C. Lutz, "Musonius Rufus," pp. 87–100.
2. Hierocles, *Peri gamou*, in Stobaeus, *Florilegium*, 21, 17.
3. Musonius Rufus, *Reliquiae*, XIII A, pp. 67–68.
4. Ibid., XIV, pp. 70–71.
5. Hierocles, in Stobaeus, *Florilegium*, 22.
6. Aristotle, *Politics*, I, 2, 1252a. See also the *Nicomachean Ethics* (VIII, 12), where he employs the word in connection with the relation between husband and wife.
7. See Diogenes Laertius, *Lives of Eminent Philosophers*, VII, 1, 121.
8. Epictetus, *Discourses*, III, 7, 19–20, 26, and 28.
9. Ibid., 36.
10. Hierocles, in Stobaeus, *Florilegium*, 22.
11. Musonius Rufus, *Reliquiae*, XIV, p. 70.
12. Epictetus, *Discourses*, III, 22, 47.
13. Ibid., 70–71.
14. Ibid., 73.
15. Ibid., 67–68.
16. Aristotle, *Nicomachean Ethics*, VIII, 12.
17. Musonius Rufus, *Reliquiae*, XIV, pp. 74–75.
18. Hierocles, in Stobaeus, *Florilegium*, 21.
19. Musonius Rufus, *Reliquiae*, XIV, pp. 73–74.
20. Pliny the Younger, *Letters*, VII, 5.
21. Hierocles, in Stobaeus, *Florilegium*, 24.
22. Pliny the Younger, *Letters*, IV, 19.
23. Musonius Rufus, *Reliquiae*, XIII B, pp. 69–70.
24. Antipater, in Stobaeus, *Florilegium*, 25.
25. Plutarch, *Marriage Precepts*, 34, 142e–143a.
26. Ibid., 20, 140e–141a.

Chapter 2: The Question of Monopoly

1. See *The Use of Pleasure*, Part Three; Plato, *Laws*, VI, 779e–780a.
2. Seneca, *Consolation to Marcia*, 24.
3. Dio Chrysostom, *Discourses*, VII.

4. Marcus Aurelius, *Meditations*, I, 17.
5. Epictetus, *Enchiridion*, XXXIII, 8.
6. Epictetus, *Discourses*, II, 8, 12–14.
7. Musonius Rufus, *Reliquiae*, XII, pp. 63–64.
8. Ibid.
9. Ibid., XV, p. 78. This text is cited and commented on by J. T. Noonan, *Contraception: A History of Its Treatment by the Catholic Theologians and Canonists*, pp. 48–49.
10. Clement of Alexandria, *The Pedagogue*, II, 10.
11. See *The Use of Pleasure*, Part Three.
12. Epictetus, *Discourses*, II, 4, 2–3.
13. Ibid.
14. Seneca, *Letters to Lucilius*, 94, 26.
15. Musonius Rufus, *Reliquiae*, XII, p. 66.
16. Aristotle (attributed), *Economics*, III, 2.
17. Ibid., III, 3.
18. Plutarch, *Marriage Precepts*, 44, 144c–d.
19. Ibid., 50, 140b.

Chapter 3: The Pleasures of Marriage
1. Musonius Rufus, *Reliquiae*, Hense ed., XIV.
2. Plutarch, *Dialogue on Love*, 759e–f.
3. Seneca, *Fragments*, 85.
4. Plutarch, *Marriage Precepts*, 47, 144f–145a; see also 17, 140c.
5. Ibid., 29, 142a–c.
6. Seneca, *Fragments*, 85.
7. Clement of Alexandria, *Stromateis*, II, 143, 1; Saint Francis of Sales, *Introduction to the Devout Life*, III, 39.
8. Aristotle (attributed), *Economics*, III, 3.
9. Seneca, *Consolation to Helvia*, 13, 4.
10. Musonius Rufus, *Reliquiae*, XII, p. 64.
11. Plutarch, *Marriage Precepts*, 13, 139e.
12. Ibid., 10, 139c.
13. Ibid., 46, 144e–f.
14. See also Plutarch, *Bravery of Women*, 242b.
15. Plutarch, *Marriage Precepts*, 18, 140c.
16. Ibid., 2, 138d–e.
17. Ibid., 2, 138f.
18. See Part Six.

19. Plutarch, *Marriage Precepts,* 39, 143e.
20. Ibid., 38, 143d.
21. Plutarch, *Dinner of the Seven Wise Men,* 156c.
22. Ibid., 156d.
23. D. Babut, *Plutarque et le stoïcisme,* p. 109.

PART SIX: BOYS

Introduction
1. J. Boswell, *Christianity, Social Tolerance, and Homosexuality,* p. 61 ff.
2. P. Veyne, "L'Homosexualité à Rome," p. 77.
3. Quintilian, *Institutio oratoria,* II, 2.
4. Maximus of Tyre, *Lectures,* 24, 1; 25, 1.
5. Ibid., 25, 2–4.

Chapter 1: Plutarch
1. H. Martin, *Plutarch's Early Writings and Early Christian Literature,* ed. H. D. Betz.
2. Plutarch, *Dialogue on Love,* 771e.
3. Ibid., 749a.
4. Ibid., 754c.
5. Plutarch, *Life of Solon,* 20, 5.
6. Plutarch, *Dialogue on Love,* 752e–f.
7. Ibid., 749d; 755d–e.
8. Plutarch, *Love Stories,* 2, 772e; 3, 773f.
9. Plutarch, *Dialogue on Love,* 754d.
10. Ibid., 751a; 752b.
11. Ibid., 750c–d.
12. Ibid., 750d–e.
13. Ibid., 750c; 752b–c.
14. Ibid., 750e.
15. Ibid., 751d–e.
16. Ibid., 751f; 751e.
17. Ibid., 751e–f.
18. Ibid., 766e.
19. Ibid., 766e–767a.
20. Ibid., 767b–c.
21. Ibid., 767d–e.
22. Ibid., 752b.

23. Ibid., 751d–e.
24. Ibid., 768d.
25. Ibid., 751c.
26. Ibid., 751d.
27. Ibid., 769a.
28. Plutarch, *Life of Solon,* 20.
29. Plutarch, *Dialogue on Love,* 769a–b.
30. Ibid., 769e–f; see also *Marriage Precepts,* 142e–143c.
31. Plutarch, *Dialogue on Love,* 769d.
32. Ibid., 769d–e.

Chapter 2: Pseudo-Lucian

1. M. D. MacLeod, "Introduction" to Loeb edition of *Affairs of the Heart;* F. Buffière, *Éros adolescent,* p. 481. See also R. Bloch, *De Pseudo-Luciani Amoribus,* 1907.
2. Lucian (attributed), *Affairs of the Heart,* 16.
3. Ibid., 19–28.
4. K. Praechter, *Hierokles der Stoiker,* p. 148; Bloch, *De Pseudo-Luciani Amoribus.*
5. Lucian (attributed), *Affairs of the Heart,* 19.
6. Ibid., 20–21.
7. Ibid., 22.
8. Ibid., 32.
9. Ibid., 33–35.
10. Ibid., 36.
11. Praechter, *Hierokles der Stoiker;* Bloch, *De Pseudo-Luciani Amoribus.*
12. Lucian (attributed), *Affairs of the Heart,* 25–26.
13. Ibid., 27.
14. Ibid.
15. Ibid., 28.
16. Ibid.
17. Ibid., 39–42.
18. Achilles Tatius, *Leucippe and Clitophon,* II, 38.
19. Ovid, *The Remedies for Love,* v. 345–348.
20. Ibid., v. 411–418.
21. Lucian (attributed), *Affairs of the Heart,* 44–45.
22. Achilles Tatius, *Leucippe and Clitophon,* II, 38.
23. Lucian (attributed), *Affairs of the Heart,* 46.
24. Xenophon, *Symposium,* VIII, 18.

25. Lucian (attributed), *Affairs of the Heart,* 48.
26. Ibid., 53.

Chapter 3: A New Erotics

1. On this subject, see M. Grant, *The Climax of Rome,* p. 117 ff., and T. Hägg, *Narrative Technique in Ancient Greek Romances.*
2. Achilles Tatius, *Leucippe and Clitophon,* I, 10.
3. Ibid., II, 37.
4. Heliodorus, *Ethiopica,* II, 33.
5. Ibid., III, 17.
6. Achilles Tatius, *Leucippe and Clitophon,* VIII, 5; V, 20; see also VI, 16.
7. Heliodorus, *Ethiopica,* V, 4.

CONCLUSION

1. T. Zahn, *Der stoiker Epiktet und sein Verhältnis zum Christentum.*
2. A. Bonhöffer, *Epiktet und das Neue Testament.*

BIBLIOGRAPHY

Classical authors' names and works are given in the form familiar in English, with the edition Foucault used listed first and that used by the translator (if different) cited in brackets. Modern sources are given in the language Foucault consulted.

Achilles Tatius. *Leucippe and Clitophon.* French trans. P. Grimal. Paris: Gallimard, La Pléiade, 1963. [English trans. S. Graselee. *The Adventures of Leucippe and Clitophon.* Loeb Classical Library. Also: Anonymous English trans. *The Loves of Cleitophon and Leucippe.* Athens: Athenian Society, 1897.]

Allbut, C. *Greek Medicine in Rome.* London, 1921.

Antipater. In Stobaeus, *Florilegium,* vol. III. Ed. A. Meinecke. Leipzig, 1860–1863, pp. 11–15.

Apuleius. *On the God of Socrates.* French ed. and trans. J. Beaujeu. Collection des universités de France. [English trans. T. Taylor. In *The Metamorphosis, or Golden Ass, and Philosophical Works, of Apuleius.* London: J. Moyes, 1822.]

Aretaeus. *On the Causes and Signs of Acute and Chronic Diseases.* In *Corpus Medicorum Graecorum,* II. Berlin, 1958. French trans. L. Renaud. Paris, 1834. [English trans. T. F. Reynolds. Philadelphia: Haswell, Barrington, & Haswell, 1841.]

———. *On the Cure of Chronic Diseases.* [English trans. F. Adams. In *The Extant Works of Aretaeus, the Cappadocian.* London: Sydenham Society, 1856.]

Aristides. *The Roman Oration.* English trans. J. H. Oliver. In *The Ruling Power: A Study of the Roman Empire in the Second Cen-*

tury A.D. through the Roman Oration of Aelius Aristides.
Philadelphia: American Philosophical Society, 1953.

Aristotle. *The Nicomachean Ethics.* English ed. and trans. H. Rackham. Loeb Classical Library. French trans. R.-A. Gauthier and J.-Y. Jolif. Louvain-Paris, 1970.

———. *The Politics.* English ed. and trans. H. Rackham. Loeb Classical Library. French trans. J. Tricot. Paris, 1982.

Aristotle (attributed). *Economics.* French ed. and trans. A. Wartelle. Collection des universités de France. [English trans. G. C. Armstrong. *Oeconomica,* III. Loeb Classical Library.]

Artemidorus. *The Interpretation of Dreams.* French trans. A.-J. Festugière. Paris, 1975. English trans. R. J. White. Park Ridge, N.J.: Noyes Press, 1975.

Babut, D. *Plutarque et le stoïcisme.* Paris: Presses Universitaires de France, 1969.

Behr, C. A. *Aelius Aristides and the "Sacred Tales."* Amsterdam, 1968.

Betz, H. D. *Plutarch's Ethical Writings and Early Christian Literature.* Leiden, 1978.

Bloch, R. *De Pseudo-Luciani Amoribus.* Strassburg, 1907.

Bonhöffer, A. *Epiktet und das Neue Testament.* Giessen, 1911.

———. *Epiktet und die Stoa.* Stuttgart, 1890.

———. *Die Ethik des Stoikers Epiktet.* Stuttgart, 1894.

Boswell, J. *Christianity, Social Tolerance, and Homosexuality.* Chicago: University of Chicago Press, 1980.

Bowersock, G. W. *Greek Sophists in the Roman Empire.* Oxford: Clarendon Press, 1969.

Broudehoux, J.-P. *Mariage et famille chez Clément d'Alexandrie.* Paris: Beauchesne, 1970.

Buffière, F. *Éros adolescent: La Pédérastie dans la Grèce antique.* Paris: Les Belles Lettres, 1980.

Caelius Aurelianus. *On Chronic Diseases.* [English trans. I. E. Drabkin. Chicago: University of Chicago Press, 1950.]

Canguilhem, G. *Études d'histoire et de philosophie des sciences.* Paris: Vrin, 1968.

Celsus. *De Medicina.* English ed. and trans. W. G. Spencer. Loeb Classical Library. French trans. A. Vedrenes. Paris, 1876.

Chariton of Aphrodisias. *The Adventures of Chaereas and Callirhoe.* French ed. and trans. G. Molinié. Collection des universités de France.

Cicero. *Tusculan Disputations.* French ed. and trans. G. Fohlen and J. Humbert. Collection des universités de France.

Clement of Alexandria. *The Pedagogue.* French ed. and trans. M. Harl and C. Mondésert. Paris. Collection Sources Chrétiennes, 1960–1965.

———. *Stromateis.* French ed. and trans. C. Mondésert. Paris: Coll. Sources Chrétiennes, 1951–1954.

Crook, J. A. *Law and Life of Rome.* London, 1967.

Dio Cassius. *Dio's Roman History.* English ed. and trans. E. Cary. Loeb Classical Library.

Dio Chrysostom. *Discourses.* English ed. and trans. J. W. Cohoon. Loeb Classical Library.

Diogenes Laertius. *Lives of Eminent Philosophers.* English ed. and trans. R. D. Hicks. Loeb Classical Library. French trans. R. Genaille. Paris: Garnier-Flammarion, 1965.

Epictetus. *Discourses.* French ed. and trans. J. Souilhé. Collection des universités de France. [English trans. W. A. Oldfather. Loeb Classical Library. Also: English trans. P. E. Matheson. In *The Stoic and Epicurean Philosophers.* New York: Random House, 1940.]

———. *Enchiridion* (or *Manual*). French trans. É. Brehier. In *Les Stoïciens.* Paris: Gallimard, La Pléiade, 1962. [English trans. T. W. Higginson. Indianapolis: Bobbs-Merrill, 1955.]

Epicurus. *Letters and Maxims.* French ed. and trans. M. Conche. Villiers-sur-Mer, 1977. [English trans. R. M. Geer. *Letters, Principal Doctrines, and Vatican Sayings.* Indianapolis: Bobbs-Merrill, 1964.]

Ferguson, J. *Moral Values in the Ancient World.* London, 1958.

Festugière, A.-J. *Études de philosophie grecque.* Paris: Vrin, 1971.

Francis of Sales, Saint. *Introduction to the Devout Life.* French ed. C. Florisoone. Collection des universités de France.

Gagé, J. *Les Classes sociales dans l'empire romain.* Paris: Payot, 1964.

Galen. *On the Affected Parts.* In *Opera omnia,* vol. VIII, ed. C. G. Kühn. French trans. C. Daremberg, vol. II. English trans. R. E. Siegel. Basel: S. Kargel, 1976.

———. *On the Passions and Errors of the Soul.* In *Opera omnia,* ed. C. G. Kühn. French trans. R. Van der Helst. Paris: Delagrave, 1914. [English trans. P. W. Harkins. Columbus, Ohio: Ohio State University Press, 1963.]

———. *On the Usefulness of the Parts of the Body*. In *Opera omnia*, vol. II, ed. C. G. Kühn. Reprinted Hildesheim, 1964–1965. French trans. C. Daremberg. In *Oeuvres anatomiques, physiologiques et médicales de Galen*. Paris, 1856. English trans. M. T. May. Ithaca: Cornell University Press, 1968.

Grant, M. *The Climax of Rome: The Final Achievements of the Ancient World*. London, 1968.

Grilli, A. *Il problema della vita contemplativa nel mondo greco-romano*. Milan-Rome, 1953.

Grimal, P. *Sénèque ou la conscience de l'empire*. Paris, 1978.

Hadot, I. *Seneca und die griechisch-römische Tradition der Seelenleitung*. Berlin, 1969.

Hadot, P. *Exercices spirituels et philosophie antique*. Paris: Études Augustiniennes, 1981.

Hägg, T. *Narrative Technique in Ancient Greek Romances: Studies of Chariton, Xenophon, Ephesius and Achilles Tatius*. Stockholm, 1971.

Heliodorus. *The Ethiopica*. French trans. P. Grimal. Paris: Gallimard, La Pléiade, 1963. [English trans. Sir Walter Lamb. *Ethiopian Story*. London: J. M. Dent & Sons, 1961.]

Hierocles. In Stobaeus, *Florilegium*, Vol. III. Ed. A. Meinecke. Leipzig, 1860–1864, pp. 7–11.

Hijmans, B. L. *Askēsis: Notes on Epicetetus' Educational System*. Utrecht, 1959.

Kessels, A. H. M. "Ancient Systems of Dream Classification." *Mnemosyné*, series 4, no. 22 (1969).

Liebeschütz, J. H. *Continuity and Change in Roman Religion*. Oxford: Oxford University Press, 1979.

Lucian. *Hermotimus*. English ed. and trans. K. Kilburn. Loeb Classical Library.

Lucian (attributed). *Affairs of the Heart*. English ed. and trans. M. D. MacLeod. Loeb Classical Library.

Lutz, C. "Musonius Rufus." *Yale Classical Studies*, vol. X (1947).

MacMullen, R. *Roman Social Relations, 50 B.C. to A.D. 284*. London-New Haven: Yale University Press, 1974.

Marcus Aurelius. *Meditations*. French ed. and trans. A.-I. Trannoy. Collection des universités de France. [English trans. G. M. A. Grube. Indianapolis: Bobbs-Merrill, 1963.]

Maximus of Tyre. *Lectures*. Latin ed. Paris, 1840.

Meslin, M. *L'Homme romain, des origines au 1ᵉʳ siècle de notre ère: Essai d'anthropolgie.*

Musonius Rufus. *Reliquiae.* Ed. O. Hense. Leipzig, 1905. ["Should All Children Born Be Brought Up?" Trans. J. T. Noonan. In *Contraception: A History of Its Treatment by the Catholic Theologians and Canonists.* Cambridge, Mass.: Harvard University Press, 1966. *Trans. note:* All other Musonius quotations are translated from Foucault's French.]

Noonan, J. T. *Contraception et mariage, évolution ou contradiction dans la pensée chrétienne* [*Contraception: A History of Its Treatment by the Catholic Theologians and Canonists*]. French trans. M. Joussa. Paris: Éditions du Cerf, 1969.

Oribasius. *Collection of Greek and Latin Physicians.* Ed. and French trans. U. C. Bussemaker and C. Daremberg. Paris, 1851–1876.

Ovid. *The Art of Love.* French ed. and trans. H. Bornecque. Collection des universités de France. [English trans. R. Humphries. Bloomington, Ind.: Indiana University Press, 1959.]

———. *The Remedies for Love.* French ed. and trans. H. Bornecque. Collection des universités de France. [English trans. R. Humphries. In *The Art of Love.* Bloomington, Ind.: Indiana University Press, 1959.]

Philodemus. *Peri parrhēsias.* Ed. A. Olivieri. Leipzig, 1914.

Pigeaud, J. *La Maladie de l'âme: Étude sur la relation de l'âme et du corps dans la tradition médico-philosophique antique.* Paris: Les Belles Lettres, 1981.

Plato. *Alcibiades.* French ed. and trans. M. Croiset. Collection des universités de France.

———. *Apology of Socrates.* French ed. and trans. M. Croiset. Collection des universités de France.

———. *The Laws.* French ed. and trans. É. des Places and A. Diès. Collection des universités de France.

———. *The Republic.* French ed. and trans. É. Chambry. Collection des universités de France.

Pliny the Younger. *Letters.* French ed. and trans. A.-M. Guillemin. Collection des universités de France. [English trans. B. Radice. Baltimore: Penguin Books, 1963.]

Plutarch. *Ad principem ineruditum* [*To an Uneducated Ruler*]. English ed. and trans. F. C. Babbitt. In *Plutarch's Moralia,* vol. X. Loeb Classical Library.

——. *Animine an corporis affectiones sint pejores.* English ed. and trans. F. C. Babbitt. In *Plutarch's Moralia,* vol. VI. Loeb Classical Library.

——. *Apophthegmata laconica.* English ed. and trans. F. C. Babbitt. In *Plutarch's Moralia,* vol. III. Loeb Classical Library.

——. *Conjugalia praecepta* [*Marriage Precepts*]. English ed. and trans. F. C. Babbitt. In *Plutarch's Moralia,* vol. II. Loeb Classical Library.

——. *De cohibenda ira.* English ed. and trans. F. C. Babbitt. In *Plutarch's Moralia.* Loeb Classical Library.

——. *De tuenda sanitate praecepta.* English ed. and trans. F. C. Babbitt. In *Plutarch's Moralia,* vol. II. Loeb Classical Library.

——. *The Dialogue on Love.* French ed. and trans. R. Flacelière. In *Oeuvres morales,* vol. X. Collection des universités de France. [English trans. W. C. Helmbold. Loeb Classical Library.]

——. *Life of Solon.* French ed. and trans. R. Flacelière, É. Chambry, and M. Juneaux. Collection des universités de France. [English trans. B. Perrin. Loeb Classical Library.]

——. *Love Stories.* French ed. and trans. R. Flacelière. In *Oeuvres morales,* vol. X. Collection des universités de France.

——. *Mulierum virtutes* [*Bravery of Women*]. English ed. and trans. F. C. Babbitt. In *Plutarch's Moralia,* vol. III. Loeb Classical Library.

——. *On Exile.* French ed. and trans. J. Hani. In *Oeuvres morales,* vol. VIII. Collection des universités de France.

——. *Praecepta gerendae reipublicae.* English ed. and trans. F. C. Babbitt. In *Plutarch's Moralia,* vol. X. Loeb Classical Library.

——. *Quomodo quis suos in virtute sentiat profectus.* English ed. and trans. F. C. Babbitt. In *Plutarch's Moralia,* vol. I. Loeb Classical Library.

——. *Regum et imperatorum apophthegmata.* English ed. and trans. F. C. Babbitt. In *Plutarch's Moralia,* vol. III. Loeb Classical Library.

——. *Septem sapientium convivium* [Dinner of the Seven Wise Men]. English ed. and trans. F. C. Babbitt. In *Plutarch's Moralia,* vol. II. Loeb Classical Library.

——. *Socrates' Daemon.* French ed. and trans. J. Hani. In *Oeuvres morales,* vol. VII. Collection des universités de France.

————. *Table-Talk.* French ed. and trans. F. Fuhrmann. In *Oeuvres morales,* vol. IX. Collection des universités de France. [English trans. P. A. Clemens. Loeb Classical Library.]

Pomeroy, S. B. *Goddesses, Whores, Wives and Slaves: Women in Classical Antiquity.* New York: Schocken, 1975.

Porphyry. *Life of Pythagoras.* French ed. and trans. É. des Places. Collection des universités de France.

Praechter, K. *Hierokles der Stoiker.* Leipzig, 1901.

Propertius. *Elegies.* French ed. and trans. D. Paganelli. Collection des universités de France. [English trans. J. Warden. *The Poems of Propertius.* Indianapolis: Bobbs-Merrill, 1972.]

Quintilian. *Institutio oratoria.* French ed. and trans. J. Cousin. Collection des universités de France. [English trans. W. M. Smail. In *Quintilian on Education.* Oxford: Oxford University Press, 1938.]

Rostovtzeff, M. I. *The Social and Economic History of the Hellenistic World.* Oxford: Oxford University Press, 1941 reprint.

Rousselle, A. *Porneia: De la maîtrise du corps à la privation sensorielle, IIᵉ–IVᵉ siècles de l'ère chrétienne.* Paris: Presses Universitaires de France.

Rufus of Ephesus. *Works.* French ed. and trans. C. Daremberg and E. Ruelle. Paris, 1879.

Sandbach, F. H. *The Stoics.* London: Chatto & Windus, 1975.

Scarborough, J. *Roman Medicine.* Ithaca: Cornell University Press, 1969.

Seneca. *Consolation to Helvia.* French ed. and trans. R. Waltz. Collection des universités de France.

————. *Consolation to Marcia.* French ed. and trans. R. Waltz. Collection des universités de France.

————. *Fragments.* [In L. Haase. *L. Annaei Senecae Opera,* vol. III. Leipzig, 1852.]

————. *Letters to Lucilius.* French ed. and trans. F. Préchac and H. Noblot. Collection des universités de France. [English trans. R. M. Grummere. Loeb Classical Library.]

————. *Naturalis Quaestiones* [*Natural Questions*]. English ed. and trans. T. H. Corcoran. Loeb Classical Library.

————. *On Anger.* French ed. and trans. A. Bourgery. Collection des universités de France. [English trans. J. W. Basore. Loeb Classical Library.]

————. *On Benefits.* French ed. and trans. F. Préchac. Collection des universités de France.

———. *On the Constancy of the Wise Man.* French ed. and trans. R. Waltz. Collection des universités de France.

———. *On the Happy Life.* French ed. and trans. A. Bourgery. Collection des universités de France.

———. *On the Shortness of Life.* French ed. and trans. A. Bourgery. Collection des universités de France. [English trans. J. W. Basore. Loeb Classical Library.]

———. *On Tranquillity of Mind.* French ed. and trans. R. Waltz. Collection des universités de France. [English trans. J. W. Basore. Loeb Classical Library.]

Soranus. *Gynecology.* In *Corpus Medicorum Graecorum,* vol. IV. Leipzig, 1927. French trans. F. J. Hergott. Nancy, 1895. English trans. O. Temkin. Baltimore: Johns Hopkins University Press, 1956.

Spanneut, M. "Epiktet." In *Reallexikon für Antike und Christentum,* 1962.

Starr, C. G. *The Roman Empire.* Oxford: Oxford University Press, 1982.

Statius. *Silvae.* French ed. and trans. H. Frère and H.-J. Izaac. Collection des universités de France. [English trans. J. H. Mozley. Loeb Classical Library.]

Stobaeus. *Florilegium.* Ed. A. Meineke. Leipzig, 1860–1864.

Syme, R. *Roman Papers.* Oxford: Oxford University Press, 1979.

Synesius. *On Dreams.* In *Works.* French trans. H. Druon. Paris, 1878. [English trans. A. Fitzgerald. In *The Essays and Hymns of Senesius the Cyrene.* Oxford: Oxford University Press, 1930.]

Thesleff, H. "An Introduction to the Pythagorean Writings of the Hellenistic Period." *Humaniora,* 24, 3, Åbo (1961).

———. "The Pythagorean Texts of the Hellenistic Period." *Acta Academiae Aboensis,* ser. A., vol. 30, no. 1.

Vatin, C. *Recherches sur le mariage et la condition de la femme mariée a l'époque hellénistique.* Paris: De Boccard, 1970.

Veyne, P. "L'Amour à Rome." *Annales E.S.C.,* vol. 1 (1978).

———. "L'Homosexualité à Rome." *L'Histoire* (January 1981).

Voelcke, A. J. *Les Rapports avec autrui dans la philosophie grecque, d'Aristote à Panétius.* Paris: Vrin, 1969.

Xenophon. *Cyropaedia.* French ed. and trans. M. Bizos and É. Delebecque. Collection des universités de France. [English trans. W. Miller. Loeb Classical Library.]

————. *Oeconomicus.* French ed. and trans. P. Chantraine. Collection des universités de France.

————. *Symposium.* French ed. and trans. F. Ollier. Collection des universités de France.

Zahn, T. *Der stoiker Epiktet und sein Verhältnis zum Christentum.* Erlangen, 1894.

INDEX

267